International Journal on Criminology

Also from Westphalia Press
westphaliapress.org

INTERNATIONAL JOURNAL ON CRIMINOLOGY

VOLUME 9, NUMBER 1
WINTER 2022

Alain Bauer, editor-in-chief

Published with the support of:

le cnam
équipe sécurité & défense
renseignement, criminologie, crises, cybermenaces

Westphalia Press
An imprint of Policy Studies Organization

INTERNATIONAL JOURNAL ON CRIMINOLOGY
VOL. 9, NO. 1 • WINTER 2022

Westphalia Press
An imprint of Policy Studies Organization
1527 New Hampshire Ave., NW
Washington, D.C. 20036
info@ipsonet.org

ISBN: 978-1-63723-913-1

Cover and interior design by Jeffrey Barnes
jbarnesbook.design

Daniel Gutierrez-Sandoval, Executive Director
PSO and Westphalia Press

Updated material and comments on this edition
can be found at the Westphalia Press website:
www.westphaliapress.org

INTERNATIONAL JOURNAL ON CRIMINOLOGY

VOLUME 9, NUMBER 1
WINTER 2022
© 2022 Policy Studies Organization

RISKS, CHAOS, RESILIENCE

Facing Total Crises: Cassandra, The State and Its Double

Alain Bauer

Professor of Criminology at the Conservatoire National des Arts et Métiers
Coordinator of the New Risks Chair
Security Defense Intelligence Criminology Cyber Threats Crises
(PSDR3C / ESDR3C)

ABSTRACT

"Risks, chaos, resilience. Facing total crises: Cassandra, the State and its double" deals with the prevention and study of threats. Indeed, since the end of the Cold War, we have witnessed a mutation of threats and dangers, as they have been taken out of the usual framework of study. It is therefore necessary to renovate strategic thinking in the face of these threats. A new way of thinking is emerging, embodying this idea: the concept of global security. It is opposed to the inability of administrations to anticipate and their tendency to analyze exclusively in a retroactive manner. The current health crisis thus highlights this inability to anticipate, characterized by a lack of communication, giving way to the massive dissemination of fake news from all sides, and undermining the relationship of social trust between the state and the population. Reacting is already a setback. The Nation must be able to foresee and anticipate, to react and prevent.

Keywords: Total crises, Forecasting, Risk management, Strategic thinking, Global Security, Public Administration

Riesgos, caos, resiliencia: frente a las crisis totales: cassandra, el estado y su doble

RESUMEN

"Riesgos, caos, resiliencia. Frente a las crisis totales: Casandra, el Estado y su doble" trata de la prevención y el estudio de las amenazas. En efecto, desde el final de la Guerra Fría hemos asistido a una mutación de amenazas y peligros, a medida que han sido sa-

doi: 10.18278/ijc.9.1.1

cados del marco habitual de estudio. Por ello, es necesario renovar el pensamiento estratégico frente a estas amenazas. Está surgiendo una nueva forma de pensar que encarna esta idea: el concepto de seguridad global. Se opone a la incapacidad de las administraciones a anticiparse y su tendencia a analizar exclusivamente de forma retroactiva. La actual crisis sanitaria pone de relieve así esta incapacidad de anticipación, caracterizada por la falta de comunicación, dando paso a la difusión masiva de noticias falsas por todos lados, y socavando la relación de confianza social entre el Estado y la población, reaccionar ya es un retroceso, la Nación debe saber prever y anticipar, reaccionar y prevenir.

Palabras clave: Crisis totales, Previsión, Gestión de riesgos, Pensamiento estratégico, Seguridad Global, Administración Pública

风险、混乱和复原力
面对全危机：预言者、国家以及对等国

摘要

《风险、混乱和复原力—面对全危机：预言者、国家以及对等国》一文分析了威胁的预防和研究。自冷战结束以来，我们确实目睹了威胁和危险的改变，正如通常的研究框架所分析的那样。因此，在面临这些威胁时革新战略思维是必要的。代表全球安全这一概念的新思维正在出现。其有别于行政部门，后者没有预测能力且往往仅以回溯的方式进行分析。当前的卫生危机因此强调了这一预测能力的缺失，其特征是缺乏沟通，无法控制巨大的假新闻传播，并削弱了国家与人民之间的社会信任关系。采取行动一事已遭遇困难。国家必须拥有预测能力并能响应和预防。

关键词：全危机（total crises），预测，风险管理，战略思维，全球安全，公共行政

Forecasters and their errors, as well as "doomsayers," are often mocked or even singled out when they fail to anticipate a dramatic event. Those who make a profession of retrospective analysis, which is far less dangerous for reputations, more or less deride the Cassandras and other *pythias*.

In Greek mythology, Cassandra is the daughter of the king of Troy, Priam, and Hecuba. She was given the gift of predicting the future by Apollo. She rejected him and the god decreed that no one would believe her predictions, even though they were correct.

After each disaster or tragedy, a commission of enquiry, whether public or less visible, analyzes the reasons for the incident. It usually begins its report by listing all the clues that should have aroused the interest of the states or those responsible for the sector concerned.

Although mistakes are not unavoidable, it is nevertheless up to researchers to continue developing mechanisms for anticipating crises and threats in order to try to prevent and avoid having to resolve them.

In an agitated and unpredictable world, the renovation of strategic thinking supported by a flexible early warning tool remains crucial. Since the end of the Cold War, terrorism and organized crime have mutated. They globalized and hybridized in ways that take these two increasingly interdependent actors far beyond the static and retrospective framework in which they were studied in the past.

A new strategic thinking, irrigated by the concept of "global security," has integrated national defense, public security, corporate protection, and environmental security. The health dimension can undoubtedly be added to this list.

In 2010, the instrument for the renovation of French strategic thinking attempted to emerge in the form of a Conseil Supérieur de la Formation et de la Recherche Stratégiques. The main part of this structure is now hosted by the Conservatoire National des Arts et Métiers, thanks to the proactive action of the Secrétariat Général de la Défense et de la Sécurité Nationale and the general administration of the CNAM.

In Europe, the United States, Russia, China, and India, the urgency of rebuilding strategic thinking has become even more pressing in the face of the need to modernize state security and defense structures and to clarify their content and missions.

The transition from the Cold War to a "hot" peace, characterized by a multiplication of destabilization operations, notably on social networks, but also in the form of threats, poisonings, kidnappings, or assassinations, is gradually forcing us to wake up from a strategic siesta marked by the illusions of the post-Berlin Wall era. After ten years of uncertainty, Russia has taken stock of an attempt to open up that was marked by a bloodletting, for which it blames the West. And China has understood that it is better to play aggressive in order to preserve its model. Empires have awakened, under the watchful but equally firm stare of the Turkish and Indian powers.

Most democratic states no longer have a structured and active strategic thinking to deal with these upheavals, despite their considerable potential.

Nonetheless, recent developments have shown that concepts cannot remain static in the face of evolving and interrelated threats. Ensuring States' security and defense requires perceiving and understanding dangers and risks.

Yet, as introduced, central or federal administrations are almost devoid of the necessary tools to understand, analyze and deal with what is currently referred to as "global security." Because of their tendency to analyze retroactively, these agencies are more able to react to the previous war than to anticipate the next one. One moves rather quickly from the Azincourt syndrome to the disaster of the Maginot Line.

A number of brilliant but isolated minds are corseted in a bureaucratic environment that slows down innovation at best and stalls it at worst.

The 2020/2021 crisis, which follows the 2010 H1N1 crisis by barely a decade and its 1918 genesis (the Kansas "Spanish" flu) by a century, has made it possible to perceive its outlines and issues.

Krisis, the Greek basis of the word crisis, does not only relate to health. Its etymology refers to distinguishing, choosing, separating, or deciding—in short, to judging. Latin transposes the term to the medical field. The word seems to have been invented to analyze the relationship between a pandemic and the state that was to combat it.

In France, the relationship between the State and the Nation is very special. While in most countries the Nation was the driving force behind the creation of the State, in France the opposite seems much more likely.

Our history is rich in great political leaders and their Palace Mayors, Missi Dominici, Imperial Commissioners, Prefects, who structured a powerful and dominant central state, wavering between the heaviness of its millennial past and the excitement of its young conquerors. Aware of the risk of disintegration of a diverse and multilingual country with many traditions and a wide range of religions, politically astute leaders and brilliant administrators joined forces. With patience and determination, they built a state that is now called "deep state."

Alas, this evil hidden ghost that would block any evolution or reform is no more. It is structurally buried in a bureaucratic and accounting gangue, which it has patiently helped to build and which has literally submerged it. Today, it seems to be on life support.

Until now, for each major crisis, a savior or an icon has miraculously emerged from the people or the elite: Charlemagne, Louis XI, Joan of Arc, Henri IV, Bonaparte . . . The deficiency of politics was saved by the genius of the military (De Gaulle), Sully, Colbert, or Pompidou taking care of economic, financial, or industrial aspects. Everyone will add to this list his favorite heroes or heroines.

The COVID crisis was a grim revelation of this situation. While doctors and politicians were slowly shifting from skepticism to panic mode, exposing ten years of dismantling of the public hospital, the media, disoriented and overwhelmed by the magnitude of an event that is nevertheless recurrent in the history of the world, trapped in the moment, disturbed by the absence of consensus in the small world of media experts and TV sets' "experts of everything," contributed largely to the dissemination of the original sin of this crisis: the lie by ignorance or omission, much more than by manipulation

Political communication was ridiculed, both on the issue of masks and tests, and on the high-profile transfers between hospitals or the culpable ignorance of the capacities of the private hospital sector and especially of laboratories.

However, until 2016, France had a remarkable tool for pandemic prevention, the establishment for the preparation and response to health emergencies (EPRUS). The country also had a stockpile of life-saving masks it could have mobilized without closing the country's borders. Political leaders, e.g., parliamentarians, deputies and senators, experts and scientific actors, public administrators and government officials, from the President to the Ministers concerned, had done their job well in investigating, preparing, and informing the population on virus prevention.

Alas, others, curiously aided by the atony of the supervisory administrations, have since taken ten years to deconstruct with determination what could undoubtedly have prevented this major crisis. Other states have also decided on the "zero Covid" option rather than choosing to live with it.

It was the honor of the highest officers of the State to impose the sense of a necessary continuity on policies such as major industrial programs, the creation of national champions or building a sense of the future and its challenges and actors. For a long time, our leaders invested in a future called Ariane, Airbus, Renault-Nissan, Sanofi, Veolia, Total, etc.

The problem is that the industrial sector has been largely sacrificed to globalization, characterized by the relocation of commercial giants and the privatizations of the 1980s, but also by the lure of stock options, the often-incestuous relationships that have slowly but strongly developed with uprooted investment funds. These different dynamics changed the nature of patrimonial capitalism to transform it into a pure speculative tool in high frequency in the long term. The "Holy Alliance" between the State and the Capital, which had strengthened the country, was seriously handicapped by this competition of allegiances.

Worse still, many training structures, particularly academic ones, continued to form and train graduates that had succeeded in developing start-ups or headed companies that managed to develop effective vaccines in a short time outside France. This has not been the case for the French national champion.

The health crisis has thus revealed a clueless and immobilized State, paradoxically unable to restore confidence in communication, a tool that generally survives when all else seems lost.

In failing to take responsibility for their own redemption after their risky statements, which are the joy of retrospectives on social networks, politicians, but also permanent guests on 24-hour news channels, have created and spread a crisis of truth that initially only affected the political and media world. This phenomenon has also spread to the scientific sphere, posing a crucial problem of social trust between the population and these spheres.

In 1919, Jacques Bainville foresaw the coming crises by indicating what the effects of the signed peace agreements would be in "Les conséquences politiques de la Paix." History proved him right. In 1946, posthumously, Marc Bloch's "L'étrange défaite" (The Strange Defeat) was the autopsy of a methodically constructed disaster. Replacing "military" with "sanitary" would almost be enough to republish this work in 2022 to methodically analyze the erratic management of this COVID crisis.

Michel Rocard rightly explained that the State was not designed to produce, but to control. Misunderstanding or bypassing the instruction, the administration decided that it was to produce and that the rest would regulate itself naturally.

The State was unable to manage the crisis, but the Nation's "System D" made it possible to survive it.

Still, civil servants, entrepreneurs, and elected officials capable to re-establish a democratic and solidarity-based state, with order and fraternity, are still present everywhere.

Unfortunately, the current situation remains worrying: lack of capacity for prospective analysis on the part of administrations, poorly-funded university research, *almost* non-existent relations between central administration operators, universities or even economic circles, deficient information sharing, few shared priorities and therefore few precise and lasting common objectives between private and public actors, scattered strategic information, lack of evaluation and synthesis of studies, reluctance to identify real security and defense sectors, etc. Admittedly, notable progress and salutary reactions have been made, but they are still too isolated. In adversity, the national genius is more often revealed through coercion and pressure than through preventive but unheard speeches.

Training in anti-terrorism, intelligence analysis and the reactive effect of attacks claimed or assumed by the Islamic State exist in France. The dimension of New Risks has been anticipated, that of industrial and food sovereignty, and the challenges of controlling R & D discoveries have been reactivated. One can say that sovereignty is back.

In a chaotic and fragmented world, reacting is already being late. A strategic nation must constantly be able to foresee, anticipate, avoid, and prevent. This new agility obligation requires that the nation, in all of its components (the State, the world of research, the economy), be warned *in time*.

Commercial and financial liberalization, technological innovation and the development of communications are creating interdependencies. These different dynamics constitute a new geography of real and virtual territories organized around *megacities, clusters*, and communities. At the same time, they are also creating excluded people for whom globalization increases dispossession and powerlessness.

These discrepancies in development are conducive to dangers such as riots, economic migration, political instability, local conflicts over the sharing of resources, identity or religious claims and, above all, the uncontrollable development of a real criminal economy. Thus, by interweaving interests at a distance and initially limiting tensions at the global level, globalization has been able to reinforce these threats at other levels.

The new geostrategic tensions, the effects of the post-Berlin Wall "thaw," the appearance of new actors and the reappearance of old Empires, the revenge/vengeance of borders, nations, tribes, and religions, are sending us back to a decomposed past that we had wanted to forget as if it had never existed. Our amnesias seem to damage us much more than our blindness.

Crime itself has become a major player on the international scene, an economic and military operator, ultimately a danger to states and democracies. Crime operates on the model of the advanced liberal enterprise, for example through vertical and horizontal integration, the development of catchment areas, the introduction of new products, investment in R&D, and even the introduction of incentives for staff. Only the management of competition seems a little more definitive than elsewhere. Also, the use of the virtual world makes organized crime even more transnational, freeing it from the constraints of border crossing or ransom delivery.

The cyber virus has spread rapidly, combining purely financial operations with political manipulation. Indeed, among its aberrations we find the dissemination of alternative truths, "fake news" (while waiting for the much more dangerous Deep Fake), but also the "Trollisation" of the Internet space, marked by the creation of an immense outlet for hatred and anger, a sort of "Rageosphère"[1] unprecedented in its power. This space is defined by its cumulative capacity for action, the lack of control over impulses and the absence of accountability of the users.

In addition, and on a more worrying level, different elements could together or separately lead to major explosions. For example, an uncontrolled military escalation from a local conflict, the search for a diversion from internal tensions

---

1   Notion developed by the author that could be literally translated as "rage-sphere."

7

in an external adventure, the exact or false perception of a decisive technological advantage, a cyber-attack under false pretenses, etc.

The reflection process is almost clinical: a shared diagnosis (the least successful stage to date), a discussed prognosis and an affirmed therapy.

This is indeed a real Cassandra's work. Analysts of the future will long be astonished by our difficulty in anticipating crises that have been written down, dramas that have been announced, and attacks that have been proclaimed.

Those who did not want to read *Mein Kampf*, those who did not translate the Declaration of War to America, those who did not want to read the terrorist propaganda, those who did not analyze the risk posed by cyberspace without its guidelines, can still be surprised by events. But there are few that could not be predicted.

As the master of criminologists, Sherlock Holmes, reminded us: "When you have eliminated the impossible, whatever remains, however improbable, must be the truth."

This concludes the eleven meetings of the Professors of the Conservatoire National des Arts et Métiers with ALLIANZ within the framework of the New Risks Chair created in 2019 and which continues its journey of enlightenment, exchanges, and dialogues.

The New Risks 2021 annual report will include most of the contributions in the fall of 2021.

Criminology, Facts and Data

Xavier Raufer

ABSTRACT

The article highlights the doctrine of stigmatisation, stating that it is a 'catch-all' concept, which means everything and nothing. Used to explain that there is no such thing as crime, it suggests that there is no such thing as a criminal being, if not just a label. At the heart of the doctrine of minimal intervention, it allows crime and criminals to flourish. It must therefore be countered, and crime control policies put in place to prevent social disorder. Far from discriminating, this measure restores civic rights to the place they need to guarantee social peace. Like stigma, the role of prisons remains controversial, although essential.

Keywords: Criminology, Doctrines, Stigmatization, Social disorder, Prison, Police

Criminología, hechos y datos

RESUMEN

El artículo destaca la doctrina de la estigmatización, afirmando que es un concepto 'cajón de sastre', que significa todo y nada. Usado para explicar que no existe el crimen, sugiere que no existe un ser criminal, sino solo una etiqueta. En el corazón de la doctrina de la intervención mínima, permite que florezcan el crimen y los criminales. Por lo tanto, debe contrarrestarse y establecer políticas de control del delito para prevenir el desorden social. Lejos de discriminar, esta medida devuelve los derechos ciudadanos al lugar que necesitan para garantizar la paz social. Al igual que el estigma, el papel de las prisiones sigue siendo controvertido, aunque esencial.

Palabras clave: Criminología, Doctrinas, Estigmatización, Desorden social, Prisión, Policía

犯罪学、事实和数据

摘要

本文强调了污名化教条，认为其是一个"笼统"的概念，即包含所有却又没有具体的被包含物。被用于解释没有犯罪这

doi: 10.18278/ijc.9.1.2

一概念，其暗示没有罪犯，如果后者不只是一个标签的话。位于最小干预原则的核心，其允许犯罪事件和罪犯的快速发展。因此，其必须被制约，并且需要犯罪管控政策来预防社会混乱。与歧视完全相反的是，该措施将恢复公民在"需确保社会和平的地点"方面的权利。与污名类似的是，监狱发挥的作用仍然具有争议性，尽管其是关键的。

关键词：犯罪学，教条，污名化，社会混乱，监狱，警察

Doctrines and ideas in criminology:

- Stigma,

- Crime and social disorder,

- The prison, "school of crime"?

- "Abolish the police"?

Complements of previous articles or studies:

- The Grey Wolves

- The Aum Shinrikyo sect

Reminder: organized crime and criminal procedure

Texts on crime by Karl Marx, Oscar Wilde, and Friedrich Nietzsche

---

Doctrines and ideas in Criminology

- *"Stigmatization"?* [1]

For a decade now, the media and politicians have had a new key semantic narrative that they use to their heart's content: "stigmatization." But once again, this "caste" is limited to rummaging (via the daily newspaper *Libération*, whose business it is) in the bins of the Californian anarcho-capitalism of the 1960s, where it draws most of its "ideas."

"Social stigmatization": together with "labeling" and the "criminal's stereo-type," one of the three main concepts of the "interactionist" doctrine (interactions

---

1   D. Chapman, "Sociology and the stereotype of the criminal," Tavistock, London, 1968; S. Shoham "The mark of crime," Oceana Publication, 1970; Jean Pinatel, "Le phénomène criminel," MA Éditions, 1987; E. Lemert, "Primary and secondary deviation in delinquency, crime and social process," Harper & Row, NY, 1969.

its author is incarcerated. The inertia between these two moments suggests that prisons continue to fill up when crime decreases—but this illusory phenomenon is only momentary; once the temporal inertia has been caught up, prisons then empty—all the more quickly as they catch up with a temporal gap. Foucault did not see this—or did not want to see it.

- "Abolish the police?" Two concrete cases of what happens then[4]

Since the 19th century, one of the favorite projects of anarchists has been to abolish the police and replace them with social workers. However, this has happened several times in History (strikes, collective arrests, etc.) and the result of this temporary evaporation of the police from the public highway was not exactly what the dreamers, naïve or extremists, had hoped for. Here is a look at two well-known cases in Denmark and Brazil.

DENMARK 1944 - At dawn on September 19, 1944, the German occupation forces set out to arrest all the Danish police, massively committed to resisting German occupation. Out of approximately 10,000 police officers, 1,700 were deported to Germany; three-quarters were hidden by sympathizers or fled to neighboring Sweden. The result, in any case, was that there were no more policemen in (nonetheless peaceful) Denmark. Thefts, rapes, etc.: a raging wave of crime immediately ravaged the country, further aggravated by the exactions of militias of collaborators.

BRAZIL 1997 - Recife, capital of the state of Pernambuco; at that time, 2 million inhabitants. The salary of the ± 18,000 local police officers was then 210 € per month (2021 equivalent); some had not been paid for months. On July 16, 1997, the city's police unanimously decided to go on an illegal strike. In three days, the city's homicide rate *tripled*; no one respected red lights anymore; armed gangs looted shopping centers and drugstores; 8 bank robberies in 48 hours; hospitals were overflowing with wounded people (from knives or firearms). Deployed in haste, the army could not do anything. And when the State agreed to increase the salaries of the police, it took weeks to restore calm.

Addition of previous articles or studies

- "GREY WOLVES"[5] - looking back at two fundamentals

The Turkish-Islamic synthesis

The "Grey Wolves" are the (pre-Islamic) totem of the Turkish nationalist cur-

---

4   *International Herald Tribune* - 24/07/1997 "Crime sweeps Brazil as police strike," *The New York Times* 31/01/1981; "Denmark Nazi-inspired crime wave of 1944." *Journal of criminal law and criminology*, 1972, Vol. 63, Issue 1, "Crime in Denmark, a statistical history."

5   *CEMOTI* - Cahiers d'études sur la Méditerranée orientale et le monde turco-iranien - N°13, 1992 "La droite nationaliste dans les milieux turco-immigrés" - *Hérodote*, 1st quarter 1992, N°64 "Le rêve du Loup Gris : les aspirations turques en Asie centrale. "

rent—Carl Schmitt would say, of the "political theology" expressed by the formula "Türk-Islam-Ülküsü," the "Turkish-Islamic synthesis" (national myth = *ülkü* in Turkish). Those who advocate for this synthesis are the *Ülkücüler*, the idealists. For these so-called Grey Wolves, Islam is thus one (but only one) of the components of the patriotic ideal.

For the "idealists," the Turkish nation is over a thousand years old. Its symbolic birth dates back to the battle of Malazgirt (Manzikert in medieval Greek), won in 1071 by the Turkish leader Alparslan and his cavalry, a prelude to the conquest of then-Byzantine Anatolia, and the ultimate capture of Constantinople in May 1453.

At the time of the guide-founder of their movement, the slogan of the "idealists" was "Our guide, the Quran, our goal Turan,[6] our leader, Türkes." More than a classical Islamism, "Muslim Brotherhood" type,[7] Turkish "idealism" is rather a nationalism with a strong religious dimension.[8] Hence, the double orientation of this current:[9]

- ethnic patriotism with sometimes racist connotations,[10]

- deep distrust, even detestation, of European neighbors (seen as degenerate due to the influence of pornography, drugs, alcohol, and other "vices"); and Arabs.

ETHNIC PATRIOTISM - Pride in being Turkish, loyalty to the Turkish cultural area, to the culture and civilizations of the steppes of Central Asia and Siberia, to the medieval nomadic Turkish empires. The "Turks of the outside" are "brothers of race," "members of the family," and the Turks of Turkey, their "big brother": those of the Silk Road, as far as Chinese Turkestan, the Azeris, Kazakhs, Turks of Greece, Crimea, ex-Yugoslavia, the Caucasus and Turkmens of Iraq only to name a few. A constant demand of the "idealists" is that of the creation of a specific ministry for the Eurasian Turkish diaspora.

ANTI-WESTERN AND ANTI-ARABIC FEELING—distrust and hostility towards the "traitors" in the Middle East who took territory from the Ottomans and handed it over to the Jews. Like "Islam is too precious to be entrusted to Bedouins," a thinly veiled demand for the return to Istanbul of a new caliphate. The "ideal"

---

6   *Turan*: the original settlement area of the then nomadic Turks, in the steppes of Central Asia; what we more or less call today the "stans."

7   Represented in Turkey by the Milli Gorüs current or by the Refah Partisi, ancestor of the present AK Partisi, of President R. T. Erdogan.

8   Clearly distinct from the origin of Atatürk's patriotism: in 1944, Alparslan Türkes, then an army officer, was thus tried for "racism. "

9   Abundantly defended and illustrated by the nationalist daily *Türkiye* (Turkey), circulation ± 150 000 copies, close to the "idealist" theses.

10 We take this term here in its strict sense: belief in the superiority of one race over another (s); not in the media sense, a simple insult intended to disqualify any opponent.

Great National-Islamic Turkey would be destined to protect the Muslim world from the Christian West, from Zionism, from idolatrous India and other imperialisms—starting with Armenia, the "new Christian Israel."

For the Grey Wolves, Islam strengthens Turkey, which must thus be the fortress and shield of the faith—from there to asserting Turkish supremacy over the Islamic *ummah*, it is not far. Let's listen to Alparslan Türkes, founder and leader of the National Movement Party (MHP), the political-identity expression of the "idealist" current: "Islam and Turkish nationalism are inseparable . . . Our nation is the sword, shield and armor of Islam. The non-Muslim Turkish societies and those who have abandoned Islam have been annihilated. But the Turkish societies that remained faithful to Islam were able to protect themselves and continue to live."

Grey Wolves in Europe

Noticeable in Germany, in Belgium, and in the Netherlands, the "idealist" movement of Europe is discrete, even hidden everywhere else, notably in France. In a strict and disciplined atmosphere, the "idealists" animate a crowd of small cultural, friendly, family, mutual aid or sports structures, frequenting common premises, associative tearooms, etc. Outside of these places, there are no distinctive signs of the Grey Wolves, neither posters nor banners. The rooms rented to municipalities or parishes are rented by anodyne and apolitical associations.

The people who frequent these places and events tend to be modest and conservative immigrants from the underprivileged, rural Anatolia. In the three above-mentioned countries, important political or electoral meetings (sometimes gathering thousands of participants) are organized during elections, around MHP leaders; in normal times, we have rather concerts of "idealistic singers." Since the formation of the AKP-MHP coalition in Turkey, this "idealistic" associative nebula serves quite efficiently as a transmission belt to the power of Ankara.

THE AUM SECT[11]— New developments

On March 20, 1995, members of the (initially Buddhist) Aum Shinrikyo sect released deadly sarin poison gas in the Tokyo subway. Not having been able to manufacture an effective aerosol, the fanatics brought this liquid gas (visually similar to lighters) in a plastic bag, punctured with the end of an umbrella. This technical shortcoming limited the tally to 12 victims (at the point of spraying) and about 5,000 wounded; those who fled in panic from the epicenter of the attack carried sarin under their soles, poisoning passers-by in the subway corridors.[12]

---

11 *The Sun* - 23/05/2020 "Japanese cult bought 1 million acres of land in Australia outback to test nerve agent on sheep before poisoning commuters."

12 At the time, Japanese National Police officials told the author that an effective aerosol can, which propelled the deadly sarin gas into the air ducts of the Tokyo subway, would have killed 50,000 passengers.

Chizuo Matsumoto (known as Guru Shoko Asahara executed in Tokyo in July 2018) founded the "Supreme Truth" (Aum Shinrikyo) cult in 1984. At its peak, this cult has tens of thousands of followers—not all of them very mentally stable: they buy US$ 300 a bottle of the Guru's bath water to "spiritually strengthen" themselves. Ever more delirious, Asahara declared himself in 2012 the "new Christ" and "Lamb of God." From then on, his public preaching hides a secret project: to start a third world war, nuclear of course, after which only his followers will survive. A rather classic goal: it was more or less the same as that of Charles Manson to perpetrate his massacre in August 1969, 26 years earlier.

But how to start this 3rd World War? By causing a huge disaster in the Tokyo subway, which (Asahara's sick brain imagines) will trigger a military escalation, then war. All this is known, but recently declassified information (in Australia) reveals more about the preparations for the attack.

In April 1993, two Aum executives, Kiyohide Hayakawa and Yoshihiro Inoue, bought an abandoned property in the middle of the Australian Outback, a 14-hour drive north-east of Perth. Named Banjawarn, the property is absolutely isolated: Kalgoorlie (a mining city of 30,000 inhabitants), and the nearest inhabited place, is 350 km away. In September 1993, Asahara arrived in Perth with 25 followers, all Japanese, including 7 underage girls. The Australian customs were surprised by his large luggage, including strange bottles of "liquid soap," laboratory equipment, etc.

Installed in the property, the group sets up a complete chemical laboratory there; after which it returns in majority to Japan. In August 1994, Asahara sold his property at a loss; seven months later, he was attacked. The investigation then established that sheep in Banjawarn had been poisoned with sarin gas, a preliminary test before the act.

REMINDER - Organized Crime and Criminal Procedure

We often talk about organized crime, without fully knowing its scope in French criminal law; hence this reminder of what criminal procedure includes in this concept.

Légifrance - Code de procédure pénale - ORGANIZED CRIME OFFENCES

TITLE XXV - Criminal procedure applicable to organized crime and delinquency

Article 706-73 - Amended by LAW N°2017-1510 of October 30, 2017 - art.9

The procedure applicable to the investigation, prosecution, trial, and adjudication of the following crimes and misdemeanors shall be as provided in this code, subject to the provisions of this title:

1° Crime of **murder** committed in an organized gang as provided for in article 221-4 of the penal code;

2° Crime of **torture and acts of barbarism** committed in an organized gang as provided for in Article 222-4 of the penal code;

3° Crimes and offences of **drug trafficking** provided for by articles 222-34 to 222-40 of the penal code;

4° Crimes and offenses **of kidnapping and sequestration** committed in an organized gang as provided for in article 224-5-2 of the penal code;

5° Aggravated crimes and offences of **trafficking in human beings** provided for in articles 225-4 to 225-4-7 of the Criminal code;

6° Aggravated crimes and offences of **pimping** provided for in articles 225-7 to 225-12 of the penal code;

7° Crime of **theft committed in an organized gang**, provided for in article 311-9 of the penal code;

8° Aggravated crimes **of extortion** provided for in articles 312-6 and 312-7 of the penal code;

9° Crime of **destruction, degradation and deterioration of property** committed in an organized gang, provided for by article 322-8 of the penal code;

10° Crimes of **counterfeit money** provided for in articles 442-1 and 442-2 of the penal code;

11° Crimes and offences constituting acts of **terrorism** provided for in articles 421-1 to 421-6 of the penal code;

11° bis Crimes **against the fundamental interests of the nation** provided for in Title 1 of Book IV of the Criminal code;

> 12° ... 13°... 14° ... 15° ... 16° (various **offenses**: in matters of weapons and explosives, provided for in various codes; ... aiding the illegal entry, movement and residence of a foreigner in France, in an organized gang; ... money laundering or concealment of the products, income and things provided for in the preceding articles 1 to 13; ... criminal association, in the case of preparation of one of the above-mentioned offenses; ... non-justification of resources coming from the above-mentioned offenses) ;

17° Crime of **hijacking of aircraft**, ship or any other means of transport committed in an organized gang, as provided for in Article 224-6-1 of the criminal code;

18° Crimes and offenses punishable by ten years' imprisonment, contributing to the **proliferation of weapons of mass destruction** and their means of delivery falling within the scope of Article 706-167;

19° Offence **of exploitation of a mine** or disposal of a mining substance without an exploitation title or authorization, accompanied by environmental damage, committed in an organized gang, as provided for by Article L. 512-2 of the Mining Code, when it is related to one of the offences mentioned in 1° to 17° of this article.

Great texts on crime

- KARL MARX "In Praise of Crime"

Excerpt from Volume 4 of *Capital* "The theories of surplus value."

("In praise of crime" is of course ironic, bordering on pastiche, even self-mockery)

"The philosopher produces ideas, the poet poems, the clergyman sermons, the professor treatises . . . The criminal produces crimes. To look more closely at the relations existing between this last branch of production and the society as a whole, frees from many prejudices. The criminal does not only produce crimes: he produces the criminal law, therefore the professor of criminal law, and therefore the inevitable treatise in which the professor records his lectures, put on the market as "merchandise."" The result is an increase in national wealth, not to mention the inner satisfaction that, according to Professor Roscher, an authorized witness, the manuscript of the treatise gives its author.

More: the criminal produces the whole police and judicial apparatus; police officers, judges, executioners, jurors, etc., and all these various professions, forming so many categories of the social division of labor, develop various faculties of the human mind and create at the same time new needs and new means to satisfy them. Torture alone has given rise to the most ingenious mechanical discoveries, the production of which provides work for many honest craftsmen.

The criminal creates a sensation that participates in the moral and the tragic, and in doing so he provides a "service" by stirring the moral and aesthetic feelings of the public. It does not only give rise to treatises on criminal law, criminal codes and, therefore, criminal law legislators; but also, to art, belles-lettres, even tragedies; witness not only Müllner's *La Faute* and Schiller's *Les Brigands* but also *Oedipus* and *Richard III*. The criminal breaks the monotony and the daily security of bourgeois life, thus shielding it from stagnation and creating that incessant tension and agitation without which the spur of competition itself would dull. It thus stimulates the productive forces.

At the same time that crime removes a surplus part of the population from the labor market, and thus reduces competition between workers, helping to prevent wages from falling below the minimum, the fight against crime absorbs another part of this same population. Thus, the criminal operates one of those "natural compensations" which create equilibrium and give rise to a multitude of "useful" occupations. The influence of criminals on the development of the productive forces can be demonstrated in detail: without thieves, would locks have reached their present stage of perfection? Without counterfeiters, the manufacture of banknotes? Without fraudsters, would the microscope have penetrated the spheres of ordinary commerce? Does not applied chemistry owe as much to fraud and its repression as to legitimate efforts to improve production?

- OSCAR WILDE: a classic of angelism and the "culture of apology"

The soul of man under socialism, Avatar Publishing, 1990

"When one reads history, not in redacted versions written for schoolchildren and diploma candidates, but in texts established by the authorities of each era, one is sickened, not by the account of the crimes committed by the wicked, but by that of the punishments inflicted by the good; and a community is a thousand times more bruised by the habitual use of punishment than by the accidental presence of crime. It is obvious that the more punishment is inflicted, the more crime is created; and most contemporary legislators have understood this so well that they have made it their duty to reduce punishment to the extent that they think they can. Wherever the penal system has been really softened, the results have been excellent. The less punishment there is, the less crime there is.

When there is no punishment at all, either crime will cease to exist, or, if it occurs, it will be treated by doctors as a distressing form of insanity, which they will try to cure by care and kindness. For those whom we call criminals today are not criminals at all. Misery, not perversity, is the mother of contemporary crime. This is in fact the reason why our criminals, as a category, are absolutely psychologically devoid of interest. They are not wonderful Macbeths, and terrible Vautrins.

They are only what respectable ordinary people would become if they did not have enough to eat. When private property has been abolished, crime will no longer be necessary, it will no longer have a reason to exist; it will cease to exist. Of course, not all crimes are aimed at property, although it is these crimes that English law, attributing more value to a man's possessions than to that man himself, punishes most severely and horribly (if we except homicide and judge death worse than penal servitude—a point of view which our criminals, I think, do not share).

But although some crimes may not be directed against property, they may arise from a state of unhappiness, rage, depression, engendered by our bad system of property distribution; so, when that system is abolished, these crimes will disappear."

- FRIEDRICH NIETZSCHE: "Progress" and Crime

Beyond Good and Evil (1886) On the Natural History of Morality

"Finally, in periods of long and deep peace, there is always less opportunity and less obligation to train one's feelings to severity and harshness; from then on, this severity, even in justice, begins to bother consciences; one is almost offended by the haughty and hard aristocrat who claims responsibility for himself and his actions, he awakens distrust; the lamb and even more so the bleating sheep gain in consideration. There is a point in history of sickly softening and decay where society goes so far as to take sides, seriously and sincerely, for the one who wrongs it, for the criminal.

Punishment seems unfair to her—at the very least, the idea of punishment and the obligation to punish makes her suffer and frightens her. 'Is it not enough to put him out of action? What is the point of punishing him on top of that? To punish is terrible!' Thus, the morality of the herd, the morality of fear, draws its last consequences. Supposing that we could abolish the danger, the reason to fear, we would have abolished this morality: it would not be necessary anymore. It would no longer consider itself necessary. If we examine the conscience of the modern European, it is always the same imperative that we will flush out from the thousand folds and recesses of morality, the imperative of the fear of the herd: we want that one day there will finally be nothing more to fear. One day, one beautiful day—the will and the path that lead to it, that is what is called "progress" everywhere in Europe today."

International Journal on Criminology • Volume 9, Number 1 • Winter 2022

Cryptocurrency and National Security

Carolyn Alfieri

Abstract

The article takes cryptocurrency as an example of how criminals and terrorist groups seek to weaken national security. The decentralized nature of virtual currency along with the lack of regulations foster clandestine operations and illegal activities. Illegal business on dark net marketplaces as well as money laundering can thus be conducted far from law enforcement. Cryptocurrency also serve terrorism financing with the examples of Hamas, al-Qaeda, and ISIS. After analyzing US policy on the matter, this article offers recommendations. Adapting legislation to technological developments appears essential to take back control of cyberspace.

Keywords: Cryptocurrency, National Security, Cyberspace, Financial Crime, Terrorism

Las criptomonedas y la seguridad nacional

Resumen

El artículo toma las criptomonedas como ejemplo de cómo los delincuentes y grupos terroristas buscan debilitar la seguridad nacional. La naturaleza descentralizada de la moneda virtual, junto con la falta de regulaciones, fomentan operaciones clandestinas y actividades ilegales. Los negocios ilegales en los mercados de la red oscura, así como el lavado de dinero, pueden realizarse lejos de la aplicación de la ley. Las criptomonedas también sirven para financiar el terrorismo con los ejemplos de Hamas, al-Qaeda e ISIS. Luego de analizar la política estadounidense al respecto, este artículo ofrece recomendaciones. Adaptar la legislación a los avances tecnológicos parece fundamental para recuperar el control del ciberespacio.

Palabras clave: Criptomoneda, Seguridad Nacional, Ciberespacio, Delitos Financieros, Terrorismo

 doi: 10.18278/ijc.9.1.3

加密货币与国家安全

摘要

本文以加密货币为例，展示罪犯和恐怖主义集团如何试图削弱国家安全。虚拟货币的去中心化性质以及相关监管的缺乏为秘密行动和非法活动创造适宜条件。暗网上的非法交易和洗钱因此能在远离执法的情况下进行。加密货币还为哈马斯、基地组织和伊斯兰国等提供恐怖主义融资。本文分析了美国在该事务上的政策，并提供了相关建议。将法律适应于技术开发一事似乎对夺回网络空间控制权而言至关重要。

关键词：加密货币，国家安全，网络空间，金融犯罪，恐怖主义

Introduction

In recent years, cryptocurrency has emerged as a unique national security challenge with its increasing popularity and profitability around the world. Cryptocurrency attracts technological innovators and investors, as it becomes more mainstream and integrated into the legitimate economy. However, cryptocurrency also appeals to illicit actors, such as criminals and terrorist groups who seek to weaken national security and operate within cyberspace to evade law enforcement. Cryptocurrency offers these malicious groups an opportunity to generate revenue from illegal activities and fund their operations in an increasingly clandestine manner. The decentralized nature of virtual currency makes it easier for bad actors to engage in crime without the regulations or detection mechanisms of the traditional banking system. In addition, the ability to conduct financial transactions anonymously or pseudo-anonymously provide enhanced privacy to virtual illicit activities.[1] These two key factors aid criminals and terrorists in conducting illegal operations and undermining national security through the use of cryptocurrency.

The recent popularity, increasing profitability, and growing acceptance of cryptocurrency across different legitimate sectors forces policymakers to address the illegitimate uses of digital currency. This paper will analyze how cryptocurrency has a significant and growing use in different areas of crime and terrorism. By examining U.S. policy towards cryptocurrency, we can better understand how the U.S. should address digital currency as a national security concern, as well as identify challenges to implementing policy. As the threat landscape continues to evolve due to expanding technological innovations in cyberspace, cryptocurrency poses a unique national security threat because of its role in ransomware attacks, illicit activities, and terrorism financing.

Background

Cryptocurrency is a decentralized form of digital currency, meaning that no institution or organization controls or regulates it. The peer-to-peer exchanges are logged in the blockchain, which cryptocurrency expert, Dr. Diana Dolliver, referred to as the encrypted foundation where cryptocurrency exists.[2] The blockchain is a public ledger that records and maintains a history of cryptocurrency transactions. However, the publication, "Fistful of Bitcoins: Characterizing Payments Among Men with No Names," explains that while the blockchain is public, the records are based on the pseudonyms of the users.[3] Real-life identities are not necessary to conduct crypto transactions, allowing users to protect their privacy behind one, or sometimes, multiple pseudonyms with ease. The use of digital wallets also allows users to maintain their privacy, as well as their own crypto.

Digital wallets are a type of software that allows users to store their cryptocurrency. Each user has a wallet address that provides them with pseudo-anonymity.[4] The types of wallets range from hardware to mobile apps, or even a simple piece of paper with a QR code. Some of the mobile apps used to store crypto, such as Coinbase or Binance, also function as an exchange platform, which allows users to buy and sell virtual currencies.[5] As one of the most popular exchanges, Coinbase has an estimated 43 million users and traded over $455 billion dollars of volume.[6] With over 5,500 different cryptocurrencies in existence, licit users can invest in cryptocurrency as a financial asset or use it as a means to purchase legitimate commodities.

Many users choose to invest in cryptocurrency, as its profitability and value have skyrocketed despite its volatility. For example, at the end of 2017, one Bitcoin was valued at around $17,400.[7] One year later, it was worth about $3,212. In March of 2020, Bitcoin garnered attention in the financial sector as its value exceeded $57,000.[8] Months later, the cryptocurrency's value dropped to around $35,000.[9] Unlike fiat money, which is government-issued and regulated, the value of virtual currencies is not in the amount one has. Instead, the value is determined by how much consumers are willing to pay for cryptocurrency using fiat money.[10]

Cryptocurrency can also be used to purchase goods, the same way that much of society uses fiat money. Its increasing popularity appears to be leading to a more mainstream acceptance of its uses. Today, a growing number of companies are creating and improving systems to allow payments using crypto, typically Bitcoin.[11] For example, in June 2020, Mastercard announced its partnership with Bitpay, a bitcoin payment platform in creating a debit card tied to cryptocurrency that could be used at thousands of vendors around the world.[12] Mastercard explained the reasoning for this new debit card was due to the increasing interest and investments in crypto, and that in some countries, up to 20% of the population owns cryptocurrency.[13] In addition, Microsoft, AT&T, and Home Depot are among the major companies working towards or currently implementing Bitcoin payment systems. This trend will likely continue if the popularity of cryptocurrency continues its current trajectory.

The primary properties of cryptocurrency attract both good and bad actors. Decentralized currencies are not subject to inflation, exchange rates, or international transaction fees because there is no central authority. Also, an absence of regulation means that users are not required to provide information about their identities, which is appealing to those who highly value privacy. Different types of cryptocurrencies have varying levels of anonymity. For example, the two most popular cryptocurrencies, Bitcoin and Ethereum, are nearly pseudo-anonymous.[14] According to the Council on Foreign Relations, this means that while the blockchain does not document names or real addresses, if a wallet's owner is identified, the transactions can be tied back to the user.[15] Other cryptos, such as Monero and Zcash have enhanced security to protect the privacy of users and increase anonymity. While it is not completely impossible to trace a crypto transaction to the user, these layers of privacy protection make it increasingly challenging.[16] Chainalysis's "The 2021 Crypto Crime Report" states that cryptocurrency is attractive to criminals because of its pseudo-anonymity and the ability to transfer money around the world with ease.[17] Although bad actors make up a small portion of crypto transactions, cryptocurrency plays a role in criminal activities that undermine national security.

Cryptocurrency and Ransomware

Ransomware is a type of cyberattack that allows malicious actors to encrypt data and computer systems until the victim pays the ransom for decryption. Ransomware threatens public and private networks around the world and can result in "data loss, privacy concerns, and cost billions of dollars a year," according to the U.S. Cybersecurity and Infrastructure Security Agency (CISA).[18] When ransomware first emerged, hackers would demand money via online cash payment systems. However, this placed a constraint on ransomware hackers who could only conduct these attacks in locations where the cash payment systems were available.[19] For this reason, hackers turned to cryptocurrency, as it offered a way around this limitation. CISA advises ransomware victims against paying the ransom because it funds cybercriminals and incentivizes further ransomware attacks.[20] However, the cost of the ransom is frequently less expensive than the cost of redeveloping systems and data. Therefore, malicious actors often profit off of ransomware attacks, as statistics from the past few years demonstrate.

A number of research reports examining the link between cryptocurrency and ransomware conclude that the use of crypto in this type of cyberattack is becoming more frequent. It also provides malicious actors with an opportunity to generate a significant amount of revenue. The 2018 academic article "Tracking

Ransomware End-to-End" studied the broader structure of ransomware attacks over a two-year period. It was estimated that from 2015-2017, hackers extorted over $16 million from about 20,000 ransomware victims.[21] After hackers receive payments via cryptocurrency, they were able to cash out through a crypto exchange for fiat currency. To further hide their identities, some hackers deposited their funds into "mixers," which are services that disguise the source of crypto by mixing the transaction pathways with other transactions from different origins.[22]

Chainalysis's crime report explains how ransomware had a higher growth rate in 2020 than every other category of crypto-related crime, including dark net marketplaces and scams.[23] The total amount that ransomware victims paid "increased by 311% . . . to reach nearly $350 million worth of cryptocurrency."[24] This is partially due to the COVID-19 pandemic as people around the world migrated to telework and distance learning. Ransomware attacks provide malicious actors, including state-sponsored hackers and cybercriminals, with the opportunity to generate profits through the extortion of victims for cryptocurrency.[25]

The Democratic People's Republic of Korea (DPRK) utilizes ransomware attacks and other cybercrimes as a means to steal money. The *New Yorker* article, "The Incredible Rise of North Korea's Hacking Army," explains the growing cyber threat from the isolated country. North Korea is the only nation in the world that executes hacking operations and cybercrimes for the sole purpose of earning revenue.[26] Ironically, less than 1% of North Korean citizens have access to the internet, yet the government has recruited and trained some of the best hackers in the world.[27] Kim Jong Un believes that advanced cyber capabilities are essential for a strong defense arsenal. He even stated that cyber capabilities are an "all-purpose sword that guarantees the North Korean People's Armed Forces ruthless striking capability, along with nuclear weapons and missiles."[28]

North Korea's military intelligence agency, the Reconnaissance General Bureau (RGB), is trained to conduct a variety of cybercrimes, including ransomware attacks and the theft of cryptocurrency from exchanges. In 2017, North Korean hackers carried out the WannaCry 2.0 ransomware attack that impacted 200,000 victims in 150 countries, demonstrating North Korea as a true cyber threat.[29] WannaCry 2.0 impacted several industries around the world, including Boeing, the National Health Service in Britain, and Germany's railways.[30] The hackers exploited a vulnerability in the WindowsXP operating system and demanded $300 worth of cryptocurrency to unlock the system. Overall, about $143,000 in Bitcoin was paid to the hackers.[31]

In February 2021, three North Korean hackers were indicted by the U.S. District Court in Los Angeles in connection to the WannaCry 2.0 ransomware incident. The three hackers were also indicted for a range of other cybercrimes related to cryptocurrency, such as the "creation and deployment of malicious cryptocurrency applications" and "targeting of cryptocurrency and theft of cryptocurrency" from a number of companies.[32] Theft of crypto exchanges is the most dependable source of income for the country.[33] In 2017, the hackers stole $75 million from a Slovenian cryptocurrency company and in 2018, stole $24.9 million from an Indonesian cryptocurrency company.[34] In total, theft from crypto exchanges have earned North Korea an estimated $1.75 billion in digital currency.[35] This alone could pay for about 10% of North Korea's defense budget.[36] In addition, a United Nations report claims that the $2 billion generated from North Korea's cybercrime activities was allocated to its weapons of mass destruction program to enhance its nuclear capabilities.[37] This demonstrates how state-sponsored crypto-related crime undermines national security by worsening existing security threats. Ransomware hackers can also weaken the security of critical infrastructure.

Ransomware incidents targeting critical infrastructure have increased in recent years, however the identities and state-alliances of these hackers are often unknown. The potential for high rewards incentivizes criminals to engage in this relatively low risk illicit cyber activity. For example, in 2019 hackers locked the municipal computer systems of Lake City, Florida and demanded around $460,000 worth of Bitcoin to release them.[38] The attack, which froze the email accounts of city workers and hindered the ability for residents to pay their bills online, forced the city to send a Bitcoin payment to an anonymous wallet. This type of attack on municipalities is not uncommon. In 2019, hackers targeted the municipal computer networks of Atlanta, Baltimore, Albany, and smaller towns in Florida, Georgia, and Massachusetts.[39] Although U.S. federal agencies urge victims not to pay the ransom so as not to provide incentives for future hackers, recovery efforts frequently cost significantly more than the initial demand. In Atlanta, hackers demanded $51,000 in cryptocurrency for the decryption of its files. Although the city refused to pay the ransom, reconstruction efforts totaled an estimated $17 million.[40] Baltimore faced a similar situation when the refusal to pay a $76,000 ransom cost the city over $18 million by the end of its recovery.[41] While ransomware attacks have been on the rise, 2020 saw an especially high number of incidents partially due to the COVID-19 pandemic and the migration to telework and distance learning.

The dramatic shift in the reliance on virtual private networks and online systems left data and computer networks vulnerable to exploitation by malicious actors. According to Chainalysis, this is demonstrated in the 60% increase in the average ransom payment between the first quarter and the second quarter of 2020. During the second quarter, the average ransom payment increased from $111,605 to $178,254.[42, 43] The education and healthcare sectors were particularly vulnerable, as hackers capitalized on society's desperate reliance for school systems and healthcare facilities to operate effectively. For this reason, there was greater opportunity in these two areas for cybercriminals to maximize their revenue.

Recently, ransomware attackers have targeted other essential sectors in the U.S. In May 2021, the cybercrime group, DarkSide, executed a ransomware attack against Colonial Pipeline, a major U.S. pipeline operator.[44] The attack shut down the company's computer systems and led to gasoline price hikes, panic buying, and fuel shortages along the East Coast.[45] To resume its stalled operations, the pipeline company paid the hackers about 75 Bitcoin, which at the time valued almost $5 million.[46] Since the attack, U.S. investigators tracked a number of electronic transactions linked to DarkSide and were able to seize around $2.3 million worth of Bitcoin from the hackers.[47] A *New York Times* article explains how the Eastern European cybercrime group has potential links to Russia, as DarkSide provides ransomware services and earn a portion of the extorted profits.[48] DarkSide's possible connection to Russia grants the Russian government "a layer of plausible deniability" regarding cyberattacks, such as the Colonial Pipeline incident, while also providing protection to cybercriminals.[49]

Weeks after the ransomware attack on Colonial Pipeline, JBS, the world's largest meat processor, was also impacted by a cyberattack, demonstrating another recent case of ransomware disrupting the supply and production chains of vital U.S. commodities.[50] The attack targeting JBS, which processes about one-fifth of the U.S.'s meat supply, forced a temporary shutdown of all nine of JBS's beef plants located in the U.S. The shutdown led to production changes for its poultry and pork plants, as well as canceled shifts for around 2,500 employees.[51] To prevent further price spikes and meat shortages, JBS paid a ransom of $11 million in Bitcoin.[52] Similar to the ransomware attack on Colonial Pipeline, there are suspicions that the unnamed cybercriminal group had connections to Russia. White House Deputy Press Secretary, Karine Jean-Pierre, stated that the ransom originated from "a criminal organization likely based in Russia."[53] These two cases show how cybercriminals with potential nation-state connections can generate cryptocurrency through extorting important U.S. industries.

The use of cryptocurrency in ransomware attacks provide state and non-state cybercriminals an additional layer of anonymity as it is extremely difficult to identify the actors and track payments. In addition to the expense of recovery efforts, cryptocurrency's role in ransomware attacks weakens the security of essential infrastructure. As COVID-19 forced large populations to work and learn from home, the education and healthcare sectors experienced tremendous stress. In addition, recent ransomware attacks demonstrate how cybercriminals are willing to disrupt the supply and production chains of vital U.S. commodities. The pressure to function efficiently and continuously makes these sectors attractive, and potentially profitable targets for ransomware attacks. The possible connections to Russia in the Colonial Pipeline and JBS ransomware attacks exemplify how a U.S. adversary can use cybercriminals to its advantage to extort critical industries for cryptocurrency and weaken U.S. security. On a larger scale, the North Korean case demonstrates how state-sponsored hackers can utilize ransomware and cryptocurrency to fund the DPRK's nuclear program. This not only severely undermines U.S. national security, but the security of nations around the world.

Cyrptocurrency and Illicit Activity

There is a considerable amount of debate surrounding the scale of cryptocurrency's involvement in criminal activity. A *New York Times* article explains that although only 1% of Bitcoin transactions is linked to crime, there are a few concerning trends.[54] First, while 1% is an extremely small portion of transactions, this is actually an increase from the previous year, indicating a growing criminal use of Bitcoin. Second, the amount of criminal activity linked to Bitcoin remains relatively unchanged by fluctuations in value.[55] This means that despite Bitcoin's volatility, criminals continue to use it. Additionally, the anonymity provided by both cryptocurrency and the dark net makes it extremely challenging to estimate how much cryptocurrency is connected to illicit activity compared to its overall usage. Criminals use crypto to their advantage in the illegal drug trade on dark net marketplaces and to launder money due to the lack of oversight and regulations. The use of cryptocurrency in various illicit activities undermines the broader threat landscape by facilitating and expanding transnational crime.

The Illegal Drug Trade

Criminal activity on the dark net is able to stay out of the public eye with unique software, such as Tor. According to Mark Goodman, Tor is the "closest thing to actual anonymity on the internet." [56] Tor reroutes web connections through thousands of computer servers to disguise the origin and destination of the web traffic, preventing anyone, including law enforcement, from tracing the web traffic back to the user.[57] Tor and other anonymizing software make it possible for criminals to access dark net marketplaces with a lesser risk of detection and identification. Similarly, when marketplaces use this software, their site is only accessible to those who also use it. The use of cryptocurrency, combined with Tor, further protects the identities of the criminals engaged in the buying and selling of illicit goods.

Dark net marketplaces, also referred to as cryptomarkets, are primary examples of the intersection between cryptocurrency and illicit activity. These illegitimate marketplaces provide an opportunity for criminals to buy and sell an extraordinary supply and range of unlawful products. Buyers can find an extremely wide variety of weapons, explosives, illegal wildlife parts, child pornography, hitmen, cybercrime products, and much more.[58] In particular, drug sales have had tremendous success on dark net marketplaces. The first major dark net marketplace, Silk Road, elevated the drug trade and the use of cryptocurrency to a higher level of transnational crime.

Silk Road was founded in 2011 by 29-year-old Ross Ulbricht, who operated under the pseudonym "Dread Pirate Roberts."[59] While the site sold almost every illicit product imaginable, it was most well-known for its sale of illegal drugs. Marijuana was the most popular drug on Silk Road, with transactions worth over $46 million.[60] Cocaine accounted for 82,582 transactions amounting to $17.4 million.[61] Heroin followed marijuana and cocaine with sales worth an estimated $8.9 million.[62] The combined sales of other popular drugs including meth, LSD, ecstasy, and narcotics, such as oxycodone and fentanyl, generated an estimated $19.2 million.

Silk Road was the largest online criminal marketplace for the two and a half years that it operated. During its lifetime, Silk Road brought in approximately 9.5 million Bitcoin in revenue.[63] The site intentionally only accepted Bitcoin as payment. The combination of Bitcoin and Tor software was purposely designed to hide the site from law enforcement and align with Ulbricht's libertarian beliefs. A Department of Justice press release states that the use of cryptocurrency "served to facilitate the illegal commerce conducted on the site, including by concealing the identities and locations of users transmitting and receiving funds through the site."[64] Ulbricht earned an estimated $13 million through the illicit sales until the FBI seized the site in 2013.[65] Ulbricht was arrested and convicted of seven offenses, including distributing narcotics by means of the Internet, engaging in a continuing criminal enterprise, and conspiring to commit money laundering. Ulbricht was sentenced to life in prison.[66] Unfortunately, Silk Road was only the beginning of the rise in dark net marketplaces.

Other dark net marketplaces quickly emerged to fill the void left by Silk Road. Silk Road 2.0 was developed about 5 weeks after Silk Road's takedown and was essentially identical to the first version. Similar to its predecessor, the site consisted overwhelmingly of drug listings. The site operated for about one year and brought in around $8 million a month in illicit sales until the FBI shut down the site.[67] While Silk Road was the first marketplace of its kind, AlphaBay surpassed Silk Road as the largest dark net marketplace for drugs. AlphaBay was about 20 times larger than Silk Road, with approximately 350,000 listings for illicit goods and services.[68] Shortly prior to its shutdown, AlphaBay had over 21,000 listings for opioids and more than 4,100 for fentanyl and similar substances.[69] Law enforcement seized AlphaBay in the summer of 2017. In the time that AlphaBay operated, the site conducted transactions worth over $1 billion in Bitcoin and other forms of digital currency.[70]

Dark net marketplaces have given users easy access to the buying and selling of unlawful products. Law enforcement has seen a significant increase in drug-related overdoses since the existence of these marketplaces. According to a *New York Times* article on the U.S. opioid crisis, the sale of drugs via the internet, including over dark net marketplaces, has greatly increased the accessibility of illegal substances, such as fentanyl and other potent synthetic opioids.[71] Not only is the increased volume of distribution a major challenge for law enforcement, but the role of cryptocurrency hinders efforts to combat the illegal drug trade. The use of cryptocurrency on these marketplaces is a tactical strategy to protect the identities of those engaged in illicit activities. Countless dark net marketplaces emerge faster than law enforcement can shut them down. In addition, cryptocurrency's role in conducting unlawful transactions presents another significant challenge for law enforcement, as it already struggles to address criminal activity on the dark net.

Money Laundering

There are a number of instances of Silk Road users laundering hundreds of millions of dollars generated from illicit activities through cryptocurrency.[72] One example involves 60-year-old Hugh Haney. Haney was a member of a collection of drug vendors on Silk Road who engaged in the large-scale trafficking of narcotics, including OxyContin, heroin, and fentanyl.[73, 74] Silk Road's payment system functioned in a manner where each user had to have a Bitcoin account internal to the site to conduct transactions.[75] Vendors could then transfer profits from their Silk Road Bitcoin address to their personal Bitcoin address once transactions were complete. This allowed Haney to launder his illegal drug profits with cryptocurrency.

According to a Department of Justice press release, Haney transferred his Silk Road Bitcoin profits to an account with a cryptocurrency exchange.[76] Through the exchange, Haney converted the Bitcoin to cash and falsely asserted that the Bitcoin came from his own crypto mining activity. In total, Haney laundered an estimated $19 million with cryptocurrency from his Silk Road drug transactions.[77] In 2020, Haney was sentenced to three and a half years in prison for money laundering charges.[78] Cryptocurrency-based money laundering is not uncommon and criminals outside of dark net marketplaces also engage in this illicit activity.

Organized crime groups use cryptocurrency to launder their criminal profits. For example, a 2020 *Reuters* article explains how cryptocurrency-based money laundering is increasing among Latin American drug cartels. The article states that smuggling drug profits to cartels is the "only thing tougher than smuggling drugs."[79] Large amounts of cash are difficult to transport due to the weight of the bulk. It also increases the risk of detection when moving money internationally due to the regulations of financial institutions.

The head of Mexico's financial ministry's financial intelligence unit, Santiago Nieto, explained how these criminals usually deposit small amounts of illicit profits into several bank accounts to minimize the risk of raising red flags.[80] Then, they use the money in these accounts to purchase small amounts of Bitcoin. Purchasing Bitcoin makes it even more difficult to track the illicit funds while making it easier for these crime groups to send money internationally throughout their networks. According to the Drug Enforcement Administration (DEA), the number of cash seizures decreased over the past few years. In 2011, cash seizures totaled $741 million but fell to $234 million in 2018.[81] The DEA partly attributes this decrease to cryptocurrency-based money laundering. It is expected that cartels and other transnational criminal organizations will increasingly use cryptocurrency to launder illicit profits.[82]

Cryptocurrency's involvement in illicit activities, including the selling and purchasing of drugs on the dark net, and as a means to conduct money laundering, undermines national security as well as the security of communities. Modernizing the drug trade via dark net marketplaces can have devastating effects far beyond the transaction between the buyer and seller. Although the same argument could be made for drug transactions involving cash, the use of cryptocurrency on dark net marketplaces allows for the transport of significantly more volume at a much lesser risk. For example, about 20% of drug users in the U.S. purchased narcotics on Silk Road when the site was at its peak, demonstrating the prevalence of purchasing drugs via Silk Road.[83] Cryptocurrency makes it increasingly difficult for law enforcement to counter the rapid and large-scale movement of drugs, while criminals are able to expand their networks and send money internationally with ease and little risk.

Chainalysis calls money laundering the "key to cryptocurrency-based crime."[84] Cryptocurrency-based money laundering undermines national security, as it gives criminals the opportunity to generate funding, hide its sources, and operate outside of regulatory authorities. Money laundering, whether through more traditional channels or through crypto, helps keep criminals in business by ensuring financial stability and the ability to reinvest their "clean" funds to continuously expand their profits, networks, and operations. Cryptocurrency adds additional layers of anonymity to money laundering and makes it easier for criminals to hide capital around the world while evading law enforcement. Cryptocurrency-based money laundering also undermines the legitimate economy, banking systems, borders, and the rule of law. The benefits of using cryptocurrency for illicit activities, such as purchasing drugs on the dark net and money laundering, suggests that criminal groups will continue using crypto to their advantage.

Cryptocurrency and Terrorism Financing

Similarly to how cryptocurrency's anonymous and decentralized nature attracts cybercriminals, dark net drug dealers, and money launderers, crypto also appeals to terrorist groups. As the U.S. prioritized counterterrorism efforts after 9/11, revenue streams financing terrorist operations began to dissolve. As a result, terrorist groups were forced to adapt and diversify their activities by engaging in other criminal activities and soliciting donations from supporters. The article, "Illicit Trade and Terrorism," states that cryptocurrency serves as a facilitator for terrorism financing.[85] Last year, law enforcement organizations around the world detected and prosecuted a record number of cryptocurrency-related terrorism financing cases.[86] In the U.S. alone, over $1 million was recovered from Bitcoin addresses linked to terrorist groups.[87] While terrorist attacks themselves cost a relatively small amount of money, terrorist groups require a significant amount of funds for operational costs, such as recruitment, training, weapons, bribes, and payments to families of suicide bombers.[88] Cryptocurrency provides terrorist groups a way to send and receive funds around the world quickly, often with little chance of detection. Groups engaging in crypto-related terrorism financing include Hamas's military branch, an al-Qaeda affiliate, and ISIS.[89]

Hamas's military branch, the Izz ad-Din al-Qassam Brigades (AQB) was behind "one of the largest and most sophisticated cryptocurrency-based terrorism financing campaigns ever seen," according to Chainalysis.[90] In 2019, AQB attempted to solicit donations from supporters using Bitcoin and adapted its methods each time law enforcement impeded its efforts. AQB requested donations from supporters via a QR code on the group's website that directed the user to a Bitcoin address. However, after a short time, law enforcement was able to freeze the account and investigate its owner and the account's activities. AQB adjusted and replaced the QR code Bitcoin address with one that was connected to a private wallet. Although AQB believed this private wallet increased anonymity, Chainalysis explains that analysts were able to trace the wallet's transactions and donations to the group.[91] The wallet was eventually shut down.

AQB once again changed its method of collecting Bitcoin donations. This time, the website created an individual Bitcoin address for each donor to send money.[92] The website even had an instructional video to guide donors on how to contribute while maintaining maximum anonymity. The instructions included two donation options: hawala or a private Bitcoin wallet.[93] Hawala is an informal money transfer system founded on trust.[94] If they chose this option, they could provide the Bitcoin address and the donated amount in fiat currency. The hawala would then send the fiat currency amount in Bitcoin to the address. The video also informed donors that they could create a private Bitcoin wallet, choose from a recommended crypto exchange to purchase Bitcoin, and then transfer their donation.[95] This complex system made it increasingly difficult to trace funds. AQB earned over $10,000 in donations until U.S. authorities seized the donation campaign webpage in 2020.[96] AQB not only used crypto to its advantage, but it demonstrated its ability to adapt when law enforcement impeded its efforts. ISIS and an al-Qaeda affiliate also relied on cryptocurrency schemes to generate funds.

In September 2020, 29 people were arrested by French authorities for a cryptocurrency-related terrorism financing scheme for groups in Syria, including ISIS and an al-Qaeda affiliate. The cryptocurrency scheme had been active since 2019 until French government authorities uncovered a web of financial transactions sent to French extremists in Syria.[97] The scheme involved the purchase of cryptocurrency coupons. Recipients in Syria were sent the details of the coupons and then used the details to collect money through cryptocurrency exchanges.[98] Prosecutors explained that dozens of people located in France anonymously purchased cryptocurrency coupons worth 10 to 150 euros or $11 to $165.[99] The crypto coupons were credited to accounts abroad that were opened by extremists who could then convert the credited amount into cryptocurrency. It is believed that this scheme allowed members of ISIS and the al-Qaeda affiliate hiding in Syria to collect hundreds of thousands of euros.[100] This crypto scheme demonstrates another case where terrorists use the ease and anonymity of cryptocurrency to their advantage for the purpose of funding their extremist operations.

In addition to the two cases discussed above, there are also instances of al-Qaeda and affiliated groups laundering cryptocurrency and soliciting crypto donations through social media.[101] There was another case where a 27-year-old from Leicestershire, England, transferred Bitcoin abroad for the purpose of helping ISIS members escape from prisons controlled by the Kurds in Northern Syria.[102] ISIS also capitalized on the COVID-19 pandemic by selling counterfeit personal protective equipment (PPE) to generate revenue. A Department of Justice press release explains how Murat Cakar, an ISIS facilitator, operated the website, Face-MaskCenter.com.[103] The site claimed to have an ample supply of FDA-approved N95 respirator masks, as well as other PPE, despite shortages.[104] The scheme also involved the use of Facebook pages in order to help facilitate sales of the counterfeit products.[105] This case, along with al-Qaeda and affiliated groups soliciting cryptocurrency donations on social media platforms and the AQB donation campaign, resulted in the "largest-ever seizure of cryptocurrency" related to terrorism financing.[106] U.S. authorities seized millions of dollars and more than 300 cryptocurrency accounts, as each terrorism financing campaign made use of digital currency. In response to the seizure, Attorney General William Barr stated, "it should not surprise anyone that our enemies use modern technology, social media platforms and cryptocurrency to facilitate their evil and violent agendas."[107] Cryptocurrency not only aids in financing extremism abroad, but it is suspected of playing a role in funding a domestic extremist incident in the U.S.

On January 6, 2021, growing domestic tensions reached a boiling point when alt-right groups stormed the U.S. Capitol to protest the certification of the 2020 election results. A single Bitcoin transaction worth approximately $522,000, is under investigation by the FBI for its potential connection to the event. On December 8, 2020, the transaction transferred Bitcoin to 22 crypto addresses, many of which belong to far-right activists.[108] Chainalysis notes that the popular alt-right internet personality and podcaster, Nick Fuentes, received the largest donation of $250,000.[109] The donor was allegedly a French computer programmer who committed suicide the same day the donation was made. According to a suicide note published on his personal blog, the man seemingly committed suicide due to health issues. However, he also highlighted a number of alt-right viewpoints in his note, such as the decline of Western civilization and the hatred of Western "ancestors and heritage."[110] Given that international extremists use cryptocurrency to fund their activities, it is not impossible for domestic groups to do the same.

There is evidence that domestic extremist groups are moving towards cryptocurrency funding, as discussed in the hearing "Dollars Against Democracy: Domestic Terrorist Financing in the Aftermath of Insurrection" conducted by the Subcommittee on National Security, International Development, and Monetary Policy of the U.S. House Committee on Financial Services. Dr. Daniel Rogers, who is the co-founder and Chief Technical Officer of the Global Disinformation Index (GDI), provided a witness testimony on the use of cryptocurrency for the financing of extremist groups. Dr. Rogers explained how hate groups not only use online platforms to spread hateful ideologies, but they also use cyberspace to garner funding to support their activities.[111] GDI examined how 73 domestic groups, some of which participated in the January 6 Capitol riots, use a variety of online platforms, including five different cryptocurrencies.[112] GDI found evidence of these cryptocurrencies being used to transfer funds to groups. The organization also noticed a trend between the level of extremism of a group and their tendency to use crypto within their fundraising strategy.[113] For example. Dr. Rogers explained how groups who were less extreme relied more on traditional fundraising methods. As the groups were censored or removed from online platforms and became increasingly extreme, they would then migrate to cryptocurrency where pseudo-anonymity protected the identities of these groups.[114] This trend is likely to continue as technology companies continue to confront the issue of censoring users who spread extreme hate and toxic ideology through their online platforms.

While the true extent of cryptocurrency's role in terrorism financing is unknown, it is clear that terrorist groups have the ability to adapt and use technology to further their interests and undermine national security. The various methods these groups deployed to collect Bitcoin, whether through their websites, the use of crypto coupons, or individual donors, demonstrate a clear capacity to evolve their strategies in order to generate revenue and elude law enforcement. Crypto-related terrorism financing allows terrorists to collect money through donors and supporters with a lower risk of detection. As a result, terrorists are able to carry out operations and attacks that threaten the safety of innocent civilians around the world. Well-funded extremists perpetuate conflict and destabilize regions with their violence, putting both national and international security at significant risk. In addition, the suspected connection of Bitcoin to the January 6 Capitol riots demonstrates how crypto could help fund hostile groups within the U.S.

U.S. Cryptocurrency Policy

The decentralized nature of cryptocurrency makes it extremely difficult for policymakers to address how crypto can undermine national security. Cryptocurrency continues to become increasingly valuable and attractive faster than policy can be formulated. In addition, policymakers are faced with the challenging task of countering the national security threats of crypto while understanding that too much regulation could eliminate the essence of cryptocurrency. In order to make policy recommendations related to crypto, it is important to first examine how the Trump administration and the Biden administration addressed or plan to address cryptocurrency and its appeal to criminals and terrorists.

The topic of cryptocurrency as a national security concern remained relatively unacknowledged throughout Trump's presidency. However, the Department of Justice published the 2020 Report of the Attorney General's Cyber Digital Task Force, which highlights a number of ways that cryptocurrency facilitates crime and undermines national security. The report states that although cryptocurrency has existed for a relatively short amount of time, "this technology already plays a role in many of the most significant criminal and national security threats our nation faces."[115] Yet policymakers faced pushback when the Trump administration proposed reporting requirements for cryptocurrency and digital assets.

A few weeks before the end of Trump's presidency, the Financial Crimes Enforcement Network (FinCEN), a bureau within the Department of Treasury, announced a proposal to counter money laundering for virtual currency transactions. FinCEN proposed that financial institutions, such as banks and money services businesses (MSBs), would be "required to submit reports, keep records, and verify the identity of customers" for transactions that surpass specific thresholds and involve convertible virtual currency.[116] According to the proposal, banks and MSBs would be required to gather information, such as the names and addresses of customers and the type and amount of virtual currency used. In addition, the proposed thresholds include any transfers exceeding $3,000 if the funds are sent to a private crypto wallet.[117] The Treasury Department stated that while it values "responsible innovation," greater transparency and closing loopholes that bad actors can exploit, is required in order to safeguard national security.[118]

Despite its seemingly appealing objective of combating financial crimes, the proposal faced significant pushback. Critics of this proposal include major financial service providers, such as Fidelity Investments, Union Square Ventures, and Coinbase.[119] Cryptocurrency users opposing this proposal pointed out that FinCEN's reporting requirements ultimately take aim at the very essence of digital currency. Both licit and illicit actors are drawn to crypto for the privacy and freedom it offers. Increased reporting requirements would largely remove what makes cryptocurrency attractive. Some critics complained that attempting to identify parties involved in transactions would be expensive and sometimes impossible.[120] Despite its short existence, there is clearly a vocal sector of advocates that wish to protect the freedom and privacy cryptocurrency offers despite its potential national security implications. While the previous administration hoped it would be able to move the proposal forward prior to the end of Trump's presidency, the fate of the proposal now rests with the Biden administration.

In January 2021, President Biden's nominee for treasury secretary, Janet

Yellen, suggested that policymakers "curtail" the use of cryptocurrencies due to its role in facilitating crime, signaling an objective to increase crypto regulations during Biden's presidency.[121] According to a May 2021 *Washington Post* article, the Biden administration is reviewing oversight gaps in cryptocurrency regulation that aid in the facilitation of illegal activity, including tax evasion and terrorism financing.[122] In addition, the Treasury Department released the American Families Plan Tax Compliance Agenda to increase tax revenue through enhanced compliance measures. This includes new reporting requirements for cryptocurrency transactions. The agenda requires businesses and crypto exchanges to report transactions with a fair market value exceeding $10,000 in an effort for businesses to provide the IRS with more information surrounding large cryptocurrency transactions.[123] Although the political future of the Tax Compliance Agenda is uncertain, there seems to be some expectation that the current administration will work towards increased cryptocurrency regulations for the purpose of countering national security threats and financial crimes. Also, as ransomware has become a central national security threat in recent months, it is likely that the Biden administration will, at the very least, be forced to address the role of cryptocurrency in ransomware attacks.

Policy Recommendations

The primary challenge surrounding cryptocurrency is deciding how policy can address the national security threat while balancing crypto's core principles of privacy and decentralization. Because cryptocurrency is used for a number of areas of crime that can undermine national security, there is no "one-size-fits-all" approach. For this reason, the following policy recommendations will be specific to the issues discussed in this paper.

The rise in ransomware over the past few years demonstrates how cryptocurrency plays a major role in the facilitation of cyberattacks and the extortion of victims. Government agencies and policymakers should increase their efforts through informational campaigns to inform citizens and public and private organizations of the risks of ransomware. These informational campaigns should include how to implement defensive measures to protect systems and networks from hackers. This is essential given the shift to virtual work and distance learning due to COVID-19. It is also imperative that government agencies and policymakers deter victims from paying the cryptocurrency ransom. Although CISA and the FBI recommend against paying the ransom, informational campaigns should highlight the potential national security implications if ransomware victims pay hackers. Not only is it important to highlight how paying ransoms can facilitate more crime, but it is essential to underscore how U.S. adversaries, such as North Korea and Russia, can use ransomware and cryptocurrency to their advantage. Russia's potential links to the Colonial Pipeline and JBS ransomware attacks demonstrate how Russia could be willing to disrupt and extort critical U.S. industries for millions of dollars' worth of cryptocurrency. In addition, North Korea uses ransomware and cryptocurrency as a tactic to circumvent sanctions to fund its nuclear program. This information can help citizens and organizations understand how ransomware contributes to the broader national security threat landscape. It can also dissuade victims from paying the ransom, despite the higher financial cost. Educating the public on the consequences of ransomware is particularly important as the number of incidents is likely to continue increasing as cybercriminals advance their capabilities.

To address the illegal drug trade on the dark net, policymakers should focus on curbing the demand for these unlawful products. In her book *Dirty Entanglements,* Dr. Louise Shelley notes that drugs are a unique illicit commodity in the way that the addictive substances create continuous demand.[124] For this reason, the drug market itself is a major problem. According to an article from the Council on Foreign Relations, some experts believe public health policies would be an effective method to decrease demand.[125] The approach of addressing demand could help counter the drug trade in and out of cyberspace. With the use of dark net marketplaces and cryptocurrency, cyberspace in particular has significantly aided in the facilitation of the illegal drug trade. The use of cryptocurrency hides the identities of buyers and sellers and allows drugs to be sold and distributed around the world at a much faster rate. Therefore, addressing demand could help combat the illicit use of cryptocurrency as well as drug crime on dark net marketplaces.

Countering cryptocurrency-based money laundering requires building on existing anti-money laundering legislation. FinCEN's proposal to implement anti-money laundering regulations to close loopholes signifies an effort to do so. Policymakers should incentivize cryptocurrency exchanges to comply with anti-money laundering laws to minimize the number of illicit actors using cryptocurrency and their platforms. U.S. anti-money laundering policies currently require compliance from banks. However, in the last year there have been a significant number of financial institutions faced with fines for noncompliance related to anti-money laundering regulations.[126] Therefore, policymakers should identify and apply lessons learned and best practices from the lack of compliance with traditional financial institutions. By applying these lessons to increase cooperation and compliance, policymakers and exchanges can combat the activities that allow criminals to maintain their capital and evade law enforcement.

Terrorism financing is difficult to address because terrorist groups are expanding their activities to ensure diversified streams of revenue. The use of online platforms to solicit donations and generate funds in the form of cryptocurrency requires enhanced law enforcement capabilities. Greater support for law enforcement can help to identify and seize sites that are linked to terrorism financing, as well as track down facilitators. In addition, countering terrorism financing requires international cooperation and coordination. As the cases in the U.S. and France demonstrated, terrorism financing activities occur around the world. One of the advantages of cryptocurrency is the ease at which terrorists can send money internationally. Therefore, international organizations and federal governments need to combine resources and capabilities to identify facilitators of crypto-related terrorism financing and thwart their efforts.

Conclusion

As technology advancements progress, criminals and terrorist groups will continue to capitalize on innovative capabilities to weaken national security. Cryptocurrency has grown tremendously since it first emerged, and it attracts both illicit and licit actors with its decentralization and near anonymity. It is important to underscore that cryptocurrency does have legitimate uses, especially as digital currency becomes more mainstream. Companies are developing and adopting cryptocurrency payment systems and investors view cryptocurrency as a highly valuable digital asset. However, its anonymity and lack of regulations leave too many opportunities for transnational criminals to evade law enforcement and undermine national security.

Cryptocurrency plays an important role in the extortion of ransomware victims, especially as the number of ransomware incidents has been on the rise in recent years. Ransomware attackers generate a significant amount of cryptocurrency revenue because it often costs victims more not to pay the ransom. These profits incentivize cybercriminals to continue extorting victims through ransomware. The use of cryptocurrency in ransomware attacks protects the hackers' identities and places law enforcement at a disadvantage. This is particularly true when hackers use mixer services to further disguise their transactions when cashing out their ransomware profits. Ransomware attacks can have serious repercussions on national security beyond the initial victims, as exemplified by the DPRK cases, the attacks against municipalities in the U.S, and the targeting of critical U.S. sectors. The use of cryptocurrency in ransomware undermines national security by anonymizing malicious actors, obfuscating the path of funds, and thus making it extremely challenging for law enforcement to identify, charge, and prosecute these cybercriminals.

Cryptocurrency combined with the emergence of dark net marketplaces gave the illegal drug trade and transnational crime the opportunity to expand. Silk Road generated millions of Bitcoin in revenue, largely due to the ease with which drugs could be purchased and distributed. Despite its takedown, Silk Road paved the way for future dark net marketplaces, as more appeared in its place. Although Silk Road was the first of its kind, AlphaBay far exceeded its predecessor's success in the illegal drug trade. The use of cryptocurrency on dark net marketplaces, such as Silk Road and AlphaBay, was an intentional design. Cryptocurrency protected the site and hid the identities of those engaging in the buying and selling of drugs from law enforcement. Cryptocurrency and dark net marketplaces have also aided in the facilitation of harming individuals and communities through drug addiction, as the U.S. opioid epidemic demonstrates.

Cryptocurrency-based money laundering is not an uncommon occurrence. Dark net vendors and organized criminal groups participate in crypto-based money laundering to hide their profits, avoid detection, and circumvent the regulations of traditional financial institutions. Cryptocurrency-based money laundering makes it more difficult for law enforcement to track illicit proceeds, while making it easier for transnational crime groups to distribute funds throughout their international networks. As is the case with ransomware and dark net transactions, money laundering with crypto hides the identities of criminals. Cryptocurrency-based money laundering undermines national security because it allows criminals to generate funding and disguise its sources. This provides criminals with financial stability, as they are then able to reinvest laundered funds back into their criminal activities. This form of money laundering also weakens the legitimate economy, as well as international borders, the rule of law, and regulations of traditional financial institutions.

The use of cryptocurrency demonstrates how terrorist groups adopt new methods to bring in money. Crypto allows terrorist groups to send and receive funds with ease from around the world. The cases involving Hamas, an al-Qaeda affiliate and ISIS exhibit how terrorists have turned to cryptocurrency to generate revenue through donations. Each case illustrates how terrorist groups deploy various methods to garner funds. Hamas's military branch, AQB, solicited Bitcoin donations through its website, while ISIS and an al-Qaeda affiliate created a scheme involving the purchase of cryptocurrency coupons. Although it is unclear how prevalent cryptocurrency's role is in terrorism financing, it is clear that some groups are adapting to technological developments and have the ability to use it to their advantage. Terrorism financing with cryptocurrency greatly undermines national security because it allows terrorists to generate funds for their violent activities with a relatively low risk of detection. In addition, there is a possibility that cryptocurrency may have funded prominent far-right activists who participated in the January 6 Capitol riots. Cryptocurrency's role in financing both international and domestic extremism presents a major national security concern.

Developing policy to counter criminals exploiting loopholes in crypto regulation is extremely difficult. The Trump administration's proposal to implement reporting requirements and greater regulation would essentially remove the privacy and freedom that cryptocurrency has to offer. While it would potentially combat financial crimes, it would come at the cost of the digital currency's fundamental principles. Moving forward, it is unclear how the Biden administration will confront the national security concern of cryptocurrency. However, Treasury

Secretary Janet Yellen's comments seem to suggest that the administration will at least attempt to address this issue.

Policymakers face a significant challenge in addressing the national security threat of cryptocurrency. Regarding ransomware, policymakers and federal agencies should educate the public, as well as public and private organizations on the risks of ransomware, how to implement protective measures, and highlight the national security concerns of these cyberattacks. Public awareness can deter victims from paying the cryptocurrency ransom if they have a better understanding of how ransomware can greatly undermine national security. Policymakers should address the demand for illegal drugs to combat the use of dark net marketplaces and, by extension, the use of cryptocurrency in illicit trade on the dark net. Addictive substances create a continuous demand, therefore, implementing public health policies could help alleviate the drug epidemic both in and out of cyberspace. To counter cryptocurrency-based money laundering, policymakers should build on existing anti-money laundering legislation. In addition, policymakers should incentivize cryptocurrency exchanges to comply with laws and regulations. They should also examine lessons learned from the failure of traditional financial institutions to comply with anti-money laundering regulations and apply these best practices to increase effective cooperation with crypto exchanges. Lastly, combating cryptocurrency-related terrorism financing requires enhanced law enforcement support to identify and seize sites that engage in terrorism financing. International cooperation and coordination are also required as terrorism financing activities occur throughout the world. Terrorism financing activities easily cross borders and jurisdictions. For this reason, the international community needs to combine its resources to track cryptocurrency transactions and identify terrorism financiers more effectively.

Ransomware attacks, the dark net drug trade, cryptocurrency-based money laundering, and terrorism financing all undermine national security in different ways. Therefore, policymakers cannot rely on a "one-size-fits-all" approach. Instead, policies combating crypto-related crime and the threat to national security should uniquely address each issue. The uses of cryptocurrency will likely expand in the coming years, especially as it becomes increasingly mainstream. Therefore, it is imperative that policymakers urgently address how cryptocurrency can threaten national security before criminals and terrorist groups gain too much of an upper hand.

Notes

1 Sarah Durant and Mangai Natarajan, "Cryptocurrencies and Money Laundering Operations," *International and Transnational Crime and Justice* (June 2019): 74, https://doi.org/10.1017/9781108597296.012.

2 Dr. Diana Dolliver, "Cryptocurrencies and Criminal Investigations: From Transaction to Seizure" (presentation, Criminal Investigations and Network Analysis Center, DHS Centers of Excellence, March 17, 2021), https://cina.gmu.edu/event/cina-virtual-distinguished-speaker-series-diana-dolliver-cryptocurrencies-and-criminal-investigations-from-transaction-to-seizure.

3 Sarah Meiklejohn, Marjori Pomarole, Grant Jordan, Kirill Levchenko, Damon McCoy, Geoffrey M. Voelker, and Stefan Savage, "A Fistful of Bitcoins: Characterizing Payments Among Men with No Name," *Communications of the ACM* 59, no. 4 (April 2016): 10, EBSCO.

4 Danny Yuxing Huang, Maxwell Matthaios Aliapoulios, Vector Guo Li, Luca Invernizzi, Kylie McRoberts, Elie Bursztein, Jonathan Levin, Kirill Levchenko, Alex C. Snoeren, and Damon McCoy, "Tracking Ransomware End-to-End," *IEEE Symposium on Security and Privacy (SP)* (July 2018): 619, https://ieeexplore.ieee.org/document/8418627.

5 Dr. Diana Dolliver, "Cryptocurrencies and Criminal Investigations: From Transaction to Seizure."

6 "About Coinbase," Coinbase, accessed March 29, 2021, https://www.coinbase.com/about.

7 "Bitcoin," *CoinDesk*, accessed March 30, 2021, https://www.coindesk.com/price/bitcoin.

8 Ibid.

9 Ibid.

10 Isaac Kfir, "Cryptocurrencies, national security, and terrorism," *Comparative Strategy* 39, no. 2 (March 2020): 115, https://doi.org/10.1080/01495933.2020.1718983.

11 Jacob Bernstein, "What Can You Actually Buy With Bitcoin?" *The New York Times,* February 5, 2021, https://www.nytimes.com/2021/02/03/style/what-can-you-actually-buy-with-bitcoin.html.

12 Ibid.

13 "Mastercard Accelerates Crypto Card Partner Program, Making it Easier for Consumers to Hold and Activate Cryptocurrencies," Mastercard, July 20, 2020, https://investor.mastercard.com/investor-news/investor-news-details/2020/Mastercard-Accelerates-Crypto-Card-Partner-Program-Making-it-Easier-for-Consumers-to-Hold-and-Activate-Cryptocurrencies/default.aspx.

14 Ankit Panda, "Cryptocurrencies and National Security," Council on Foreign Relations,

February 28, 2018, https://www.cfr.org/backgrounder/cryptocurrencies-and-national-security.

15 Ibid.

16 "What is Bitcoin," *CoinDesk*, December 4, 2020, https://www.coindesk.com/learn/bitcoin-101/what-is-bitcoin.

17 Kim Grauer and Henry Updegrave, *The 2021 Crypto Crime Report* (Chainalysis, 2021), https://go.chainalysis.com/2021-Crypto-Crime-Report.html.

18 "CISA Launches Campaign to Reduce the Risk of Ransomware," Cybersecurity and Infrastructure Security Agency, January 16, 2021, https://www.cisa.gov/news/2021/01/21/cisa-launches-campaign-reduce-risk-ransomware.

19 Ibid.

20 "Reduce the Risk of Ransomware Awareness Campaign," Cybersecurity and Infrastructure Security Agency, January 2021, https://www.cisa.gov/sites/default/files/publications/Fact%20sheet_Ransomware%20Awareness%20Campaign_20210119_508.pdf.

21 Huang, Aliapoulios, Li, Invernizzi, McRoberts, Bursztein, Levin, Levchenko, Snoeren, and McCoy, "Ransomware End-to-end," 13.

22 Ibid., 2.

23 Grauer and Updegrave, *The 2021 Crypto Crime Report*, 5.

24 Grauer and Updegrave, *The 2021 Crypto Crime Report*, 6.

25 Alan Brill and Eric Thompson, "Ransomware, A Tool and Opportunity for Terrorist Financing and Cyberwarfare," *Defence Against Terrorism Review* 12, (2019): 55, EBSCO.

26 Ed Caesar, "The Incredible Rise of North Korea's Hacking Army," *The New Yorker,* April 19. 2021, https://www.newyorker.com/magazine/2021/04/26/the-incredible-rise-of-north-koreas-hacking-army.

27 Ibid.

28 Ibid.

29 Arjun Kharpal, "How to tell if you're at risk from the WannaCry ransomware and what to do if you have been attacked," *CNBC,* May 15, 2017, https://www.cnbc.com/2017/05/15/ransomware-wanncry-virus-what-to-do-to-protect.html.

30 Caesar, "The Incredible Rise of North Korea's Hacking Army."

31 Ryan Browne, "Hackers have cashed out on $143,000 of bitcoin from the massive WannaCry ransomware attack," *CNBC,* August 3, 2017, https://www.cnbc.com/2017/08/03/hackers-have-cashed-out-on-143000-of-bitcoin-from-the-massive-wannacry-rans

omware-attack.html.

32 Department of Justice Office of Public Affairs, "Three North Korean Military Hackers Indicted in Wide-Ranging Scheme to Commit Cyberattacks and Financial Crimes Across the Globe," February 17, 2021, https://www.justice.gov/opa/pr/three-north-korean-military-hackers-indicted-wide-ranging-scheme-commit-cyberattacks-and.

33 Caesar, "The Incredible Rise of North Korea's Hacking Army."

34 Department of Justice Office of Public Affairs, "Three North Korean Military Hackers Indicted in Wide-Ranging Scheme to Commit Cyberattacks and Financial Crimes Across the Globe,"

35 Caesar, "The Incredible Rise of North Korea's Hacking Army."

36 Ibid.

37 Brill and Thompson, "Ransomware, A Tool and Opportunity for Terrorist Financing and Cyberwarfare," 50.

38 Ibid., 47.

39 Antonio Villas-Boas, "A Florida city was forced to use pen and paper and pay a $500,000 ransom after hackers took control of its computers," *CNBC*, June 27, 2019, https://www.businessinsider.com/lake-city-florida-ransomware-cyberattack-hackers-bitcoin-payment-2019-6.

40 Brill and Thompson, "Ransomware, A Tool and Opportunity for Terrorist Financing and Cyberwarfare," 48.

41 Ibid.

42 Boaz Sobrado, "Bitcoin Is Aiding in the Ransomware Industry," *CoinDesk*, January 19, 2021, https://www.coindesk.com/bitcoin-is-aiding-the-ransomware-industry.

43 "Ransomware Attacks Fracture Between Enterprise and Ransomware-as-a-Service in Q2 as Demands Increase," *Coveware*, August 3, 2020, https://www.coveware.com/blog/q2-2020-ransomware-marketplace-report#1.

44 Katie Benner and Nicole Perlroth, "U.S. Seizes Share of Ransom From Hackers in Colonial Pipeline Attack," *The New York Times*, June 7, 2021, https://www.nytimes.com/2021/06/07/us/politics/pipeline-attack.html?searchResultPosition=1.

45 Ibid.

46 Michael D. Shear, Nicole Perlroth, and Clifford Krauss, "Colonial Pipeline Paid Roughly $5 Million in Ransom to Hackers," *The New York Times*, June 7, 2021, https://www.nytimes.com/2021/05/13/us/politics/biden-colonial-pipeline-ransomware.html.

47 Benner and Perlroth, U.S. Seizes Share of Ransom From Hackers in Colonial Pipeline Attack."

48 Ibid.

49 Ibid.

50 Julie Creswell, Nicole Perlroth, and Noam Scheiber, "Ransomware Disrupts Meat Plants in Latest Attack on Critical U.S. Business," *The New York Times,* June 3, 2021, https://www.nytimes.com/2021/06/01/business/meat-plant-cyberattack-jbs.html.

51 Ibid.

52 Jacob Bunge, "JBS Paid $11 Million to Resolve Ransomware Attack," *The Wall Street Journal,* June 9, 2021, https://www.wsj.com/articles/jbs-paid-11-million-to-resolve-ransomware-attack-11623280781.

53 Creswell, Perlroth, and Scheiber, "Ransomware Disrupts Meat Plants in Latest Attack on Critical U.S. Business."

54 Nathaniel Popper, "Bitcoin Has Lost Steam. But Criminals Still Love It," *The New York Times,* January 28, 2020, https://www.nytimes.com/2020/01/28/technology/bitcoin-black-market.html

55 Ibid.

56 Marc Goodman, "Inside the Digital Underground," in *Future Crimes: Everything is Connected, Everyone is Vulnerable and What We Can Do About It*, (Canada: Doubleday, 2015), chap. 11.

57 Goodman, "Inside the Digital Underground," 198.

58 Erik Silfversten, Marina Favaro, Linda Slapakova, Sascha Ishikawa, James Liu, and Adrian Salas, *Exploring the use of Zcash cryptocurrency for illicit or criminal purposes*, RR-4418-ECC (Santa Monica, CA: RAND, 2020), https://www.rand.org/pubs/research_reports/RR4418.html.

59 Goodman, "Inside the Digital Underground," 197.

60 James King, "Here's a breakdown of the $1.2 billion in Silk Road drug transactions," *Business Insider,* May 29, 2015, https://www.businessinsider.com/heres-a-breakdown-of-the-12-billion-silk-road-drug-transactions-2015-5.

61 Ibid.

62 Ibid.

63 Department of Justice U.S. Attorney's Office Southern District of New York, "U.S. Attorney Announces Arrest and Money Laundering Charges Against Dark Web Narcotics Trafficker," July 18, 2019, https://www.justice.gov/usao-sdny/pr/us-attorney-announces-arrest-and-money-laundering-charges-against-dark-web-narcotics.

64 Department of Justice U.S. Attorney's Office Southern District of New York, "Ross Ulbricht, A/K/A 'Dread Pirate Roberts,' Sentenced in Manhattan Federal Court to Life in

Prison," May 29, 2015, https://www.justice.gov/usao-sdny/pr/ross-ulbricht-aka-dread-pirate-roberts-sentenced-manhattan-federal-court-life-prison.

65 Ibid.

66 Ibid.

67 "Operator of Silk Road 2.0 Website Charged in Manhattan Federal Court," Federal Bureau of Investigation, November 6, 2014, https://www.fbi.gov/contact-us/field-offices/newyork/news/press-releases/operator-of-silk-road-2.0-website-charged-in-manhattan-federal-court.

68 Louise I. Shelley, *Dark Commerce: How a New Illicit Economy is Threatening Our Future* (Princeton: Princeton University Press, 2018), 70.

69 Nathaniel Popper, "Opioid Dealers Embrace the Dark Web to Send Deadly Drugs by Mail," *The New York Times*, June 10, 2017, https://www.nytimes.com/2017/06/10/business/dealbook/opioid-dark-web-drug-overdose.html?_r=0.

70 "Darknet Takedown: Authorities Shutter Online Criminal Market AlphaBay," Federal Bureau of Investigation, July 20, 2017, https://www.fbi.gov/news/stories/alphabay-takedown.

71 Popper, "Opioid Dealers Embrace the Dark Web to Send Deadly Drugs by Mail."

72 Department of Justice, "U.S. Attorney Announces Arrest and Money Laundering Charges Against Dark Web Narcotics Trafficker."

73 Ibid.

74 Tom Huddleston Jr., "This Ohio man is accused of trying to launder $19 million of bitcoin from the dark web," *CNBC*, July 23, 2019, https://www.cnbc.com/2019/07/23/man-accused-of-laundering-millions-in-bitcoin-from-silk-road.html.

75 Department of Justice, "U.S. Attorney Announces Arrest and Money Laundering Charges Against Dark Web Narcotics Trafficker."

76 Ibid.

77 Ibid.

78 Department of Justice U.S. Attorney's Office Southern District of New York, "Dark Web Narcotics Trafficker Sentenced To 3½ Years in Prison in Connection with Laundering More Than $19 Million," February 12, 2020, https://www.justice.gov/usao-sdny/pr/dark-web-narcotics-trafficker-sentenced-3-years-prison-connection-laundering-more-19.

79 Diego Oré, "Latin American crime cartels turn to cryptocurrencies for money laundering," *Reuters,* December 8, 2020, https://www.reuters.com/article/mexico-bitcoin-insight/latin-american-crime-cartels-turn-to-cryptocurrencies-for-money-laundering-idUSKBN28I1KD.

80 Ibid.

81 Ibid.

82 Ibid.

83 Goodman, "Inside the Digital Underground," 198.

84 Grauer and Updegrave, *The 2021 Crypto Crime Report*, 9.

85 Louise I. Shelley, "Illicit Trade and Terrorism," *Perspectives on Terrorism* 14, no. 4 (August 2020): 14, JSTOR.

86 Grauer and Updegrave, *The 2021 Crypto Crime Report*, 93.

87 Ibid.

88 Louise I. Shelley, *Dirty Entanglements: Corruption, Crime, and Terrorism* (New York: Cambridge University Press, 2014), 177.

89 Grauer and Updegrave, *The 2021 Crypto Crime Report*, 94.

90 Chainalysis, "Terrorism Financing in Early Stages with Cryptocurrency But Advancing Quickly," January 17, 2020, https://blog.chainalysis.com/reports/terrorism-financing-cryptocurrency-2019.

91 Ibid.

92 Ibid.

93 Ibid.

94 Louise I. Shelley, *Dark Commerce*, 144.

95 Chainalysis, "Terrorism Financing in Early Stages with Cryptocurrency But Advancing Quickly."

96 Grauer and Updegrave, *The 2021 Crypto Crime Report*, 96.

97 "French arrest 29 in cryptocurrency scheme to finance jihadis," *AP News,* September 29, 2020, https://apnews.com/article/arrests-terrorism-archive-france-701371a367d1a e26ff057d6e3d082458.

98 Ibid.

99 Ibid.

100 Grauer and Updegrave, *The 2021 Crypto Crime Report*, 94.

101 Department of Justice Office of Public Affairs, "Global Disruption of Three Terror Finance Cyber-Enabled Campaigns," August 13, 2020, https://www.justice.gov/opa/pr/global-disruption-three-terror-finance-cyber-enabled-campaigns.

102 Grauer and Updegrave, *The 2021 Crypto Crime Report*, 94.

103 Department of Justice, "Global Disruption of Three Terror Finance Cyber-Enabled Campaigns."

104 Andy Greenberg, "ISIS Allegedly Ran a COVID-19 PPE Scam Site," August 13, 2020, https://www.wired.com/story/isis-allegedly-ran-a-covid-19-ppe-scam-site/.

105 Department of Justice, "Global Disruption of Three Terror Finance Cyber-Enabled Campaigns."

106 Ibid.

107 Ibid.

108 Grauer and Updegrave, *The 2021 Crypto Crime Report*, 101.

109 Ibid., 102.

110 Ibid., 105.

111 *Virtual Hearing – Dollars Against Democracy: Domestic Terrorist Financing in the Aftermath of Insurrection: Testimony before the Subcommittee on National Security, International Development, and Monetary Policy*, 117th Cong. (2021) (statement of Dr. Daniel Rogers, Co-Founder and Chief Technical Officer, Global Disinformation Index).

112 Ibid.

113 Ibid.

114 Ibid.

115 Department of Justice, *Report of the Attorney General's Cyber Digital Task Force: Cryptocurrency Enforcement Network* (Washington, DC: United States Department of Justice, 2020), https://www.justice.gov/archives/ag/page/file/1326061/download.

116 "The Financial Crimes Enforcement Network Proposes Rule Aimed at Closing Anti-Money Laundering Regulatory Gaps for Certain Convertible Virtual Currency and Digital Asset Transactions," U.S. Department of the Treasury, December 18, 2020, https://home.treasury.gov/news/press-releases/sm1216.

117 David Z. Morris, "Trump and Mnuchin's parting sneak attack on financial privacy," *Fortune,* January 6, 2021, https://fortune.com/2021/01/06/trump-and-mnuchins-parting-sneak-attack-on-financial-privacy/.

118 U.S. Department of the Treasury, "The Financial Crimes Enforcement Network Proposes Rule Aimed at Closing Anti-Money Laundering Regulatory Gaps for Certain Convertible Virtual Currency and Digital Asset Transactions."

119 Joe Light, "Bitcoin Storm Brewing Over Trump's Anti-Money Laundering Push," *Bloomberg*, March 5, 2021, https://finance.yahoo.com/news/bitcoin-storm-brewing-

over-trump-070000416.html.

120 Ibid.

121 Harry Robertson, "Janet Yellen suggests 'curtailing' cryptocurrencies such as Bitcoin, saying they are mainly used for illegal financing," *Business Insider*, January 20, 2021, https://markets.businessinsider.com/currencies/news/bitcoin-price-cryptocurrency-should-be-curtailed-terrorism-concerns-yellen-2021-1-1029985692.

122 Jeff Stein, "White House reviews 'gaps' in cryptocurrency rules as bitcoin swings wildly," *The Washington Post,* May 25, 2021, https://www.washingtonpost.com/us-policy/2021/05/25/biden-bitcoin-crypto-markets/.

123 Jeff Stein, "Treasury targets tax cheats, cryptocurrency in proposal it hopes will bring in $700 billion," *The Washington Post,* May 20, 2021, https://www.washingtonpost.com/us-policy/2021/05/20/biden-tax-compliance-treasury/.

124 Louise I. Shelley, *Dirty Entanglements,* 244.

125 Global Governance Monitor: Crime," Council on Foreign Relations, accessed January 24, 2021, https://www.cfr.org/global-governance-monitor/#!/crime.

126 Jaclyn Jaeger, "Fines against financial institutions hit $10.4B in 2020," *Compliance Week*, December 22, 2020, https://www.complianceweek.com/surveys-and-benchmarking/report-fines-against-financial-institutions-hit-104b-in-2020/29869.article.

International Journal on Criminology • *Volume 9, Number 1* • *Winter 2022*

Radicalization Analyzed by Social Sciences: Can the medium-range concepts already mobilized on urban riots explain the radicalization processes in France?

Éric Marlière

HDR Lecturer in Sociology at Lille University, CeRIES Research Center

ABSTRACT

The purpose of this paper is to question the concepts that social scientists use to apprehend the processes of so-called Islamic radicalization. While some academic disciplines—such as geopolitics or psychology—provide global explanations of radicalization, sociologists tend to be more hesitant or more nuanced when it comes to analyzing the phenomenon. Moreover, the notion of radicalization is debated within the discipline. In fact, in sociology, the various approaches remain too compartmentalized to produce a consensual analysis of jihadism. The purpose of this paper is therefore to offer an inventory of some of the concepts used in sociology on urban uprisings so as to take a step back from the overhanging readings of the phenomenon. The concepts presented herein may not only shed light on certain aspects of this complex subject by closely analyzing the paths of jihadists, in the sense that their combined analysis enriches our knowledge of a controversial phenomenon.

Keywords: Radicalization, Frustration, Identity denied, Moral economy, Political Commitment

La radicalización analizada por las ciencias sociales: ¿Pueden los conceptos de rango medio ya movilizados en disturbios urbanos explicar los procesos de radicalización en Francia?

RESUMEN

El propósito de este trabajo es cuestionar los conceptos que utilizan los científicos sociales para aprehender los procesos de la llamada radicalización islámica. Si bien algunas disciplinas académicas,

doi: 10.18278/ijc.9.1.4

como la geopolítica o la psicología, brindan explicaciones globales de la radicalización, los sociólogos tienden a ser más vacilantes o más matizados cuando se trata de analizar el fenómeno. Además, la noción de radicalización se debate dentro de la disciplina. De hecho, en sociología, los diversos enfoques siguen estando demasiado compartimentados para producir un análisis consensuado del yihadismo. El propósito de este artículo es, por lo tanto, ofrecer un inventario de algunos de los conceptos utilizados en sociología sobre los levantamientos urbanos para alejarse de las lecturas que sobrevuelan el fenómeno. Los conceptos presentados aquí pueden no sólo arrojar luz sobre ciertos aspectos de este complejo tema al analizar de cerca los caminos de los yihadistas, en el sentido de que su análisis combinado enriquece nuestro conocimiento de un fenómeno controvertido.

Palabras clave: Radicalización, Frustración, Identidad negada, Economía moral, Compromiso político

社会科学视角下的激进化：已用于城市暴乱的媒介范围概念能解释法国的激进化进程吗？

摘要

本文目的是质疑社会科学家用于理解所谓的伊斯兰激进化过程而使用的概念。尽管一些学术领域—例如地缘政治学或心理学—为激进化提供了全球性的解释，但社会学家往往用更为犹豫或细微的方式分析该现象。此外，激进化这一概念在该学科中存在辩论。事实上，社会学中的不同方法仍然太过于区分化，以至于无法就圣战主义达成统一的分析。本文目的因此是对关于城市叛乱的社会学中所使用的部分概念加以梳理，以期对关于该现象的大量研究进行广泛审视。通过仔细分析圣战分子的路径，本文所提出的概念可能不仅能解释该复杂主题的部分方面，即综合分析能促进我们对该争议现象的理解。

关键词：激进化，挫败，身份否认，道德经济，政治承诺

Detailed plan

1. **Introduction**

2. **Radicalization in the social sciences: a battlefield?**

   A. A total and global social phenomenon

   B. Antagonistic approaches

   C. Beyond the social and postcolonial question of the "suburbs"?

3. **The notion of relative frustration**

   A. Relative Frustration: An American Genealogy

   B. From hope to disillusionment

4. **Denied subjectivities and disdained identities**

   A. The *jihadist*: a despised youth who responds with violence

   B. In search of a short-lived but brilliant recognition

5. **"*Politicité*" to rehabilitate politics**

   A. The political commitment of the desperate

   B. Specific and isolated mobilizations

   C. To destroy oneself or to destroy society?

6. **A moral economy of radicalization?**

   A. A competition of norms and values

   B. Specific and binding standards and values.

   C. Impose your values and "convert the system"?

7. What about the concept of Habitus?

   A. Personal dispositions, structural issues and a favorable situation for the habitus of radicalized people

   B. Habitus to better understand the pathways of individuals in connection with decisive contexts

8. **Conclusion**

1. Introduction

Terrorism and political violence have a long history in France, as the phenomenon goes back to the anarchist attacks which shook the hexagon at the end of the 19th century. In the wake of the recent attacks, journalists, media experts and other "all-purpose speakers" have occupied the space of the "small window" increasingly fed by continuous news channels. Initially, psychoanalysts, psychologists and psychiatrists have focused their interpretation on the mental aspect of the problem, invoking psychological disorders that can lead to psychopathology and nihilism. Thus, individuals influenced by *jihadist* ideology continue to be the object of interpretative endeavors that consist in finding psychiatric solutions in an attempt to "de-radicalize" them. Secondly, the "orientalist" researchers that we name, admittedly unduly. These researchers and political scientists try to interpret the terrorist phenomenon with Islam as the main stake. This analysis is sometimes contradictory or even opposed, as illustrated by the studies of Olivier Roy or Gilles Kepel. A third stream, mainly composed of essayists and editorialists, emphasizes the civilizational and "ethnocultural" issue at stake. Alain Finkielkraut or Éric Zemmour are the mainstream tell bearers of a discourse focused on the "clash of civilizations," a narrative that now directly echoes the discourse invoking the "problem of the suburbs." Yet with the exception of one or two sociologists with high media profiles, sociological explanations are rarely put forward in the analysis of terrorism by the media and even newspapers (Guérandel & Marlière, 2016).

The purpose of this article is to revisit the work of sociologists on the phenomenon of radicalization, regardless of their currents and "obediences." Thus, this paper calls upon the notions or concepts elaborated by these researchers, in order to show the contributions and strengths of our discipline. Sociology, unlike other fields, does not have preconceived explanations or "omnibus" interpretations to provide to the public opinion explaining the processes that lead young people to commit attacks in France and elsewhere in the name of Islam. Nevertheless, the subject presents relevant notions to explain a set of factors, processes, or mechanisms that lead to political violence. Therefore, this article will consider the concepts that have proven their worth in the field of urban upheavals. While it is not possible to provide an overarching and definitive explanation of the *jihadist* phenomenon, sociology, with its different schools of thought, can offer a variety of complex and sometimes contradictory answers, which are undoubtedly useful for understanding events, trajectories, and situations.

In an attempt to answer this question, the main works of researchers who have tried to circumscribe the phenomenon of radicalization will be reviewed. Even though the notion is questionable and leads to controversy, and even antagonisms on the approaches to understand the phenomenon. In order to better comprehend the processes that lead to terrorism, we will then use concepts that have already been used in social sciences. Thus, we will approach the notion of social frustration put forward by Raymond Boudon and his successors. Then, we will focus on the question of the denial of subjectivity and the recognition of the logic of actors inspired by the so-called Touraine school. Also, we will try to reflect on the concept of *politicité*, introduced by Denis Merklen, around the popular radical social movements. Finally, we will also look at the notion of moral economy initiated by Edward P. Thompson and rehabilitated by Didier Fassin. We will also illustrate how the moral economy of injustice structures the social representations of a certain youth from the "suburbs" confronted with discrimination.

2. Radicalization in the social sciences: a battlefield?

A. A total and global social phenomenon

For many sociologists, radicalization or *jihadism* is a holistic social phenomenon insofar as it challenges the symbolic foundations of living together in our democratic societies (Khosrokhavar, 2018). This phenomenon prompts some researchers to question the homicidal "logics" that lead young adults to take action in free and democratic societies (Van Campenhoudt, 2017). Radicalization also challenges the growing success of a totalitarian ideology that has been emerging for more than half a century within Islam and is destabilizing not only the West, but especially the Muslim-Sunni world (Dassetto, 2018). Indeed, flabbergasting and incomprehension upset our "modern" sensibilities: how is a conservative and medieval ideology likely to lead young people to their own death in order to provoke that of others in liberal societies at the beginning of the 21st century? To what extent do suicide attacks question the responsibility of our progressive and democratic societies (Asad, 2018)? Islamic terrorism is not an entirely new phenomenon, but has grown since the attacks of September 11, 2001. It even took more worrying turns in the mid-2010s with the emergence of a proto nation-state, *Daech,* that concretizes an "utopia" into a material project through the conquest of a territory and the implementation of a governance for all the *jihadists* of the world (Atran, 2016; Luizard, 2015).[1]

While sociologists all, in their own way, refer to *jihadism* or radicalization as a prominent issue that needs to be approached with caution but urgency, the work on definitions, terminological references and sensitivities is far from consensual. The frequent use of the term radicalization goes back to the 2005 London bombings (Neuman P. R. & Kleiman S., 2013). While certain researchers defend this concept, despite its imperfections, as it enables us to move from the *why* to the *how* (Khorsokhavar, 2014; Crettiez, 2016), some of them note that this notion is too imprecise to analyze *jihadism* (Raggazi, 2014; Kundnani, 2015; Health-Kelly,

---

1   Beyond the physical, political and symbolic attributions that the territory offers, it is also a producer of financial resources and therefore facilitates a certain political and diplomatic independence (Dassetto, *op. cit.*).

2016). Others, even more severe, apprehend the overuse of the term radicalization as a "catch-all" that definitely disqualifies its use (Coolsaet, 2011; Mauger, 2016).[2] The lack of consensus is the consequence of the heterogeneity of the observed phenomenon leading to controversy or even antagonism between researchers. Similarly, the notion of terrorism, which includes more than two hundred definitions to date, remains difficult to mobilize in its current state to describe the phenomenon (Raflik, 2016). The term *jihadism* is not unanimously accepted either insofar as it reinforces the amalgam with the ordinary religious practice of everyday Muslims (Marlière, 2021). This is why sociologist Luc Van Campenhoudt recommends the use of the terminological combinations of terrorism and *jihadism* through the expression "jihadist terrorism" in order to better circumscribe the phenomenon (Van Campenhoudt, *op. cit.*: 8). We are thus, for the moment, in a semantic impasse to understand a social phenomenon that it is nevertheless essential to apprehend at the beginning of the 21st century.

B. Antagonistic approaches

If there are several currents, schools, and sensibilities, as we have just seen on the subject of radicalization, it seems important to focus on the tension between researchers who see Islam as a source of violence and others who present that political violence has always existed before *jihadism,* but in other forms. For the former, we can include researchers close to the "clash of civilizations." One of its main figures is Gilles Kepel, who prefers to seek the explanations of violence in the Muslim religion. Thus, Kepel refers to the text of Osama Bin Laden's former right-hand man, Abu Musab Al-Suri, "the architect of the global *jihad*" with his famous call for an Islamic world revolt and highlights, since 2005, the emergence of a third generation of *jihadists* (Kepel, 2015).[3] A little more nuanced, but along the same lines, the work directed by the political scientist Anne Muxel and the sociologist Olivier Galland shows through a survey in high schools, a propensity to approve or use violence among high school students "of Muslim origin" (Galland & Muxel, 2018). Finally, two very recent works by the "Kepelian movement" reactivate the idea of the "clash of civilizations." The first shows the danger that Islamism arises in the suburbs to the West (Rougier, 2020); the second book anticipates, for its part, a probable civil war in Europe caused by incarcerated *Salafo-jihadists* wishing to wage a more strategic revenge since the defeat of *Daech* (Micheron, 2020). Finally, for Dassetto, Islamism has become hegemonic in the Gramscian sense,

---

2   The notion of radicalization is not without problems in terms of scales of understanding whether in terms of micro (individual), meso (groups) and macro (society) analyses as Dutch researchers show even though the meso (peer groups or comrades in arms) plays a prominent role in radicalization processes (Doosje, Moghaddam, Kruglanski & De Wolf, 2019). Moreover, the occurrence of the terminology of deradicalization in the media has definitely blurred the cognitive perspectives of the term radicalization reduced to nothing since the unsuccessful attempts to apply it at the level of public and associative policies (Beunas, 2019).

3   For Félice Dassetto, it is rather the fifth generation (Dassetto, *op. cit.*).

progressively providing the Muslim world with "baggage of reasons and justifica-
tions that make radi... ation plausible and, from there, legitimize armed action"
(Dassetto, *op. cit.*). ...nded by the political scientist Olivier Roy is orientated rather
The the... ction. The author sees in the radical investment of current *ji-*
in the oppo... tion of a kind of "*Islamization of radicality*" (Roy, 2016). Indeed,
hadists ...erts," reject the culture and religion of their parents. They adhere to
for R... ...g people motivated to wage *jihad*, whether they are "*second gener-
...upture*" anchored in an exacerbated individualism and an ideology of
ati...m society. The "*Islamization of radicalism*" constitutes in a way a tran-
...ween the revolutionary communisms of the 1970s-1980s and the new
...s that are becoming apparent in the Middle East, Europe, and Southeast
...emaire, 2016). The disappearance of communisms as a support for social
...st has led to a lack of political outlets for anger that should undoubtedly be
...tioned today (Marlière, 2019: 98-107). Talal Asad, for his part, questions the
double ethics of modern, yet progressive, societies, which exert physical, but legal,
violence through preventive wars on Muslim populations forced to respond in
turn, due to the asymmetry of military power relations, through terrorism and
suicide bombings (Asad, *op. cit.*). Islam is not necessarily at fault in its theological
foundations, as it is the symptom of political, social, and cultural *malaise* (Liogier,
2016) and thus responds to accumulated anger, which makes the Anglo-Saxon sociologist Arjun Appadurai declare that we face a civilization of clashes rather than
a "clash of civilizations" (Appadurai, 2009).

C. Beyond the social and colonial question, and the history of "suburbs"

The paths taken by *jihadists* appear to be quite heterogeneous, as reflected in research and sociological literature. First of all, one could refer to researchers who
see *jihadism as* a historical continuity, whether in connection with the colonial
past or through the social history of working-class suburbs. Thus, François Burgat
sees in the phenomenon of radicalization a direct consequence of colonization
that is still not tolerated by the populations originating from Maghreb and Middle
Eastern countries (Burgat, 2016). He insists on the colonial, but also neo-colonial
dimension of political Islamism. Burgat shows that the return of an orthodox Islam
is to be correlated with the arrival of European powers in North Africa in the middle of the 19th century. According to him, contemporary *jihadism* is the result of
a form of neo-colonialism that prolongs past Islamic claims, but in a more radical
way, although current *jihadism* has its own dynamics and specific contemporary
issues (Dassetto, *op. cit.*). Instead, Alain Bertho highlights the historical genealogy
of urban working-class suburbs. He notes a real incapacity of the inhabitants of
the "suburbs" to be democratically represented and to defend their rights. Indeed,
since the March for Equality in 1983, through the "riots of 2005," Bertho insists

on the political disillusionment of the working-class suburb, inhabitants, leading progressively, but irremediably, to the phenomenon of di... zation among the latest generations (Bertho, 2016). Positioning themselves in... between the co- lonial past and the social history of urban working-class neigh... tions, Anglo-Saxon researchers make similar observations by su... explana- of a continuous war between Muslims and Westerners since the... the idea century (Hussey, 2015; Dély & Heargraves, 2016).

Instead, other scholars have emphasized the greater heterogeneit 19th ists' backgrounds. First of all, the historian Jenny Raflik has shown, wh... the anarchists of the 19th century, the revolutionary communists of the m... century or the *jihadists* of today, the importance of the rupture with the ins... tional, social, or family environment, which constitutes one of the common d... nominators of all terrorist paths, whatever the era studied (Raflik, *op. cit.*). Anthro- pologist Dounia Bouzar, for her part, recalls the existence of radicalized young people, both from the middle classes who are foreign to the Muslim world, and that of the "suburbs," in the deradicalization center where she conducted her in- vestigation (Bouzar, 2016). Ethnopsychiatrist Tobie Nathan, who has received a hundred radicalized youth in his practice, is surprised to see people from affluent social backgrounds as well (Nathan, 2017). For these researchers, Islam offers a regenerative framework for young people destabilized by a modern individualistic and competitive society who not only aspire to personal reconstruction, but also want to rebel against a political, cultural, social, and/or family order. Thus, not all radicalized youths come from working-class neighborhoods and Muslim families, just as not all youths from "suburbs" with an immigrant background and a Muslim background have become *jihadists* (Marlière, 2020: 45-65).

In our fieldwork of working-class neighborhoods, we began with the obser- vation that the feeling of injustice structured the social representations of many of the young people we interviewed (Marlière, 2008). The political, economic, and social capacities to respond to this feeling remain limited insofar as social inequal- ities and discrimination persist on a daily basis without the possibility or the will to remedy them in positive and constructive ways. This observation of powerless- ness accentuates bitterness and feelings of revenge (Arendt, 1972) among the new generations, both from the "suburbs" and from the middle classes in the process of being downgraded. If some researchers advocate for following the sociologist Claude Dubar on the retributive dimensions of militant commitment at the sym- bolic level in order to structure a field of research (Fragnon, 2019), it seems ap- propriate to mobilize concepts applied in the human sciences on urban revolts in order to further expand the repertoire of analyses likely to apprehend a disparate, complex and controversial total social phenomenon.

3. The notion of relative frustration

A. Relative frustration: an American genealogy

The question of social frustration seems decisive insofar as the internalization of democratic egalitarian norms is assimilated by most citizens in the West. Following Raymond Boudon and Walter Gary Runciman, the sociologist Gérald Bronner attempts to articulate the themes of discrimination and humiliation, conveying the idea that adherence to terrorism is due to the social frustrations of radicalized youth (Bronner, 2016). He develops the following point: the concept of *relative frustration* emerges in the United States in an attempt to understand the behaviour of economically disadvantaged people in a more or less prosperous society. This notion has its roots in Tocqueville (Tocqueville, 1985), who argued that democracy opens up more "possibilities" and thus hope among the people. As paradoxical as it may seem, the greater openness of means of emancipation can also be the source of feelings of disillusionment and therefore of dissatisfaction likely to lead to despair. Durkheim's analysis of suicide draws on this idea. He develops the theory that in a context of deregulation of social norms, most often in a period of improved living conditions, suicide is a social fact that most often results from unfulfilled desires causing a feeling of "emptiness" that ensues from accumulated social frustrations (Durkheim, 2007). Indeed, the concept of *relative frustration* takes into account in greater depth the importance of the social context, the economic situation and the primacy of interactions and opportunities that are offered to individuals, especially in a society perceived as free. For the sociologist Raymond Boudon, the equitable norms of democratic societies have paradoxically generated social frustration among a large number of people who have internalized egalitarian norms, but who nevertheless feel that they do not benefit from the ideals displayed by democratic societies (Boudon, 1977). Robert K. Merton insists more on the individualization of inequalities and the driving impact of the consumer society in democratic societies: these phenomena are at the origin of competition between people and accentuate the *relative frustration* at the origin of personal conflicts and multiple frustrations (Merton, 1997). The sociologist Walter Runciman analyses democratic and multicultural societies and shows that the feeling of frustration is even more acute when the individual assimilates his "failure," not through a personal prism, but as the result of discrimination experienced by the community to which he belongs (Runciman, 1966). According to Gérald Bronner, adhering to extreme ideas relieves the individual of his discomforts by giving him a clearer and simpler vision of injustices. This observation, in certain aspects, clears the suffering person of his personal failure, thus enabling him to designate an identified enemy as responsible for his misfortunes. The question of the possibilities of success in democratic societies is therefore a potential trigger for social protest, or even revolution. The most striking example of this phenomenon is the increase in protests following the end of an economic depression and "crisis" (Davies, 1962).

B. From hope to disillusionment

According to Bronner, the issue of possible adequacy between individual aspiration and personal satisfaction is at stake. If there is too great a disproportion between the two, *relative frustration* may not only determine daily representations, but also the conduct of actions (Gurr, 1971). The notion of *relative frustration* has already been developed by Dietmar Loch on the subject of urban revolts. It was applied to explain the phenomenon in France, which claims to promote and ensure egalitarian republican values, but is confronted with a large number of riots, in contrast to Germany where the relationship with Turkish immigration is much more distant. French citizens from the Maghreb, who have been socialized according to republican values, seem to not all cope well with the injustices they face, unlike the children of Turkish immigrants who have been conditioned, in a way, to accomodate to unequal situations based on their ethnic origins. Thus, since the French republican ideal of "liberty, equality, and fraternity" has been more or less internalized (Loch, 2008)[4] by young French people from working-class and underprivileged urban areas with an immigrant background. It becomes particularly intolerable when it is not respected, in contrast to Germany, where the promises of equality to the Turkish second generation do not exist as such. According to Hugues Lagrange, these young people from working-class urban suburbs originating from former colonies are more likely to compare themselves to middle-class youth from the inner cities. Thus, "feelings of being second-class citizens provoke strong reactions" (Lagrange, 2008: 377). For these authors, *relative frustration* is therefore at the root of urban violence.

However, the question of radicalization is to a certain extent more complex. Indeed, through the notion of *relative frustration*, Gérald Bronner has questioned the role of Western societies in the rise of anger, lost illusions, but also of radicalization. The author demonstrates that these societies, through a set of values such as freedom, equality, recognition, and consumption, have developed in most people a set of aspirations and dreams that very few will be able to access in their lifetime (Bronner, *op. cit.*). Anger and bitterness are therefore all the stronger for some actors, as the frustration stems from the fact that they have built themselves through the values of freedom and equality promoted by institutions.

Thus, the race for consumption and recognition is the new Holy Grail for a majority of people today: "the equation leads to an optimal rate of frustration, which is all the more inevitable because the aspiration for distinction is always relative, which means that it is not enough to get a lot to be happy, but above all to get a little more than others" (Bronner: 261). The aspiration to succeed, whatever the domains from then on internalized as inaccessible, creates resentment towards the

---

4   In the majority of the interviews conducted with young people, questions relating to democracy or equality are omnipresent when we discuss discrimination, racial profiling, access to employment, or housing.

social system and its institutions. The colonial past, ordinary discrimination, and daily stigmatization have created distinctive personalities in certain young adults who are now receptive to ideological clusters of revenge and vengeance. These ideologies are all the stronger because they emerge and develop in a democratic society that *jihadists* perceive as failing. These radicalized youths have thus gradually developed systems of thought that they believe castigate the corrupt anddeceptive nature of social systems. This enables them to rationalize the destruction of institutions and codify mass murders in the name of an extreme ideology. Indeed, for Bronner, adherence out of frustration can constitute a powerful lever for the radicalization of minds insofar as it "results from a biographical situation and from social mechanisms linked to democratic systems" (Bronner: 335). Relative frustration echoes the social, economic and cultural transformations that are nowadays occuring in Europe, notably through the increase in structural inequalities and the sidelining of a growing part of the working classes in a competitive and highly consumerist society.

4. Denied subjectivities and disdained identities

A. The *jihadist:* a despised youth who responds with violence

A second approach involves questioning the role of the subjectivity of the actor or the individual. This notion has a less extensive theoretical genealogy than the previous one. However it can also provide some answers as to why people produce violence in the name of an idea or a belief. According to the sociologist Jérôme Ferret, radicalization leads to extreme political violence and questions the nature of the social contract of late modernity, due to the appearance of new subjectivities generating their own self-referential system (Ferret, 2015). Thus, the question of multiple social representations of identity that seem to compete with each other constitutes a new issue for our societies. This is why identity-based subjectivities that are ostracised or denied existence have no other recourse than violence to make themselves heard or recognized. It raises the question of recognition for a certain number of actors who are diminished in the public space.

Following the work of Alain Touraine and Michel Wieviorka, Jérôme Ferret explains that violence is the product of a political community's inability to implement the necessary conditions for a conflictual relationship between citizens and institutions: the impossibility of developing an appropriate expression engenders symbolic and social violence for stigmatized populations, in the absence of recognized or effective institutional or organizational mediation (Ferret, *op. cit.*). For this purpose, the term terrorism is not a relevant expression. In this case, Ferret prefers referring to a "total violence understood as a deliberate strategy of mindless violence, striking the civilian population according to the principle of disjunction between the victims of the attack [...] and the intended political target"

(Ferret: 21). This violence thus questions the nature of the social contract which grounds the democratic societies in which ve evolve. It raises the issue of social relationships and everyday interactions that are at the heart of a co-construction of violence and reciprocal animosity, whether between people and institutions or between individuals. This analysis by Jerôme Ferret holds our attention insofar as it consists in apprehending two forms of violence within the social contract: 1) the state of the monopoly of legitimate violence of state institutions in modern society at the heart of globalization and the capacity to prevent competing ideas or to counter these new violent projects; 2) the foreclosure of violence in late modern societies and the appearance of new emerging subjectivities, in particular of young adults caught up in this modernity. In other words, the extremist violence of the latter is a response to the institutional violence of the State, the consequence of a reciprocity between terror, repression and negation that reaches the extremes that we know during attacks.

Jerôme Ferret's studies are interesting insofar as they introduce the idea of an operational dialectic. According to this concept, the violence of terrorists responds to the symbolic negation of institutions that do not recognize these individuals' existence as subjects: destructive violence thus responds to ordinary symbolic political violence. Thus dehumanized by the powers in place, a certain youth may despise and even repudiate the institutions and people who are supposed to represent them. They may then mount insurrections against the wearers of the uniform, or even become radicalized by committing lethal attacks against anyone perceived as an ally of a system apprehended as iniquitous and illegitimate. The reciprocal negation between these two actors (institutional actors *versus* private actors) leads to a vicious circle of violence, repression, revenge, etc. The lack of recognition of an identity and the humiliations that this entails can also offer an avenue for reflection in the framework of our research program. It can therefore be traced back to the work of Alain Touraine and present that the discriminated actor is therefore unable to act individually or collectively.

B. In search of an short-lived but striking recognition

According to the readings conducted around our object of study, we can wonder if we are not able, through the recent social, cultural, and societal mutations, to attend a kind of transformation of the processes of socialization which favors individualism. And also recognition as shown by the extent of the social networks and the attitude of the new generations concerning appearance and individual competition. We should thus seek a temporary desire for recognition in order to attract the attention of a society that despises one on a daily basis. The sociologist Didier Lapeyronnie, on the subject of the urban revolts of 2005, has demonstrated that "the riot is a kind of short circuit: it allows an individual to overcome obstacles in an instant, to become a recognized actor, even in a negative, ephemeral and illusory way, and to obtain 'gains' without being able to control and even less to negotiate either the recognition or the possible benefits" (Lapeyronnie, 2006: 445). In other words, urban riots reinvigorate the despised or denied subjectivities of certain young people in suburbs in order to take temporary revenge on the institutions, to occupy the street for a limited period of time and to momentarily attract the attention of public opinion and therefore of the authorities.

But it would seem that in the case of *jihadism*, expecting recognition is taken to the extreme. For the political scientist Olivier Roy, it is the hero quest that motivates some radicalized youth: to rebuild their self-esteem through the image of a conqueror for a cause, whether it is just or not, even if it means appearing to be a "negative hero." Olivier Roy thus insists on the narcissistic aspect of *jihadism* where the emphasis on the ego takes precedence over geopolitical or political dimensions for some young people (Roy, 2016). For sociologist Farhad Khosrokhavar this even goes beyond the desire for recognition, greed for glory and success: "The promotion of oneself into an emir, for example, which replaces the dream of being president" (Khosrokhavar, 2018: 552). For certain radicalized young people from the working classes in the West who are experiencing academic or social failure and are therefore destined for a "future without a future" or for others (young people from the declassed middle classes) destined for a "future without adventure," *Daech* ultimately represents forms of rapid social ascension, for the former, and a stimulating and exotic escape, for the latter.

5. *"Politicité"* to rehabilitate politics

A. The political commitment of the desperate

Introduced and developed recently in France by the sociologist Denis Merklen, the concept of *politicité* can also allow us to reflect on the notion of radicalization or extreme political violence. *Politicité* appears in our study as a neologism likely to offer an alternative or a complement to the analysis of the notions previously developed. Denis Merklen suggests investigating the new forms of mobilization of the working classes since the destabilization of the labour society (Castel, 1995). Analysis through the territory of the suburbs makes it possible to take into account local solidarities, the capital of autochthony and the social, territorial, and cultural supports that accompany it. *Politicité* opens up a new perspective, one that gives these terrorist phenomena an undeniably political dimension. Indeed, within the working classes, whether in France or Argentina, Denis Merklen traces the seeds and configurations in the changes in political behavior that are becoming more radical, hence the notion of *politicité* to demonstrate that "the vast majority of democracies are faced with a resurgence of their working classes and their future is compromised by a profound crisis in the systems of social integration" (Merklen, 2009: 257).

In other words, the notion of *politicité* introduces a political and a broader social dimension that is not necessarily unanimously accepted. However, this perspective can shed additional light on the heuristic level: in fact, the author posits that this notion of *politicité* be broken down into three distinct but complementary registers: 1) survival; 2) protesting; 3) partisan action (Merklen, *ibid.*). While Denis Merklen notices a change in the relationship of the working classes regarding the elites, disqualified in their eyes. The working classes are developing new forms of political and symbolic representations, most often in a more pronounced radicality (Merklen, 2012: 55-73). Like Alain Bertho, for whom the deterioration of the living conditions of the working classes for more than thirty years in the public space is manifested by the recurrent shift to urban revolts, Denis Merklen believes that "the social movement and the politics of the working classes are entirely marked by a fundamental tension between the struggle for survival and the struggle for integration" (Merklen, ibid.). However, according to the author, the issues of survival and economic integration are at stake, hence the need to find more energetic strategies through a coherent political organization generating a more effective political antagonism to access goods and services and thus give meaning to symbolic struggles (Merklen, ibid.)

B. Particular and isolated mobilizations in Europe

In South American countries, the working classes are struggling to find their place in a neoliberal society. A radical *politicité* has therefore been structured on the scale of working-class spaces and is constantly targeting the political system and the public space so that these impoverished working classes can manifest their existence (Merklen, ibid.). In France, the fragmentation of the working classes is more pronounced and concerns part of the inhabitants of working-class urban neighborhoods. These individuals are already isolated from other working-class milieus from the point of view of their identity and ethnicity for the reasons analyzed above.[5] Due to their ethnic and social isolation, the political and social demands of these young people in working-class urban neighborhoods are totally discredited by the riotous action. Indeed, their grievances are transformed into «incivilities," even into threats to the Republic, because they are not taken into account by the political parties and the unions. Protest is thus depoliticized and most often results in forms of violence such as burning libraries (Merklen, 2015). Even if these young people, heirs to the social history of the urban working class suburbs, evolve in a country that is more comfortable from an economic and social point of view than Argentina, the strategies of resistance and organization are much less easy, as they remain a minority among the working classes in France. Thus the political situation of a part of the inhabitants of the urban working class suburbs is different from the *politicité* of the working classes analyzed in South America. The latter is more unitary in the image of the French working class in the 1960s: "The

---

5   See the example of the "yellow vests" movement.

working class *politicité* based on the figure of a worker who finds his place thanks to his effort and pain at work will thus turn on the heirs of this same working class when they are pushed aside by unemployment [...] It is within this framework that this fraction of the working classes that is constituted by the territory around the figures of the "neighborhood" and the "inhabitant" tries to reconstitute modalities of action and political participation in the face of the loss of power of the formerly dominant forms of popular mobilization" (Béroud, Bouffartigue, Eckert, & Merklen, 2016: 159).

C. Radicalization: an antagonistic dynamic

Since young people in working-class urban suburbs no longer have a clear-cut position in social relations of production, their moral and political commitment is only found in their local setting. An urban space that is, let us remember, disqualified. This political solitude, discussed above, shows that the political activity of adolescents and young adults remains circumscribed to their own perception of situations and to their territory, because it cannot be exported to the wider whole of the French working classes today. This is why the political demands made through this localized *politicité* in the neighborhood and only in these deindustrialized urban social spaces cannot be exercised elsewhere. They appear at the same time as a form of political impasse explaining the repeated riots, the "incivilities" in a loop or the chronic tensions with the institutions. This new form of territorial politics, circumscribed to urban working-class suburbs, has been oriented by dint of isolation, political recuperation (notably the Socialist Party) and various and sundry manipulations towards ethnic-religious forms, including Islam, which plays an increasingly unifying role (Piettre, 2013: 89-129). The isolation is further accentuated when certain "suburb youth" have participated directly in terrorist actions, undeniably revealing the equation between Islam and working-class suburbs. These observations show that structural conflict with institutions is therefore impossible. Faced with these repeated failures in terms of institutional recognition or political demands, Islamic radicalization appears as the ultimate recourse for civilizational, but above all social, transformation, and definitively takes over from other exhausted or ineffective forms of political mediation.

6. A moral economy of radicalization?

A. A competition of norms and values

Another interesting point of view could just as well be mobilized around moral or value issues: that of the "moral economy." The notion of "moral economy" is interesting to analyze issues surrounding morals, values, and principles. It introduces a new paradigm for the analysis of political violence and radicalization. All societies produce sets of norms and values. As societies grow bigger, the enlargement of the social fabric inherently leads to alternative, competing uses and customs to rise, leading relations between individuals and senses of belonging to become extremely complex. Our so-called "post-industrial" or "hypermodern" societies no longer create univocal norms, but plural and sometimes even contradictory ones. Individuals in such societies determine themselves according to these norms and values, thanks to which they shape their moral understanding of experiences they live. As Fassin and Eideliman put it, "they are thus led to make decisions in the name of moral criteria, sometimes encountering dilemmas, and to experience affects, and even to enter into conflict with one another" (2012: 10).

Eventually, the numerous trade-offs faced by individuals on the field of morals and values inevitably leads to at best difficult coexistence, and at worst to tensions and conflicts. Moreover, individuals are summoned to make choices between individual ethics and the (perceived) collective morality. In hypermodern, globalized, complex societies such as ours, competition between values and norms is exacerbated and faced by every social group and individual.

In line with Fassin's classification (2012: 37), we may divide the field of moral economy in two. First comes the work of Edward Thompson and James C. Scott on farmers (Thompson, 1968; Scott, 1976), whose set of morals and values the two scholars deemed to be determined as a bedrock for potential unrest, were their fundamental interest to be forgotten by the elite. Hence the formation and conservation of principles and values that would ensure the perpetuation of their lifestyle and traditions in case of a despotic government. The second trend in moral economy research rather focuses on groups' means of dealing with rules and laws, questioning individuals and entire social groups' sense of ethics and respect of morals. For Fassin, both approaches are essential to shape an effective framework of moral economy. We need to take into account the studied actors' perception of their own daily life to understand reasons for (in our case) anger, deception, unrest, as well as resistance to and avoidance of rules, norms and values. This can be cheating, concealing, sabotaging but also committing acts of violence such as terrorism.

Fassin states that the notion of moral economy includes "the production, distribution, circulation and use of emotions and values, norms and obligations in the social space" (Fassin, 2012: 37). To better understand this notion, he insists on four essential points: 1) the moral economy is moral; 2) contrary to the philosophical approach, empirical work has shown that we can associate values and norms; 3) emotions are not separate from values and norms; 4) moral economies is a valid framework to understand all social worlds both locally and globally (Fassin, ibid).

The anthropological dimension of moral economy allows us to better grasp the contexts and framework in which norms and values find meaning. The sociological dimensions provide the tool for an in-depth analysis of actors' interplay and the orientation of social movements. The author goes on stating that the sociological dimension helps to understand the *raison d'être* of individuals: "the study of moral economies implies analyzing both [*individual's*] sociology [...] and their anthropology, in the sense of transformations of values, norms, emotions, and the confrontations they foster" (Fassin, ibid.: 43). The notion of moral economy enables us to analyse actors' actions, power relations, by contextualizing them and helping us understand their meaning.

B. Specific and binding standards and values

Kokoreff and Lapeyronnie have also referred to the notion of "moral economy," although they undoubtedly focused more on Edward P. Thompson's approach on working-class suburbs and discrimination-related issues. The two scholars write that "the moral economy of these suburbs is marked by a profound rupture of the population with the political and institutional universe. A feeling of injustice and humiliation is combined with an exacerbated resentment towards institutions to produce discursive positions such as: "The Republic does not keep its promises, it is a lie for which social housing dwellers pay the price. They feel that they do not participate in social life and, even more so, that society is a foreign, hostile universe constantly sidelining and stigmatizing them. Riots are the most spectacular expressions of this phenomenon"" (Kokoreff & Lapeyronnie, 2013: 83).

Thus, a moral economy specific to the inhabitants of working-class suburbs inevitably leads to the aforementioned question of injustice. The authors additionally wish to stress the difference in focus between riots and the moral economy. They distinguish a greater focus on "civic" justice than on social justice, because that discrimination is more intolerable than social inequality (Kokoreff & Lapeyronnie, ibid.: 81), because the ethnic and identity issue prevails over the motivations linked to class membership for these populations. This is a major addition as it explains how these neighborhoods' inhabitants, especially the young ones, then fall into a mix of rhetorical postures mixing identity, religion, ethnicity as the base of their moral economy, rather than using traditional norms and rules accepted by the wider society they don't feel part of. Kokoreff articulates his understanding of urban riots according to four essential elements: "identification with the victims, being part of the neighborhood, negotiating one's place, settling accounts" (Kokoreff, 2008: 201). The moral economies that structure and steer the social representations of the young people present in our field demonstrate differences in their perception of inequalities. This strongly differentiates them from the majority of the French population. This perception inherited from the group isolates them socially, thus fostering and worsening a vicious circle of misunderstanding and bitterness.

Therefore, we can analyze radicalization thanks to the notion of a moral economy. Indeed, these radicalized young people who decide to go to Syria or to shoot with a Kalashnikov at people who came to a concert at the Bataclan also respond to standards and values. Khosrokhavar's works give us some clues in this direction by providing an extremely interesting understanding of the underlying elements motivating radicalization, although, claiming to be inspired by Husserl's phenomenology, this author does not refer to the notion of moral economy. Khosrokhavar shows that *jihadists* try to distance themselves from a Western society they consider cold, vain, flawed and purposeless. Three points are essential to determine their radicalization: 1) perceived humiliation from living in housing estates and ghettos; 2) frustration, lack of prospects for the future, perceived constant discrimination; 3) sentiment of being under attack, and correlated enhanced sense of belonging to a group and identification as a member of the *ummah*, the community of Muslims (Khosrokhavar, 2014: 26-28). The author summarizes *jihadists'* moral economy accordingly: "Radicalization overwhelmingly arises when the following pair of feeling is combined: on the one hand, humiliation and despair, and on the other, the willingness to inflict an even greater humiliation to others and the deeply-rooted conviction of being able to achieve their utopia from a "theology of mad experience" that justifies the irenic vision of a future undetermined in time on the other" (Khosrokhvar, ibid.: 32).

C. Impose your values and "convert the system?"

To conclude on this point, the notion of moral economy could allow for a better understanding of the context in which radicalization processes emerge. It would enable us to understand the factors motivating actions pursuing recognition and equality even though the institutional frame is perceived as neglecting or showing despisal for its demands (Marlière, 2018: 43-50).

These means of action may to a certain extent be divided along four lines: 1) spiritual line (quest for equality and ideal); 2) individual line in a world that they perceive as corrupt (quest for justice and reparation); 3) social line through a substitute identity (quest for recognition of a "cultural specificity" they defend focused on orthodox Islam) and, at last; 4) political line through the adherence to "Islam" as a structured and dogmatic value system that effectively confronts inequalities and injustice. These values seem in confrontation with society's main narratives and dominant sets of values.

7. What about the concept of Habitus ?

A. Personal dispositions, structural issues and a favorable situation for the habitus of radicalized people

Another concept seems essential to us in an attempt to reflect on the processes of radicalization qualified as Islamic: the one proposed by Pierre Bourdieu which is the habitus. Habitus is difficult to mobilize insofar as its ambition is to play the role of mediator between lifestyles and organic institutional structures while giving meaning to social practices. It is therefore a question of overcoming the oppositions between subjectivism and objectivism. If for many sociologists the evolution of the concept of habitus between its development in the 1960s by Bourdieu and its final use at the end of the 1990s makes its operationality delicate, nothing prevents us from looking at this concept for all that. try to reflect on the radicalization process as such. Indeed, Pierre Bourdieu has developed the concept of habitus on several occasions, but we are going to try to give a definition of it in the simplest possible way, taken up in his book *Le Sens Pratique*: existence produce habitus, systems of durable and transposable dispositions, structured structures predisposed to function as structuring structures, that is to say as generating principles of practices and representations which can be objectively adapted to their goal without assuming the aim conscious of ends and the express mastery of the operations necessary to achieve them, objectively "regulated" and "regular" without being in any way the product of obedience to rules, and, being all this, collectively orchestrated without being the product of "organizing action of a conductor" (Bourdieu, 1980, pp. 88-89). This definition is therefore likely to give us a more precise orientation of the habitus and in particular on the way in which we can use it for the phenomenon qualified as radicalization. In other words, are there socialization frameworks specific to a particular category of living conditions or social trajectories at the origin of lasting and transposable dispositions and therefore generating thoughts directing conscious practices towards a form of radicalization whose would Islam be the current medium? The permanent adjustment between objective probabilities and subjective expectations produces, according to Bourdieu, the structures of the habitus which is "the product of history" (Bourdieu, ibid., p. 90) or of a subjective and individual history. Thus habitus "produces history, habitus produces practices, individual and collective, and therefore of history, in accordance with the patterns generated by history; it ensures the active presence of past experiences which, deposited in each organism in the form of patterns of perception, thought and action, tend, more surely than all formal rules and all explicit standards, to guarantee the conformity of practices and their constancy over time" (Bourdieu, ibid., p. 90). This is why the concept of habitus in terms of the organization of the patterns of perception, thought or action of the cognitive processes leading to radicalization can be useful. Indeed, we observe that the mechanisms that lead to the violence of which Islam is the ideological support therefore correspond to specific social paths that have been internalized from childhood. Youthful journeys with interpretative schemes that are admittedly complex and sometimes contradictory due to the competition of the norms of the dominant society and those of family values, for example, but whose dialectic gradually generates a coherence according to an aim adjustable to the "Space of possibilities." However, when possibilities are limited for certain young people from working-class backgrounds due to social determinism and are reduced even further due to an uncertain economic situation, there is a disorganization of behavior and thought. Many radicalized people thus find themselves in objective insecurity by being confronted with a difficult present and a mortgaged future. The concept of habitus taking into account social positions to have little and in front of infrastructures that discriminate, downgrade or exclude, can give answers on human indignity.

B. Habitus to better understand the pathways of individuals in connection with decisive contexts

As Isabelle Sommier shows in an article already cited, the process of radicalization goes back a long way: "So radical engagement is obviously a process. First, because, unlike what common expressions such as "enter into radicalism," "go into armed struggle" or a fortiori "fall into" suggest, an individual does not "fall" into terrorism. It arrives there in successive stages which can, in fact, be difficult to date, even to identify, to the point that one could speak of a "commitment by default," consecutive to "small successive choices" of which none "appears significant in itself but which in the end, through the effects of thresholds and ratchets, make it difficult to go backwards or, in this case, to de-escalate" (Sommier, 2012, *op. cit.*, p. 23). If the author makes no mention of the concept of habitus in her article, we can clearly see through this passage here the common thread that constitutes the person's life story combining structural context, economic opportunities, and individual values. It is not a question of giving in to the biographical illusion either, but it is clear that the notion of habitus through a reconstruction of individual historical paths taking into account the contexts and issues can provide us with elements of analysis. Indeed, the processes that lead to radicalization can be confused with the concept of habitus and can only be understood through a life story in order to trace the biographical threads of the social trajectory of the person where the notions of socialization and commitment are, so to speak, essential: "Everything takes place as if habitus manufactured coherence and necessity out of accident and contingency" (Bourdieu, 1980, *op. cit.*, p. 134). But how, through this concept, to discern the mechanisms or processes likely to lead to radicalization?

Habitus is therefore a "structuring mechanism that operates agents from within, although it is not strictly speaking neither strictly individual nor, in itself, completely determining behavior" (Bourdieu & Wacquant, 2014, p. 56). But the big question then that arises at this point is whether there is an essential over-determination which leads young people to engage in terrorist activities? If the divisions of social work, of classes and of sexes direct an overdetermination in terms of bodily mobilization, in terms of class values or else according to the gendered separation of roles, it is much more difficult to be able to define within the habitus concept of the mechanisms that lead to Islamic radicalization. Now Bourdieu shows us that the habitus can manifest itself in certain circumstances or certain precise conjunctures: "the habitus is revealed only—we must keep in mind that it is a question of a system of dispositions, that is, —to say of potentialities, of potentialities—in relation to a determined situation. It must be conceived of as a kind of spring that is waiting to be triggered, and, depending on the stimuli and the structure of the field, the same habitus can generate different, even opposing practices" (Bourdieu, Wacquant, *op. cit.*, pp. 184-185). Without making any bad puns, the verb trigger turns out to be the catalyst for possible action for people whose journeys may lead at one time or another to violence. But, as Bourdieu asserts, the same habit depending on changing situations can react differently or even lead to opposite actions. It is therefore difficult at this stage to specify whether there are specific habitus leading to radicalization as the patterns incorporated according to conjunctures or circumstances may react in distinct ways in a similar context.

Depending on the surveys carried out here and there on the question of Islamic radicalization, it is very difficult to define whether there are overdeterminations favoring the passage to violence insofar as the trajectories are not only multiple between the working classes and the middle classes, between the sexes but also between the ethnico-cultural origins: only the youth constitutes an explanatory variable at the level of the "passage to the act" for the moment. It is therefore difficult, at the present time, to establish specificities in terms of habitus in terms of patterns of incorporation or disposition that lead to jihadism. But nothing prevents, as sociologist Marc Joly emphasizes, from developing "investigative and conceptualization procedures allowing for the contingency of situations, experiences and necessary concatenations that need to be implemented. "Habitus cleavages" and "cleavage habitus" appear to be inherent in differentiated and unequal human societies. They are even, probably, the most widespread psychic manifestations of domination relations" (Joly, 2018, p. 176). All that remains is to understand how our societies have become what they are and above all, for what interests us here, how certain radicalized individuals have come to commit attacks and mobilize at the risk of their existence and that of others, to fight a society they hate and consider corrupt while other young people think the opposite when they sometimes have similar backgrounds.

The concept of habitus is not only intended to promote the reading of actions, thoughts and communications between individuals since it also sets itself the function of reorienting "the scale of the bio-psycho-sociological thought regime of humanity" (Joly, *op. cit.*, p. 169). Hence the great ambition of the concept to take into account both group values but also the choices of the person as an individual within a given institutional and cyclical framework. This is why empirical studies based on the concept of habitus could guide us on the aptitudes to identify the processes, paths and trajectories likely to lead to violent political actions. They could also inform us about social contexts, economic conditions but also the structural configurations in place. This would require micro-social and detailed surveys around a few people with similar social backgrounds in order to understand the similarities but also the divergences that lead to radicalization processes among certain young people.

Conclusion

The phenomena of Islamic terrorism, *jihadism*, and radicalization question the very foundations of our modern, democratic societies. However, despite this essential critical aspect, the social processes that lead young Westerners to radicalization remain to be investigated. In order to take effective action against *jihadism* and the processes of radicalization, this article recommends endorsing a multi-disciplinary approach to overcome methodological debates between academics and scholars. Multiplying statistical surveys and empirical research could provide researchers with a detailed summary of the main trends in modern *jihadism*. This ideology has produced a complete sub-system, with its paths, sensibilities, rules, sense of belonging, social representation (Dassetto, *op. cit.*).

The concepts applied so far to urban riots and separatism cannot explain the phenomenon of Islamic radicalization in its generality. However, it could facilitate the production of classifications and typologies for specific individuals depending on their personal life paths. Gaining an empirical knowledge of personal contexts in which *jihadists* evolved would definitely facilitate an in-depth analysis of the reasons for individuals to adhere to such extreme ideologies. For example, the experience of (perceived) exclusion and subsequent frustration and anger, combined to feelings of "denied personality," may be at the roots of cognitive sensibilities to radical stances. The brutal encounter between felt injustices, urban segregation, and discriminations, with society's constant promotion of notions of consumption and competition between individuals have fed misunderstandings and dissent, the bedrock of long-term political violence. Finally, the concept of habitus could show us how the internal divisions imposed by structures, cyclical issues and socialization processes are likely to lead individuals to want to destroy institutions through a deadly ideology.

In other words, Merton's "middle range" concepts may help us to grasp how events occurring in young people's early years may turn them into *jihadists*. At this stage, we could be able to elaborate typologies of important psychological breaks that would open the way for an effective identification of the core components of radicalisation. This underlines the essential role of social sciences, thanks to its distinctive nuance, distance and reflexion, to combat *jihadism* and other radical ideologies questioning the founding precepts of our progressive and liberal societies.

Bibliography

Appadurai, A., 2009, *Geography of anger, Violence in the age of globalization*, Paris, Éditions Payot et Rivage.

Arendt, H., 1972, *Du mensonge à la violence. Essai de politique contemporaine*, Paris, Calmann-Lévy.

Asad, T., 2018, *Suicide attacks. Anthropological questions*, Kremlin-Bicêtre, Zones sensibles.

Atran, S., 2016, *The Islamic State is a Revolution*, Paris, Les Liens qui Libèrent.

Béroud, S., Bouffartigue, P., Eckert, H., & Merklen, D., 2016, *En quête des classes populaires, Un essai politique*, Paris, La dispute.

Beunas, C., 2019, "From radical to 'radicalized.' Les usages médiatiques de la notion de déradicalisation en France (2014-2017)," *Deviance and Society*, 1, 43, 2019, pp. 3-39.

Bertho, A., 2016, *Les enfants du chaos. Essai sur le temps des martyrs*, Paris, La découverte.

Boudon, R., 1977, *Effets pervers et ordre social*, Paris, PUF.

Bourdieu, P., 1980, *Le sens pratique*, Paris, Les éditions de Minuit.

Bourdieu, P., 2000, *Esquisse d'une théorie de la pratique*, Paris, Le Seuil.

Bourdieu, P., Wacquant L., 2014, *Invitation à la sociologie réflexive*, Paris, Le Seuil.

Bouzar, D., *Comment sortir de l'emprise "djihadiste?"* Paris, Les éditions de l'Atelier, 2015.

Bronner, G., 2016, *La pensée extrême. Comment des hommes ordinaires deviennent des fanatiques*, Paris, PUF.

Burgat, F., 2016, *Understanding political Islam. A research trajectory on Islamist otherness*, Paris, La découverte.

Castel, R., 1995, *Les métamorphoses de la question sociale. Une chronique du salariat*, Paris, Fayard.

Crettiez, X., 2016, "Penser la radicalisation. A processual sociology of the variables of violent engagement," *Revue française de sciences politiques*, 5, 66, 2016, pp. 709-727.

Coolsaet, R. (ed.), 2011, *Jihadi terrorism and radicalisation challenge European and American experiences*, Surrey, Ashgate Publishing.

Dassetto, F., 2018, *Jihad u Akhbar. Essai de sociologie historique dans le sunnisme contemporain (1970-2018)*, Louvain-la-Neuve, Presses universitaires de Louvain.

Daston, L., 1995, "The moral Economy of Science," *Osiris,* 2nd series, 10, *Constructing knowledge in the history of science*, pp. 2-24.

Davies, J.C., 1962, "Towards a theory of revolution," *American sociological review*, 27, pp. 5-29.

Dély, R., Hargreaves, A., 2016, "De la discrimination à la disqualification : les minorités postcoloniales et la tentation djihadistes," *in* Blanchard P., Bancel N., Thomas D. (eds.), *Vers la guerre des identités? De la fracture coloniale à la révolution ultranationale*, Paris, La découverte, pp. 239-249.

Doosje, B., Mogghaddam, F.M., Kruglanski, A.W., & De Wolf, A., "Terrorism, radicalization and deradicalization," *Current Opinion in Psychology* 11 (2016): 79-84.

Durkheim, E., 2007, *Le suicide*, Paris, PUF.

Fassin, D., 2012, "Vers une théorie des économies morales," *in* D. Fassin, J.-S. Eideliman (sous la dir.), Économies morales contemporaines, Paris, La Découverte, pp. 17-49.

Fassin ,D., Eideliman, J.S., 2012, "Introduction. Défense et illustration des économies morales," *in* D. Fassin, J.-S. Eideliman, Économies morales contemporaines, Paris, La Découverte.

Ferret, J., 2015, *Total political violence. A challenge for the social sciences*, Paris, Lemieux éditeur.

Fragon, J., 2019, "Literature review. Thinking 'radical engagement,'" *Fields of Mars*, 2, 33, pp. 115-134.

Galland, O., & Muxel A. (Sous la dir.), *La tentation radicale. Enquête auprès des lycéens*, Paris, PUF.

Guérandel, C., & Marlière, E., 2016, "Les djihadistes à travers *Le Monde*. Pluralité des analyses et impensés," *Hommes § Migrations*, 1315, pp. 9-16.

Gurr, T., 1971, *Why men rebel*, Princeton, Princeton University Press.

Heath-Kelly, C., 2016, *Death and security. Memory and mortality*, Manchester, Manchester University Press.

Honneth, A., 2006, *La société du mépris. Vers une nouvelle théorie critique*, Paris, La Découverte.

Hussey, A., 2015, *Insurrections in France. Du Maghreb colonial aux émeutes de banlieues. Histoire d'une longue guerre*, Paris, Editions du Toucan.

Joly, M., 2018, *Pour Bourdieu*, Paris, CNRS éditions.

Kepel, G. (with Jardin, A.), 2015, *Terreur dans l'hexagone. Genèse du jihad français*, Paris, Gallimard.

Khosrokhavar, F., 2014, *Radicalisation*, Paris, Maison des sciences de l'homme.

Khosrokhavar, F., 2018, *The New Jihad in the West,* Paris, Robert Laffont.

Kokoreff, M., 2008, *Sociologie des émeutes*, Paris, Payot.

Kokoreff, M., & Lapeyronnie D., 2013, *Refaire la cité. L'avenir des banlieues*, Paris, Le Seuil.

Lemaire, M., 2016, *Dans le piège de la guerre insurrectionnelle. L'Ociddent à l'*épreuve du communisme hier, de l'*islamisme aujourd'hui*, Paris, L'Harmattan.

Lagrange, H., 2008, "Emeutes, ségrégation urbaine et aliénation politique," Revue française de sciences politiques, 3, 58, pp. 377-401.

Liogier, R., 2016, *La guerre des civilisations n'aura pas lieu. Coexistence and violence in the 21ˢᵗ century*, Paris, CNRS Edition.

Loch, D., 2008, "Pourquoi n'y a- t-il pas d'émeutes urbaines en Allemagne, Les jeunes issus de l'immigration en France et en Allemagne entre (absence de) protestations et politique de la ville," *Revue suisse de sociologie*, 34, 2, pp. 281-306.

Luizard, P.J., 2015, *Le piège Daech. The Islamic State or the trap of history*, Paris, La découverte.

Kundnani, A., 2015, *A decade lost. Rethinking radicalisation and extremism*, London, Clayton.

Lapeyronnie, D., 2006, "Révolte primitive dans les banlieues françaises. Essai sur les émeutes de novembre 2005," *Déviance et société*, 4, 30, pp. 431-448.

Marlière, E., 2021, *La fabrique sociale de la radicalisation. Une contre-enquête sociologique*, Paris, Ed. Berger-Levrault.

Marlière, E., 2020, "Les radicalisé(e)s: des parcours multiples aux convergences," *in* M. Boucher (ed.), *Radicalités identitaires. La démocratie face à la radicalisation islamiste, indigéniste et nationaliste*, Paris, L'Harmattan, pp. 45-65.

Marlière, E., 2019, "From communism to Islam. Reflections on political violence," *Esprit*, 460, 12, 2019, pp. 98-107.

Marlière, E., 2018, "Pistes pour une économie morale du sentiment d'injustice parmi les jeunes des quartiers populaires urbains," *L'Année du Maghreb*, 18, 1, pp. 43-50.

Marlière, E., 2008, *La France nous a lâchés! Le sentiment d'injustice chez les jeunes de cité*, Paris, Fayard.

Mauger, G., 2016, "Reactionary rhetoric. Islamophobia (2). On Islamist radicalization," *Savoir/Agir*, 3, 37, pp. 91-99.

Merklen, D., 2009, *Quartiers populaires, quartiers politiques*, Paris, La Dispute.

Merklen, D., 2012, "Of political violence in democracy," *Cities*, 2, 50, pp. 57-73.

Merklen, D., 2015, *Why do we burn libraries*, Paris, Presses de L'Enssib.

Merton, R.K., 1997, *Elements of sociological theory and method*, Paris, A. Colin.

Micheron, H., 2020, *Le jihadisme français. Quartiers, Syrie, Prisons*, Paris, Gallimard.

Nathan, T., 2017, *Les âmes errantes*, Paris, Éditions iconoclastes, 2017.

Neuman, P.R., & Kleiman, S., 2013, "How rigorous is radical research," *Democracy and securitization*, 9, 4, pp. 360-382.

Piettre, A., 2013, "Islam (im)politique et quartier (im)populaire. Retour critique sur les émeutes de novembre 2005," *L'Homme et la société*, 1, 187-188, pp. 89-129.

Raflik, J., 2016, *Terrorism and globalization. Approches historiques*, Paris, Gallimard.

Raggazi, F., 2014, *"Towards a police multiculturalism?". La lutte contre la radicalisation en France, aux Pays-Bas et au Royaume-Uni*, Sciences-Po, CERI-CNRS, Paris, Les études du CERI n°206.

Rougier, B. (under the direction), *Les territoires conquis de l'islamisme*, Paris, PUF.

Roy, O., 2016, *Jihad and Death,* Paris, Le Seuil.

Runciman, W.G., 1966, *Relative deprivation and social justice: A study of attitude to social inequality in twentieth-century England*, London, Routlege and Kegan Paul.

Scott, J., 1976, *The Moral Economy of the Peasant. Rebellion and Subsistence in Southeast Asia*, Yale University Press, New Haven.

Sommier, I., "Engagement radical, désengagement et déradicalisation. Continuum et lignes de fractures," *Lien social et politique*, 68, 2012, pp. 15-35.

Thompson, E.P., 1968, *The making of the English Working Class*, Penguin Books, London.

Tocqueville, A., 1985, *L'Ancien Régime et la révolution*, Paris, Gallimard.

Van Campenhoudt, L., 2017, *How did they get there? Les clés pour comprendre le parcours des jihadistes*, Paris, A. Colin, 2017.

International Journal on Criminology • Volume 9, Number 1 • Winter 2022

The Impacts of Organizational Structure on Salafi-Jihadist Terrorist Groups in Africa

By Mahmut Cengiz, PhD and Huseyin Cinoglu, PhD

Abstract

Africa has become a haven for jihadist terrorist organizations that run the gamut from local groups fighting to avenge political and economic grievances to splinter groups affiliated with the Islamic State in Iraq and Syria (ISIS) or al-Qaeda. Jihadist groups that left Syria and moved into the Sahel region of Africa after ISIS was defeated have only increased the threat of terrorism in the region. The organizational structure of these groups has made efforts to counter their operational capacity extremely difficult. While some of these groups, such as Boko Haram and Al-Shabaab, are organizationally independent, others, such as ISIS and Qaeda affiliates, are organizationally dependent and rely on either a hub-spoke or an all-channel group structure. The leaders of these dependent groups seek the endorsement of or assignments from the group to which they are affiliated. The results of this study show that organizationally dependent groups target military and state institutions exclusively and perpetrate fewer terrorist incidents than other jihadist organizations in the region.

Keywords: al-Shabaab, Boko Haram, Africa, organization structure, organizational models, al Qaeda, ISIS franchises, JNIM

Los impactos de la estructura organizativa en los grupos terroristas salafistas yihadistas en África

Resumen

África se ha convertido en un refugio para las organizaciones terroristas yihadistas que van desde grupos locales que luchan para vengar agravios políticos y económicos hasta grupos disidentes afiliados al Estado Islámico en Irak y Siria (ISIS) o al-Qaeda. Los grupos yihadistas que abandonaron Siria y se mudaron a la región africana del Sahel después de que ISIS fuera derrotado solo han aumentado la amenaza del terrorismo en la región. La estructura

doi: 10.18278/ijc.9.1.5

organizativa de estos grupos ha hecho extremadamente difíciles los esfuerzos para contrarrestar su capacidad operativa. Si bien algunos de estos grupos, como Boko Haram y Al-Shabaab, son independientes desde el punto de vista organizativo, otros, como los afiliados de ISIS y Qaeda, son dependientes desde el punto de vista organizativo y se basan en una estructura de grupo central o de todos los canales. Los líderes de estos grupos dependientes buscan el respaldo o las asignaciones del grupo al que están afiliados. Los resultados de este estudio muestran que los grupos organizativamente dependientes se dirigen exclusivamente a las instituciones militares y estatales y perpetran menos incidentes terroristas que otras organizaciones yihadistas de la región.

Palabras clave: al-Shabaab, Boko Haram, África, estructura organizativa, modelos organizativos, al Qaeda, franquicias ISIS, JNIM

组织架构对非洲萨拉菲-圣战主义恐怖集团产生的影响

摘要

非洲已成为圣战主义恐怖组织的避风港，这些组织的规模范围包括从"为报复政治不满和经济不满而战"的地方集团，到与伊斯兰国（ISIS）或基地组织有关联的小集团。离开叙利亚，并在伊斯兰国被击败后进入非洲撒哈拉区域的圣战分子集团仅仅增加了该地区的恐怖主义威胁。这些集团的组织架构让那些对抗其操作能力的举措变得极为困难。尽管例如博科圣地和索马里青年党等集团在组织上是独立的，然而，伊斯兰国和基地组织分支等却在组织上具有依赖性并且需要轴辐式或全方位的集团架构。这些非独立集团的领导试图获取其所属集团的支持或任务。本研究得出的结果表明，依靠组织的集团专门以军事组织和国家组织为目标，并且比该区域其他圣战组织参与更少的恐怖主义事件。

关键词：索马里青年党，博科圣地，非洲，组织架构，组织模型，基地组织，伊斯兰国分支，"支持伊斯兰与穆斯林"组织（JNIM）

Introduction

Counterterrorism efforts in the world have failed to stem the tide of bombings and killings that contribute to the roughly 8,000 terrorist incidents each year that various databases have documented.[1] Efforts to transform terrorist breeding grounds by crushing and containing the groups' operatives and leaders, destroying their defenses, delegitimizing their standing among members and sympathizers, and implementing diversion tactics[2] have been to no avail, as many terrorist groups bounce back from disruptive events, survive intact, and increase their attacks. Recent discussions on terrorist organizations have focused on the longevity and resilience of these groups and what is contributing to their increasing capacity to cause devastative harm and destruction.

Africa is one of the major hot spots for terrorist organizations. National and multinational military efforts have been no match for the resilience of Al-Qaeda and ISIS-affiliated groups on the continent. In 2019, for example, countries in Africa endured roughly 3,500 terrorist attacks—double the number of militant jihadist-group attacks—in 2013.[3] The attacks were perpetrated by dozens of groups operating in 14 countries[4] and resulted in the death of 10,000 people. Terrorism trends in Africa indicate that salafi-jihadist[5] groups that left Syria have sought refuge in African countries, mostly in the Sahel region.

Al-Qaeda's focus on *localization* and ISIS's focus on *expansion through loose ties* with clusters of like-minded individuals gave birth to multiple affiliated groups whose members made their way to and reconstituted their intergroup structure in Africa. Some of these groups—such as Boko Haram and Al-Shabaab—have declared loyalty to and are ideologically affiliated with either al-Qaeda or ISIS, but have not forsaken their independence. Other groups pledge their allegiance to and are organizationally dependent on and under the command of either ISIS (e.g., ISIS-West Africa Province and ISIS-Greater Sahara Province) or Al-Qaeda (e.g., Hay'at Tahrir al-Sham and Jama'a Nusrat ul-Islam wal-Muslimin). This study compares two groups of dependent terrorist organizations (i.e., one ISIS and one al-Qaeda-affiliate groups) and one group of independent terrorist organizations

---

1   According to the Global Terrorism Trends and Analysis Center (GTTAC) database, the number of terrorist incidents was 8,093 in 2018 (Annex of Statistical Information Country Reports on Terrorism 2018, p. 5); Global Terrorism Database (GTD, 2019) reported it as 7,553.

2   Gaines and Kremling, *Homeland Security and Terrorism,* 136.

3   *African Center for Strategic Studies,* "Threat from African Militant Islamist Groups Expanding, Diversifying."

4   Ibid.

5   Salafi jihadism reflects the strict interpretation of the Qur'an and the Hadiths and seeks to advocate for Islamic ideological goals by violent means. According to Maher, "there are five essential and irreducible features of the Salafi Jihadi movement: tawhid [the unity of God], hakimiyya [sovereignty], al-wala' wa-l-bara' [loyalty and disavowal], jihad and takfir [excommunication, declaring someone an unbeliever]." Maher, *A History of Salafi-Jihadism: The History of an Idea,* 13-14.

(i.e., Boko Haram and al-Shabaab) in terms of number of attacks, fatality rate, target type, group-leader ascension, and intergroup structures.

Organizational Structure in Terrorist Groups

Terrorist groups simultaneously operate under two basic organizational structures: intragroup and intergroup. The intragroup structure represents how group members are connected to each other inside the group, while the intergroup structure reflects how different groups are networked to each other. The models used within those structures vary from one terrorist group to another. For example, some terrorist groups refine the basic structure with what one researchers calls *chain networks; all-channel networks*; and *star, hub, or wheel networks*.[6] Williams and Godson describes the refinement in terms of five models: *market, enterprise, cultural, ethnic network*, and *social network*,[7] whereas Taylor and Swanson identify six organizational models: lone wolf, cell, network, hierarchical, umbrella, virtual model.[8]

Other researchers prefer the terms *bureaucracy, hub-spoke, all-channel, and market* to describe the organizational structure of terrorist groups. Groups with a *bureaucratic structure* have "clear departmental boundaries, clear lines of authority, and detailed reporting mechanisms."[9] Hezbollah is an example of a *bureaucratic structure* because each department in the group has its own specialization.[10]

Groups with a *hub-spoke structure* have a central actor to whom members must go before communicating with others in the group.[11] This type of group structure includes franchises.[12] Groups affiliated with ISIS are examples of the hub-spoke group structure. According to the U.S. State Department's 2018 Annex of Statistical Information, ISIS has affiliates[13] in 26 countries, including groups such as ISIS-Khorasan in Afghanistan, Jamaah Ansharut Daulah in Indonesia, and ISIS-West Africa in Nigeria, Niger, and Chad.[14] The group leader in these and other hub-spoke terrorist organizations do not have central command and control.

---

6   Martin, *Understanding Terrorism: Challenges, Perspectives, and Issues*, 264.

7   Williams and Godson, *Anticipating Organized and Transnational Crime*, 2002.

8   Taylor and Swanson, *Terrorism, Intelligence & Homeland Security*, 143.

9   Joshua, "A Basic Model Explaining Terrorist Group Organizational Structure."

10   Ranstorp, "Hizbollah's Command Leadership: Its Structure, Decision-Making and Relationship with Iranian Clergy and Institution."

11   Arquilla and Ronfeldt *Networks and Netwars: The Future of Terror, Crime, and Militancy.*

12   Joshua, "A Basic Model Explaining Terrorist Group Organizational Structure," 813.

13   The U.S. State Department's Annex of Statistical Information defines affiliated group as "pledging allegiance, declaring loyalty, breaking away from the group but still linked by finance, communications, technical, HR, or being a splinter/offshoot organization" (Annex of Statistical Information Country Reports on Terrorism, 2018, 5).

14   Annex of Statistical Information Country Reports on Terrorism 2018, 5 & 6.

Groups with an *all-channel structure* are loosely organized around a leader with no central control and no functional differentiation among the group's members. Tupamaros[15] and Irish Republican Army are examples of the all-channel group structure because members of the group operate as cells of an umbrella organization. The all-channel model also is applicable to umbrella terrorist groups, where several terrorist groups convene and form a big incorporating group. Terrorist groups affiliated with Al-Qaeda[16] also operate under an all-channel structure. These groups are aligned with the larger Al-Qaeda organization.

Groups that use a *market structure* have no distinct leadership or functional differentiation.[17] They are decentralized and symbolize classic leaderless resistance.[18] American militia groups, such as Sovereign Citizens, and violent American domestic groups, such as the Ku Klux Klan, are examples of market group structure.

At least one study has found that the organizational structure a terrorist organization chooses to adopt depends on both external variables (e.g., per-capita gross domestic product, freedom house, and polity durability) and internal variables (e.g., hard-target selection, group goals, and type of terrorist group).[19] The study finds that, while wealthy and democratic states host terrorist groups with a decentralized structure, poor and autocratic states host terrorist groups with a centralized structure.[20] The study also finds that religious groups are more likely to be decentralized and have an all-channel or hub-spoke group structure.[21] Religious groups that adopt instead a bureaucratic structure have one or more of the following features: a nationalist element, participation in state politics, and operations in a weak or failed state.[22]

Jihadist groups primarily adopt bureaucratic structures for their intragroup administration, a preference that arises from their Islamic ideology. It is an ideology that requires subordinates to obey their leader. The result is a leader-oriented and top-down hierarchical group structure. The leaders of such groups, therefore, frequently stress the importance of obeying the caliph and caliphate in their public and private rhetoric.

---

15   White, *Terrorism and Homeland Security,* 231.

16   According to the U.S. State Department's *Annex of Statistical Information* (p. 5), Al-Qaeda had affiliated groups in 15 countries. These groups include, for example, Hay'at Tahrir al-Sham in Syria and Laskhar-e Tayyiba in India and Pakistan.

17   Powel, "Neither Market nor Hierarchy: Network Forms of Organization," *Research in Organizational Behavior,* 297.

18   Beam, "Leaderless Resistance."

19   Joshua, K., "A Basic Model Explaining Terrorist Group Organizational Structure," 814-817.

20   Ibid., 823.

21   Ibid., 824.

22   Ibid., 824.

When it comes to intergroup relations, jihadist groups' loyalty is less uniform. Some jihadist groups pledge allegiance to groups that are more powerful and more popular their own, while some are linked ideologically only to popular groups. In either case, the jihadist groups do not change their group structure, and the leader of each group operates independently. Other jihadist groups, however, not only pledge allegiance ideologically but also link themselves organizationally to the more popular group. The result is a dependent intergroup structure where the leader of smaller group is under the command of the larger group to which the smaller group chose to affiliate.

Independent Organizational Models: Al-Shabaab and Boko Haram

The groups in this category are not organizationally under the command of any other large group, although they may declare loyalty to the larger. For example, Al-Shabaab has pledged allegiance to al-Qaeda, while Boko Haram has pledged allegiance to ISIS.

al-Shahaab

Terrorist groups flourish in areas where the state lacks the means to oust the groups, and counterterrorism efforts have been ineffective.[23] Harakat al-Shabaab al-Mujahideen or, simply Al-Shabaab (i.e., "The Youth"), is a salafi-jihadist group that arose from the remnants of a failed state and now operates in the Horn of Africa.[24] With aspirations of becoming a regional and global leader, the organization's head, Ahmed Abdi Godane, opened the doors to international jihadists in 2009, causing internal strife within the group. To quell the uproar, Godane declared loyalty to al-Qaeda and killed his rivals.[25]

al-Shabaab has an independent intergroup structure and a bureaucratic and hierarchical intragroup structure comprised of several units under a central leader. A 10-member cabinet provides guidance and council to the leader. A shura majlis, or consultative council, comprised of junior amirs, serves under the group's leader. Al-Shabaab also has regional political and military representatives (such as those for Bay and Bokool and for South-Central Somalia and Mogadishu) who are free to engage in independent actions without the approval of the shura. Three sub-amir from the shura majlis oversee the Politics Division, the Media Division, and Military Operations.[26]

---

23 Piazza, "Do Democracy and Free Markets Protect Us from Terrorism?"

24 White, *Terrorism and Homeland Security*, 168 & 169.

25 Ibid., 170.

26 Shuriye, "*Al-Shabaab's Leadership Hierarchy and Its Ideology.*"

In Somalia, al-Shabaab has pioneered a subject network model that uses ethnic, historical, and religious dynamics to create an elastic network. Thanks to this model, the organization benefits from the weaknesses of the failed Somalian government and the elusive against counterterrorism efforts of United States and the Western world.[27]

al-Shabaab is the most active terrorist group in Africa, being the perpetrator of 535 attacks and killing 3,585 people in 2018.[28] The group mostly targets Somali military, police, and the African Union Mission in Somalia (a regional peacekeeping mission operated by the African Union with the approval of the United Nations) as well as government buildings, government officials, and civilians. It operates in south and central Somalia. A small group of al-Shabaab members operates in the Bari region of Puntland state. In 2018, al-Shabaab used weapons that ranged from firearms and explosives to melees and incendiary devices.[29] Armed assault is the primary mode of the attack and includes bombings, assassinations, and suicide attacks. For example, al-Shabaab was involved in 51 assassinations and conducted 33 terrorist attacks in 2018.[30] That same year, the group also targeted foreigners in the country, killing a U.S. service member and wounding others in an attack in Lower Jubba.[31] In another attack, al-Shabaab fired mortars at a Turkish military base in the Somali capital, Mogadishu.[32]

al-Shabaab has numerous leaders who are tasked by the organization to attack Western targets.[33] The group also has targeted Kenya after the Kenyan government joined international forces seeking to counter al-Shabaab. Until then, al-Shabaab had maintained a close relationship with Kenyan Muslims who had provided logistical support to the organization.[34] The al-Shabaab group based in Kenya increased its attacks there in late 2019, killing three Americans at an airbase, striking schools, and killing civilians.[35]

The organization's independent bureaucratic structure has made al-Shabaab the most effective terrorist organization in the region—especially when the effectiveness of a terrorist organization is measured in terms of media and political attention, impact on the media audience, the ability to force concessions, the disruption of normal routines, and the ability to provoke the host state to overreact.[36]

---

27 Allen, "Al-Shabaab and the Exploitation of the Subject Network Model."

28 Annex of Statistical Information Country Reports on Terrorism, 2018, 9.

29 Ibid., 15

30 Ibid., 12.

31 UPI, "U.S. Service Member Killed in Al-Shabaab Attack in Somalia."

32 Grada World, "Somalia: Al-Shabaab Fires Mortars at Turkish Military Base in Mohadishu."

33 Allen, "Al-Shabaab and the Exploitation of the Subject Network Model."

34 White, J., *Terrorism and Homeland Security,* 170.

35 National Public Radio, "In Kenya, A Rise in Attacks by Islamist Al-Shabaab Insurgents."

36 Martin, *Understanding Terrorism: Challenges, Perspectives, and Issues,* 281 & 282.

Indeed, al-Shabaab was the terrorist group that the U.S. media covered the most in 2018.[37]

Boko Haram

The group Jama'atu Ahlus-Sunnah Lidda'Awati Wal Jihad, also known as Boko Haram, is a salafi-jihadist group that operates in northern Nigeria. The organization believes that politics have been seized by corrupt Muslims and therefore it must create a pure Islamic state ruled by sharia law.[38] Among terrorist groups worldwide in 2018, Boko Haram ranked fourth for the number of terrorist incidents committed that year. It also was the second most violent group in 2018 with a worldwide fatality rate of 5.96[39] and, at 17% was ranked first in terms of the percentage of attacks that involved bombers.[40] The group was the perpetrator of many notable attacks. In March 2012, for example, Boko Haram burnt down 12 schools in one night and forced 10,000 pupils out of education.[41] In 2014, the group kidnapped more than 250 schoolgirls[42] and, in 2018, kidnapped 104 schoolgirls.[43] Unlike Al-Qaeda in the Islamic Maghreb (in northwestern part of Africa and in West Africa) and Al-Shabaab, Boko Haram is not bent on targeting Western interests.[44] Its victims in 2018, for example, were predominantly civilians and military personnel.[45]

In its early years, Boko Haram maintained a decentralized and fluid leadership structure under its founder and leader, Salafist-trained Muhammad Yusuf. Intermediaries in the group, however, shared a common ideology and a transnational agenda.[46] After Yusuf was executed, Abubakar Shekau took the leadership reins and radicalized the organization. The group had two other significant and authoritative leaders: Maman Nur (ideological leader) and Khalid al-Barnawi (operational leader).[47] Nur, a Cameroonian, introduced Shekau to Yusuf and was third in command under Yusuf's leadership. Nur led Boko Haram temporarily in 2009 when Yusuf was killed and Sheaku was imprisoned.[48] The inhumane killing of Muslims by some members of Boko Haram incensed Nur and others in the group.

---

37   Timmons and O'shea, "What Makes a Terrorist Attack Notable? Determinants of U.S. Media Coverage"

38   Walker, "What Is Boko Haram."

39   Annex of Statistical Information Country Reports on Terrorism 2018, 9.

40   Ibid., 13.

41   Walker, "What Is Boko Haram," 6.

42   Zenn, "Boko Haram and Kidnapping of Chibok Schoolgirls."

43   Abubakar, "Boko Haram 104 of 110 Kidnapped Schoolgirls."

44   Walker, "What Is Boko Haram," 9.

45   Annex of Statistical Information Country Reports on Terrorism 2018, 18.

46   Zenn, "Leadership Analysis of Boko Haram and Ansaru in Nigeria."

47   Zenn, "Leadership Analysis of Boko Haram and Ansaru in Nigeria."

48   Counterextremism Project, "Mamman Nur."

Some of the opponents defected and formed Ansaru, which operated mostly in Chad and Cameroon.[49]

Boko Haram relies on a bureaucratic and hierarchical organizational structure.[50] The leader, at the top of the organizational pyramid, sets goals and has final authority over all decisions and actions. Under the leader are well-organized layers and cells that support the organizational structure: two deputies; a 30-member Shura council (which supervises state and local operational commanders and strategists and variety of operational cells). Other responsibilities of the council include overseeing the group's internal support and external publicity, terrorist missions, and financial acquisitions. All of the operational commanders and strategists operate independently to maintain the confidentiality of the group's activities. Courier messengers are used for direct and confidential communication.[51]

Boko Haram also has a permeable group structure akin to that of two other jihadist groups: Islamic State in West Africa Province (ISWAP) and Ansaru (in Nigeria). Boko Haram and Ansaru eschewed rivalries between their two groups because they wanted to avoid unnecessary strife and because some militants have undertaken operations for both groups.[52] Likewise, Boko Haram and ISWAP do not target each other.

Dependent Group Models

Unlike jihadist groups that pledge ideological allegiance but retain their organizational structure, some terrorist groups change their organizational structure after declaring loyalty to a larger group. These smaller groups then become dependent on the larger group and lose the ability to choose their leader. Instead, the leader of the larger group assigns a leader to the affiliated groups. Jihadist groups in this category adopt either a hub-spoke or an all-channel organizational structure.

Hub-Spoke Groups in Africa: ISIS and Its Franchises

Western leaders say that ISIS has been defeated in Iraq and Syria because the terrorist group has lost its territories; however, it is too early to speak about victory over ISIS. According to the *United States 2018 Annex of Statistical Information* report, ISIS is second only to the Taliban in terms of the number of terrorist incidents committed.[53] The ISIS franchise in Afghanistan, ISIS-Khorasan, is the 10th

---

49   White, 166 & 167.

50   Stratfor Global Intelligence "Nigeria: Examining Boko Haram."

51   Ibid.

52   Zenn, "Leadership Analysis of Boko Haram and Ansaru in Nigeria."

53   ISIS perpetrated 647 terrorist incidents, resulting in the death of 3,585 people and the wounding 1,791 others (Annex of Statistical Information Country Reports on Terrorism 2018, 9).

most active terrorist group and the most lethal group with a fatality rate of 12.65.[54] The report also emphasizes that ISIS is the most prevalent terrorist group in the world with franchises in 26 countries.[55] These franchises operate on provincial basis and they are loyal to the organization's "core," and its Caliph.[56]

ISIS had become a popular organizational model for other jihadist groups for three main reasons: First, the group was able to control territory in Iraq and Syria. Second, the group had the capacity to direct terrorist attacks in the Middle East and inspire self-radicalized individuals to carry out attacks in their home countries. Third, ISIS won groups in many regions of the world through being pledged allegiance or declared loyalty to itself, which ISIS treated them as the group's provinces.[57] These franchises have presented credibility and created perception on how ISIS is a globalized organization, after the organization lost its power in the territories in Iraq and Syria.[58]

Groups that want to join ISIS or become an ISIS franchise must have territorial authority in a specific country or region and be willing to alter their internal organizational structure and strategic decision-making processes to meet the demands of ISIS.[59] In return, ISIS provides tactical support to its provincial affiliates. For example, ISWAP received media equipment and tactical support for up-armored suicide vehicles used to transport improvised explosives devices.[60]

ISIS has an impact on the organizational structure on its provincial franchises in a number of ways. For example, the group assigns leaders to its affiliates, orders the foot soldiers of those affiliates to join the organization (as it did with ISWAP), and requires its provincial leaders to support a more moderate theological leadership approach.[61] ISIS also uses its influence and authority to give orders to its provincial leaders. For example, ISIS ordered the execution of two female workers for a Muslim nongovernmental organization in 2018.[62] As of March 2020, ISIS recognized eight provinces in Africa, taking advantage of ongoing conflicts and exploiting economic and political grievances of the people in those areas, as shown in Figure 1.

---

54   ISIS-Khorasan killed 1,278 people in 101 incidents (Annex of Statistical Information Country Reports on Terrorism 2018, 9).

55   Annex of Statistical Information Country Reports on Terrorism 2018, 9.

56   Zenn, "The Islamic State's Provinces on the Peripheries Juxtaposing the Pledges from Boko Haram in Nigeria and Abu Sayyaf and Maute Group in the Philippines."

57   Ibid., 87.

58   Ibid., 87.

59   Ibid., 88.

60   Ibid., 92.

61   Ibid., 93.

62   Ibid., 93.

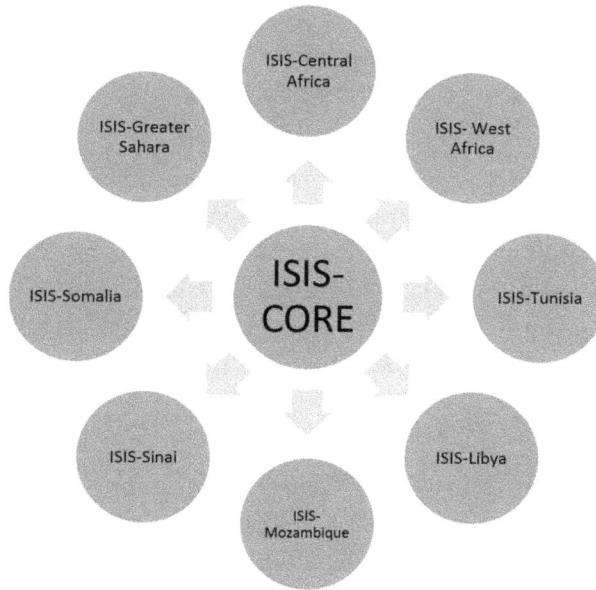

Figure 1: ISIS and Its Franchises in Africa

ISIS Provinces in Sahel

Extremist groups are gaining strength in the Sahel region of Africa, an area in Africa between the Sahara to the north and the Sudanian Savanna to the south, despite U.S.-led military operations, drone strikes, and efforts by the governments in the region. Since 2015, the extremist groups have doubled and perpetrated more than 700 violent episodes in 2019 alone.[63] ISIS-West Africa and ISIS-Greater Sahara are two ISIS provinces operating in the Sahel region of Africa.

ISIS West Africa was formed in 2016 by defectors of Boko Haram and operates primarily in Nigeria and the Lake Chad region with 5,000 fighters.[64] Boko Haram leader Sheaku pledged allegiance to ISIS in 2015, but Sheaku's indiscriminate violence targeting Muslims (and anyone outside of the group[65]) prompted the ISIS leadership to replace Sheakau with Mus'ab al Barnawi in 2016.[66] Like ISIS-core, Barnawi favored a more "hearts and minds" approach that called for targeting collaborators and military forces.[67] ISIS-West Africa perpetrated 22 terrorist incidents in 2018, resulting in the death of 160 individuals.[68] Boko Haram, meanwhile,

---

63   Gramer, "U.S. to Ramp Up Counterterrorism Efforts in Sahel Region."

64   State of New Jersey Office of Homeland Security and Preparedness, "ISIS West Africa Posturing for Prolonged Insurgency."

65   *Reuters,* "Islamic State Ally Stakes Out Territory around Lake Chad."

66   Iaccino, "ISIS Replaces Abubakar Shekau with New Boko Haram Leader Abu Musab al-Barnawi."

67   *Sundiatapost,* "Al-Barnawi Faction and Nigeria's Timeless Boko Haram War."

68   Annex of Statistical Information Country Reports on Terrorism 2018, 5.

continued to target civilians indiscriminately. Those attacks helped to make Boko Haram one of top five terrorist groups in terms of the number of civilian victims in 2018.[69] ISIS-West Africa, on the other hand, was more discriminating, targeting Christian civilians and bypassing Muslim civilians.

ISIS-Greater Sahara came to prominence in 2015 when al-Mourabitoun, a group affiliated with al-Qaeda, pledged allegiance to ISIS.[70] The group operates primarily in Mali and has claimed responsibility for attacks such as the killing of four U.S. soldiers and five Nigerian soldiers in Tongo region. The U.S. State Department subsequently designated al-Mourabitoun as a terrorist organization.[71] The size of the group fluctuates between 200 and 300 militants.[72]

ISIS Provinces in the Northern Theater

ISIS's provincial franchises in Libya, Tunisia, and Egypt perpetrated 347 terrorist incidents in 2019, up slightly from 345 incidents in 2018.[73] Libya is a failed state where conflicts are occurring at the local, regional, and national levels.[74] The country has teetered on the brink of collapse amid deteriorating security and increased lawlessness since Muammar Qadhafi was ousted in October 2011.[75] Qaddafi's strongholds were transformed into bases for ISIS and, of the foreign jihadists Libya hosted, most of them joined ISIS groups that had come into the country from Tunisia in Libya.[76] *ISIS-Libya* emerged in Derna, a port city in eastern Libya, in 2014 when a group of 300 former Libyan members of the Battar Brigade returned to their country after fighting in Syria and allied with the Ansar al-Sharia terrorist group. Immediately after Ansar al-Sharia pledged its allegiance to ISIS leader Abu Bakr al-Baghdadi, ISIS recognized and announced the formation of three branches of the Islamic State in Libya.[77] While the number of ISIS attacks in Libya has decreased since 2014, the terrorist organization still holds a presence in the country, targeting checkpoints and urban police stations and kidnapping local notables for potential prisoner exchanges or ransom.[78]

Unlike Libya, Tunisia successfully transitioned to democracy after the Arab Spring in the early 2010s. Tunisia, however, has the largest contingent of foreign

---

69   Annex of Statistical Information Country Reports on Terrorism 2018, 18.

70   Warner, "The Islamic State's Three New African Affiliates."

71   Department of State, "State Department Terrorist Designations of ISIS in the Greater Sahara."

72   Warner and Hulme, "The Islamic State in Africa: Estimating Fighter Numbers in Cells Across the Continent."

73   African Center for Strategic Studies, "Threat from African Militant Islamist Groups Expanding, Diversifying."

74   Engel, "The Islamic State's Expansion in Libya."

75   Engel, "Libya as a Failed State: Causes, Consequences, and Options."

76   Kahlaoui, "What Is Behind the Rise of ISIS in Libya?"

77   Engel, "The Islamic State's Expansion in Libya."

78   Inga, "Islamic State in Libya: From Force to Farce," 25.

fighters in Iraq and Syria.[79] According to the Tunisian government, around 3,000 Tunisians[80] have fought in Iraq and Syria for ideological and economic reasons and to support the expansion of the Salafist movement in both countries.[81] *The ISIS-Tunisia* branch emerged in 2015 when the group was involved in attacks in Sousse, Tunisia, including the targeting of the Bardo Museum.[82] ISIS-Tunisia has maintained its capacity to carry out attacks in the country, where the group executed two suicide attacks in 2019.[83]

In Egypt, which also hosts many jihadist terrorist groups, most of the attacks by these groups have occurred in the northern Sinai area. *ISIS-Sinai* was to blame for 320 terrorist attacks between 2013 and 2017.[84] This ISIS franchise originated from the Sunni Salafist Ansar Bayt al-Maqdis (ABM) terrorist group that declared war against the Egyptian government immediately after the ouster of President Mohamed Morsi in a July 2013 military coup.[85] ABM emerged in 2011 when the government collapse created power vacuums in northern regions of the country. ABM had a loose affiliation with al-Qaeda in its early years and was designated as a terrorist group by United States in 2014.[86] In 2014, ABM pledged allegiance to ISIS and began using the name of ISIS-Sinai. Since then, ISIS-Sinai has grown into the most coordinated and most operationally effective terrorist group in Egypt.[87] Many of the group's attacks in Egypt have been quite notable. For example, ISIS-Sinai has claimed responsibility for the bombing of a Russian Metrojet flying out of Sharm El-Sheikh, an Egyptian resort town between the desert of the Sinai Peninsula and the Red Sea.[88] ISIS-Sinai has been referred to as one of the most resilient ISIS franchises because the group has survived intact despite many years heavy fighting with the Egyptian military.[89] That resiliency can be attributed at least in part to its weaponry, which the group receives through illegal weapons transfers from Libya.[90]

ISIS-Somalia

The origin of the ISIS's Somalian franchise dates to 2012 when Al-Shabaab assigned

79   Lounnas, "The Tunisian Jihad: Between Al-Qaeda and ISIS."

80   Raghavan, "No Nationality Heeded the Call to Come Fight for ISIS Like Tunisians Did. Now They're Stuck."

81   Counter Extremism Project, "Tunisia: Extremism & Counterextremism."

82   Jane's Defense Weekly, "Islamic State Attack on Ben Guerdane Indicates Shift in Group's Tunisia Strategy, to Trigger Insurgency."

83   Counter Extremism Project, "Tunisia: Extremism & Counterextremism."

84   World Data, "Terrorism in Egypt."

85   AIPAC, "ISIS in the Sinai Peninsula."

86   Gomez, "Islamic State-Sinai Province: What Is the ISIS-Linked Terrorist Group?"

87   Gomez, A., "Islamic State-Sinai Province: What Is the ISIS-Linked Terrorist Group?"

88   Ibid.

89   Ibid.

90   Mazel, "ISIS in Sinai: The Libyan Connection."

Abdul Qadir Mumin to operate in its remote outpost in Puntland in northeastern Somalia. Mumin took control of the Puntland group in 2014 immediately after the Al-Shabaab regional group leader defected to the government. Mumin left al-Shabaab and began to consider himself an independent terrorist. He pledged allegiance to ISIS in 2015.[91] ISIS-Somalia has around 150 members.[92] Similar to other ISIS franchises, ISIS-Somalia primarily targets military troops and Al-Shabaab fighters. In 2018 and 2019, Several clashes between Al-Shabaab and ISIS-Somalia occurred in 2018 and 2019.[93]

ISIS-Central Africa

ISIS-Central Africa emerged in 2017 in the Democratic Republic of Congo (DRC) when militants from a new brand of the rebel group Allied Democratic Forces (ADF) known as the City of Monotheism and Monotheists leaned towards ISIS. The ADF is an Islamist group that has fought against the governments of the DRC and Uganda for several years.[94] The group recently adopted symbols similar to those of global jihadists groups.[95] Given the poorly equipped and formless structure of ADF, some scholars believe that it is not realistic to believe that an ISIS province exists in the Central African region.[96] Other scholars point out that the leader of ISIS announced in 2018 that it did have a provincial group in the region[97] and that ISIS claimed responsibility for several attacks in the DRC in 2019. In one of those attacks, eight soldiers were killed.[98]

ISIS-Mozambique

Mozambique's experience with violence by Islamic extremists began when Al Sunna wa Jama'ah (ASWJ)[99] popped up in the eastern part of the country in 2017. Referred to by locals as al-Shabaab, the group's grievances included dissatisfaction with widespread poverty and inequality, frustration over the government's ineffective policies for addressing those issues, and the expansion of Salafist ideology with support from the Gulf States in the form of funding for mosques, social programs, and young students who wanted to study abroad and propagate Wahhabi Islam. The rising influence of Wahhabism led to conflict with Sufi Muslims in the country, resulting in the death of 300 people and the displacement of thousands

---

91 Warner, "Sub-Saharan Africa's Three 'New' Islamic State Affiliates."

92 Browne, "U.S. Airstrikes Kills ISIS-Somalia's Second in Command."

93 Weiss, "Islamic State Claims Clashes with Shabab in Somalia."

94 West, "Has Islamic State Really Entered the Congo and Is an IS Province There a Gamble?"

95 Congo Research Group, "Inside the ADF Group."

96 West, "Has Islamic State Really Entered the Congo and Is an IS Province There a Gamble?" 9.

97 Weiss, "Islamic State-Loyal Group Calls for People to Join the Jihad in the Congo."

98 Wembi and Goldstein, "ISIS Claims First Attack in the Democratic Republic of Congo."

99 Postings, "Islamic State in Mozambique Further Complicates Cabo Delgado Violence."

of others. By 2019, the terrorist group Al Sunna emerged and was acknowledged by ISIS as one of its affiliates. Similar to other ISIS provincial franchises, Al Sunna selectively targeted military troops.[100]

All-Channel: Jama'a Nusrat ul-Islam wa al-Muslimin (JNIM)

Jama'a Nusrat ul-Islam wa al-Muslimin (JNIM) is an example of an all-channel network operating in the Maghreb (in the northwestern part of Africa) and West Africa. JNIM was formed by the merger of four Al-Qaeda organizations: Ansar Dine, the Macina Liberation Front, Al-Mourabitoun, and the Saharan branch of Al-Qaeda in the Islamic Maghreb (AQIM), as shown in Figure 2.[101] The group has between 1,000 and 2,000 members and is active in Mali, Burkina Faso, and Nijer.[102]

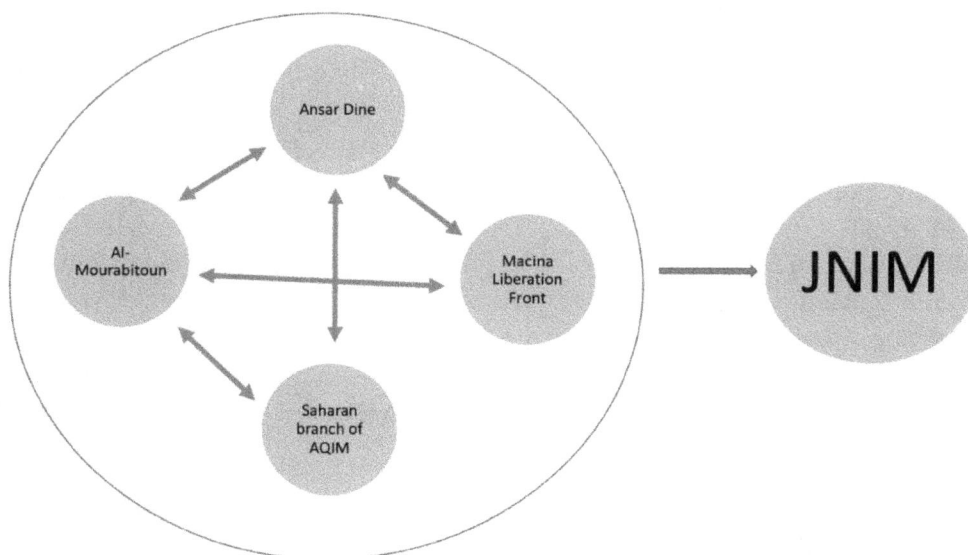

Figure 2: The Formation of Jama'a Nusrat ul-Islam wal-Muslimin (JNIM)

JNIM became an official branch of Al-Qaeda in the Maghreb and West Africa after four of the group's leaders declared loyalty to Al-Qaeda leader Ayman al Zawahiri in 2017.[103] Zawahiri welcomed the affiliation as it helped to fulfill his organization's localization policies. Inspired by the formation of Hay'at tahrir al Sham, which was created from the merger of Al-Qaeda-affiliated groups in Syria, Zawahiri sought to expand Al-Qaeda's influence with a network of allied terrorist groups. Unlike ISIS, which continued to create loose ties with its franchises,

---

100 Chua, "Challenges within Mozambique."

101 Buchanan, "Mali: Terror Threat Spreads after Sahel Groups Join Forces."

102 Center for Strategic & International Studies, "Jama'at Nasr al-Islam wal Muslimin."

103 Gaffey, "African Jihadi Groups Unite and Pledge Allegiance to Al-Qaeda."

Al-Qaeda focused on shoring up its roots in the locations where the group histor-ically has been active.[104]

Iyad Ag Ghaly, the leader of Ansar Dine, became the leader of the merged terrorist organization. Ghaly believed that group unity serves multiple purposes, such as strengthening the jihadist cause, expanding the influence of Al-Qaeda, making the group insurmountable by Western forces, and preventing ISIS's at-tempts to attract potential defectors.[105] The structural reorganization of JNIM was influenced by three Al-Qaeda's policies in Sahel. First, Al-Qaeda policy prohib-its members of merger groups from leaving the Al-Qaeda network to join a rival group. The policy was necessary because when members left, they tended to join ISIS. Second, Al-Qaeda policy requires that all members maintain the organiza-tion's ethno-political dynamics espoused by Ghaly, who had become the symbol for the nomadic Tuareg people. The Tuareg people make their home across the Sa-hara Desert, including in the North African countries of Mali, Niger, Libya, Alge-ria, and Chad. Third, Al-Qaeda policy calls for seizing opportunities to invigorate insurgency in the region.[106]

Similar to ISIS franchises in Africa, JNIM acts like a state and primarily targets national and multinational posts and soldiers.[107] In a video released by JNIM in 2018, al-Qaeda leader Zawahiri gave a speech about how he targeted multinational forces in Mali. Zawahiri explained that JNIM targeted the airport in Timbuktu, Mali, wounding United Nations peacekeepers and French soldiers.[108] The group, however, tries to avoid the targeting of civilians. When a landmine accidentally killed civilians in central Mali in September 2019, JNIM expressed its condolences and apologies and promised to compensate the victims' families.[109]

Discussion

Table 1 shows how affiliation with either ISIS or Al-Qaeda affects the or-ganizational structure of terrorist groups in Africa. Al-Shabaab and Boko Haram are examples of groups that are organizationally independent. Their leaders are not assigned by the groups to which they declare their loyalty. All of the other groups listed in the table are examples of groups that are organizationally de-pendent. For its organizationally dependent structure, Al-Qaeda uses an all-chan-nel arrangement because its policies focus on the localization operations. ISIS, on

---

104 Perkins, "Local vs. Global – Al-Qaeda's Strategy for Survival."

105 Joscelyn, "Analysis: Al-Qaeda Groups Reorganize in West Africa."

106 Zelin, "Jihadist Groups in the Sahel Region Formalize Merger." *Jihadology*.

107 Wikipedia listed the incidents that were perpetrated by JNIM between 2017 and 2019. Wikipedia Database, "Jama'at Nasr al-Islam wal Muslimin."

108 The Defense Post, "Mali Militants Disguised as Peacekeepers Attack French and U.N. Bases Killing One, Injuring Dozens."

109 Long War Journal, "JNIM Apologizes for Killing Civilians in Central Mali."

the other hand, prefers a hub-spoke organizational structure because it allows for the creation of provincial groups that remain connected to the larger organization. The hub-spoke and the all-channel organizational structures have been beneficial to not only the larger organizations but also their affiliates. For example, the leaders of some of the affiliates are endorsed by and allowed to continue in that role (i.e., beneficial to the affiliate), while the leaders of other affiliates are appointed by the larger organization (i.e., beneficial to the larger organization). More importantly, though, affiliate groups that are part of a hub-spoke or an all-channel network work to implement the strategies of the larger organization (i.e., beneficial to the larger organization).

Table 1: Description of the Organizational Structure of Salafi-Jihadist Terrorist Groups in Africa

Group	Organization to Which the Group Is Affiliated	Country of Operation	Organizationally Inter-Group Structure	Leader Assigned by the Group Affiliated to?
Al-Shabaab	Al-Qaeda	Somalia	Independent	No
Boko Haram	ISIS	Nigeria	Independent	No
JNIM	Al-Qaeda	Mali and Burkina Faso	Dependent-All-Channel	Yes
ISIS-Sinai	ISIS	Egypt	Dependent-Hub-spoke	Yes
ISIS-Greater Sahara	ISIS	Mali and Burkina Faso	Dependent-Hub-spoke	Yes
ISIS-West Africa	ISIS	Sahel	Dependent-Hub-spoke	Yes
ISIS-Somalia	ISIS	Somalia	Dependent-Hub-spoke	Yes

Table 2 uses data from the U.S. State Department's 2019 Annex of Statistical Information[110] to show how an affiliated terrorist group's organizational dependence on Al-Qaeda or ISIS affects the operational capacity of the affiliated group. The number of terrorist attacks made by organizationally independent groups are incomparably higher than the number of attacks made by organizationally dependent groups. The large gap stems from who and what the groups target. Organizationally *independent* groups (e.g., Al-Shabaab, Boko Haram) are *indiscriminate* in their choice of targets, while organizationally *dependent* groups (e.g., ISIS-Sinai, ISIS-Greater Sahara) are *discriminate* (i.e., selective) in their choice of targets. For example, organizationally *dependent* groups may choose to target only national or multinational military forces, collaborators, or Christian civilians, while organiza-

---

110 Annex of Statistical Information Country Reports on Terrorism 2018.

tionally *independent* groups will target anything or anyone. Because dependent affiliates such as ISIS-Greater Sahara and ISIS-West Africa, are under the command of ISIS (with its dependent structure), they act if they are part of a state and adhere to a "hearts and minds" policy that prohibits the targeting of Muslim civilians. Examples include the ISIS-Greater Sahara and JNIM, which targets only national and French military forces in Mali. Discriminate targeting results in fewer attacks. In 2018, for example, JNIM made only a handful of terrorist attacks. Terrorist groups that operate under a hub-spoke or all-channel organizational structure, therefore, typically perpetrate fewer terrorist attacks than terrorist groups operate under an independent organizational structure.

Table 2: The impacts of organizational structure on the operational capacity of jihadist groups

Group	Organization to Which the Group Is Affiliated	Number of Incidents Perpetrated	Target Type	Total Number of Deaths	Fatality Rate
Al-Shabaab	Al-Qaeda	535	Indiscriminate	2,062	3.85
Boko Haram	Al-Qaeda	220	Indiscriminate	1,311	5.96
JNIM	Al-Qaeda	26	Discriminate	121	4.65
ISIS-Sinai	ISIS	56	Discriminate	485	8.66
ISIS-Greater Sahara	ISIS	18	Discriminate	79	4.39
ISIS-West Africa	ISIS	22	Discriminate	160	7.27
ISIS-Somalia	ISIS	17	Discriminate	27	1.70

When it comes to the number of casualties at the hands of dependent and independent groups, no distinctive pattern emerges. Given that it may be riskier and more difficult to target national and multinational military forces, the high fatality rates from attacks by ISIS and Al-Qaeda-affiliated groups indicate that members of both terrorist organizations are well-trained and capable of inflicting heavy losses among their targets. ISIS-affiliated groups, however, have higher fatality rates than Al-Qaeda-affiliated groups.

Conclusion

Salafi-jihadist groups continue to pose a grave threat to countries in all parts of the world either from the formation of new jihadist groups or the evolution of local Muslim groups into jihadist groups. Africa has been exposed to these trends more than any other region. A number of groups affiliated with al-Qaeda or ISIS have operated in Africa today. The debate continues over what has created a favorable environment for these jihadist groups to flourish in Africa and how these groups have been able to increase their resilience, longevity, and operational capacity. Organizational structure plays a key role in the groups' rise and impenetrability to government efforts to defeat them; therefore, it is essential that government officials understand how terrorist groups structure their organizations and how those structures can inform effective counterterrorism strategies.

Al-Qaeda and ISIS have changed their strategies since they first appeared on the world stage. Al-Qaeda, for example, switched to an all-channel structure that involves the use of affiliated terrorist groups in keeping with its policy of localization. These affiliated groups, however, are allowed to remain organizationally dependent. ISIS, on the other hand, switched to a hub-spoke structure to expand its reach through loose ties with affiliate terrorist groups that become organizationally dependent on the terrorist organization to which they have pledged their allegiance. This study concludes that terrorist organizations that use a hub-spoke or an all-channel structure commit fewer terrorist attacks compared with terrorist organizations who remain organizationally independent (al-Shaabab and Boko Haram). This conclusion also is based on the observation that ISIS adheres to a "hearts and minds policy" that requires the organization to target only national and multinational military forces—unlike al-Shaabab and Boko Haram, which chooses its targets indiscriminately. Further research is needed to analyze the effects of group structure in a global context.

References

Abubakar, S. A. "Boko Haram 104 of 110 Kidnapped Schoolgirls." *USA Today.* https://www.usatoday.com/story/news/world/2018/03/21/boko-haram-returns-kidnapped-schoolgirls-witnesses-say/444611002/.

African Center for Strategic Studies. "Threat from African Militant Islamist Groups Expanding, Diversifying." https://africacenter.org/spotlight/threat-from-african-militant-islamist-groups-expanding-diversifying/

Allen, W. "Al-Shabaab and the Exploitation of the Subject Network Model." *Small Wars Journal.* https://smallwarsjournal.com/jrnl/art/al-Shabaab-and-exploitation-subject-network-model

Annex of Statistical Information Country Reports on Terrorism 2018. *State Department.* https://www.state.gov/wp-content/uploads/2019/10/DSG-Statistical-Annex-2018.pdf

APIC. "ISIS in Sinai Peninsula." https://www.aipac.org/-/media/publications/comms/mounting-threats-isis.pdf.

Arquilla, John, and David Ronfeldt. *Networks and Netwars: The Future of Terror, Crime, and Militancy.* Santa Monica: RAND Corporation, 2001.

Beam, Louis. "Leaderless Resistance." *The Seditionist,* http://www.louisbeam.com/leaderless.htm.

Browne, R. "U.S. airstrikes kills ISIS-Somalia's second in command." *CNN.* https://www.cnn.com/2019/04/15/politics/us-airstrike-isis-somalia/index.html.

Buchanan, Elsa. "Mali: Terror threat spreads after Sahel groups join forces." *International Business Times.* https://www.ibtimes.co.uk/mali-terror-threat-spreads-after-sahel-groups-join-forces-create-new-jihadist-alliance-1615105.

Center for Strategic & International Studies. "Jama'at Nasr al-Islam wal Muslimin." https://www.csis.org/programs/transnational-threats-project/terrorism-backgrounders/jamaat-nasr-al-islam-wal-muslimin.

Chua, Marc. "Challenges within Mozambique." *Small Wars Journal,* https://smallwarsjournal.com/jrnl/art/challenges-within-mozambique.

Congo Research Group. "Inside the ADF Group." https://insidetheadf.org/wp-content/uploads/2018/11/Inside-the-ADF-Rebellion-14Nov18.pdf

Counterextremism Project. "Mamman Nur." https://www.counterextremism.com/extremists/mamman-nur

Counter Extremism Project. "Tunisia: Extremism & Counterextremism." https://www.counterextremism.com/countries/tunisia.

Crenshaw, M. "How Terrorism Ends." In *How Terrorism Ends,* by Jon Alterman. Washington D.C.: United States Institute for Peace, 1999.

Department of State. "State Department Terrorist Designations of ISIS in the Greater Sahara." https://www.state.gov/state-department-terrorist-designations-of-isis-in-the-greater-sahara-isis-gs-and-adnan-abu-walid-al-sahrawi/

Engel, Andrew. "The Islamic State's Expansion in Libya." *Washington Institute.* https://www.washingtoninstitute.org/policy-analysis/view/the-islamic-states-expansion-in-libya

Engel, Andrew. "Libya as a Failed State: Causes, Consequences, and Options." *Washington Institute.* https://www.washingtoninstitute.org/uploads/Documents/pubs/ResearchNote24_Engel-3.pdf

Gaffey, Conor. "African Jihadi groups Unite and Pledge Allegiance to Al-Qaeda." *Newsweek.* https://www.newsweek.com/al-qaeda-groups-unite-sahel-563351.

Gaines, L., and J. Kremling. *Homeland Security and Terrorism.* New York: Pearson, 2019.

Gomez, Alan. "Islamic State-Sinai Province: What is the ISIS-linked terrorist group?" *USA Today.* https://www.usatoday.com/story/news/world/2017/11/24/islamic-state-sinai-province-what-isis-linked-terrorist-group/892570001/

Grada World. "Somalia: Al-Shabab fires mortars at Turkish military base in Mohadishu." https://www.garda.com/crisis24/news-alerts/118246/somalia-al-Shabaab-fires-mortars-at-turkish-military-base-in-mogadishu-may-12

Gramer, R. "U.S. to Ramp Up Counterterrorism Efforts in Sahel Region." *Foreign Policy.* https://foreignpolicy.com/2019/12/20/us-ramp-up-counterterrorism-sahel-africa/.

Iaccino, Ludovica. "ISIS replaces Abubakar Shekau with new Boko Haram leader Abu Musab al-Barnawi." *International Business Times.* https://www.ibtimes.co.uk/isis-replaces-abubakar-shekau-new-boko-haram-leader-abu-musab-al-barnawi-1574054

Inga, Kristina Trauthig. "Islamic State in Libya: From Force to Farce." *International Center for the Study of Radicalization.* https://icsr.info/wp-content/uploads/2020/03/ICSR-Report-Islamic-State-in-Libya-From-Force-to-Farce.pdf.

Institute for Economics & Peace. "Global Terrorism Index 2019 Measuring the Impact." http://visionofhumanity.org/app/uploads/2019/11/GTI-2019web.pdf.

Jane's Defense Weekly. "Islamic State attack on Ben Guerdane indicates shift in group's Tunisia strategy, to trigger insurgency." https://www.janes.com/article/58682/islamic-state-attack-on-ben-guerdane-indicates-shift-in-group-s-tunisia-strategy-to-trigger-insurgency.

Joscelyn, Thomas. "Analysis: Al-Qaeda groups reorganize in West Africa." *Long War Journal,* https://www.longwarjournal.org/archives/2017/03/analysis-al-qaeda-groups-reorganize-in-west-africa.php.

Joshua, Kilberg. "A Basic Model Explaining Terrorist Group Organizational Structure." *Studies in Conflict & Terrorism* in 35:810, 2012, pp. 810-830.

Kahlaoui, T. "What Is Behind the Rise of ISIS in Libya?" *Newsweek.* https://www.

newsweek.com/understanding-rise-islamic-state-isis-libya-437931.

Long War Journal. "JNIM apologizes for killing civilians in central Mali." https://www.longwarjournal.org/archives/2019/09/jnim-apologizes-for-killing-civilians-in-central-mali.php.

Lounnas, Djallil. "The Tunisian Jihad: Between Al-Qaeda ad ISIS." *Middle East Policy* in Volume 26, Spring 2019, Number 1.

Maher, Shiraz. *A History of Salafi-Jihadism: The History of an idea.* London: Penguin Books, 2017.

Martin, Gus. *Understanding Terrorism: Challenges, Perspectives, and Issues.* Los Angeles: SAGE, 2018.

Mazel, Zvi. "ISIS in Sinai: the Libyan connection." *Jerusalem Post.* https://www.jpost.com/Middle-East/ISIS-in-Sinai-the-Libyan-connection-482149.

National Public Radio. "In Kenya, A Rise in Attacks By Islamist Al-Shabab Insurgents." https://www.npr.org/2020/02/16/806417331/in-kenya-a-rise-in-attacks-by-islamist-al-shabab-insurgents

Perkins, Brian. "Local vs Global – Al-Qaeda's Strategy for Survival." *The Jamestown Foundation Terrorism Monitor* in May 31, 2019, Volume XVII, Issue 11.

Piazza, J. "Do Democracy and Free Markets Protect Us From Terrorism?" *International Politics* in 45, 72-91 (2008).

Powel, Walter. "Neither Market nor Hierarchy: Network Forms of Organization." *Research in Organizational Behavior* 12 (1990).

Raghavan, S. "No nationality heeded the call to come fight for ISIS like Tunisians did. Now they're stuck." *Washington Post,* https://www.washingtonpost.com/world/no-nationality-heeded-the-call-to-come-fight-for-isis-like-tunisians-did-now-theyre-stuck/2019/05/10/839a942e-5d4a-11e9-98d4-844088d135f2_story.html.

Ranstorp, Magnus. "Hizbollah's command leadership: Its structure, decision-making and relationship with Iranian clergy and institution." *Terrorism and Political Violence* in (1994), 6:3, 303-339.

Reuters. "Islamic State ally stakes out territory around Lake Chad." https://www.reuters.com/article/us-nigeria-security/islamic-state-ally-stakes-out-territory-around-lake-chad-idUSKBN1I0063.

Shuriye, Abdi. "Al-Shabaab's Leadership Hierarchy and its Ideology." *SAVAP International*, in 7-11. (2012).

State of New Jersey. "ISIS West Africa Posturing for Prolonged Insurgency." https://www.njhomelandsecurity.gov/analysis/isis-west-africa-posturing-for-prolonged-insurgency

Stratfor Global Intelligence. "Nigeria: Examining Boko Haram." https://worldview.stratfor.com/article/nigeria-examining-boko-haram

Sundiatapost. "Al-Barnawi Faction and Nigeria's Timeless Boko Haram War." https://sundiatapost.com/2018/03/22/dapchi-girlsal-barnawi-faction-and-nigerias-timeless-boko-haram-war-by-moses-ochonu.

Taylor, Robert, and Swanson, Charles. *Terrorism, Intelligence & Homeland Security.* New York: Pearson, 2019.

Timmons, Liam, and Tim O'Shea. "What makes a terrorist attack notable? Determinants of U.S. Media Coverage." *Rise to Peace,* https://www.risetopeace.org/2018/07/05/attack-characteristics-determinants/.

The Defense Post. "Postings, Robert "Islamic State in Mozambique further complicates Cabo Delgado violence."

The Defense Post. "Mali militants disguised as peacekeepers attack French and UN bases killing one, injuring dozens." https://thedefensepost.com/2018/04/15/mali-attack-france-un-bases-disguised-timbuktu/.

UPI. "U.S. service member killed in al-Shabab attack in Somalia." https://www.upi.com/Top_News/World-News/2018/06/08/US-service-member-killed-in-al-Shabab-attack-in-Somalia/4141528494386/

Walker, A. "What is Boko Haram." *United States Institute of Peace.* https://www.usip.org/publications/2012/05/what-boko-haram

Warner, Jason. "Sub-Saharan Africa's Three "New" Islamic State Affiliates." *CTC Sentinel* in January 2017, Volume 10, Issue 1, pp. 28-32.

Warner. Jason, and Charlotte Hulme. "The Islamic State in Africa: Estimating Fughter Numbers in Cells Across the Continent." August 2018, Volume 11, Issue, 7, pp. 21-28.

Weiss, Caleb. "Islamic State-loyal group calls for people to join the jihad in the

Congo." Long War Journal. https://www.longwarjournal.org/archives/2017/10/isl amic-state-loyal-group-calls-for-people-to-join-the-jihad-in-the-congo.php.

Weiss, Caleb. "Islamic State claims clashes with Shabaab in Somalia." *FDD's Long War Journal.* https://www.longwarjournal.org/archives/2018/12/islamic-state-clai ms-clashes-with-shabaab-in-somalia.php

Wembi, S., and Joseph Goldstein. "ISIS Claims First Attack in the Democratic Republic of Congo." *New York Times.* https://www.nytimes.com/2019/04/19/world/ africa/isis-congo-attack.html.

West, Sungua. "Has Islamic State Really Entered the Congo and is an IS Province There a Gamble." *The Jamestown Foundation,* Terrorism Monitor, May 31, 2019, Volume XVII, Issue 11, pp. 7-9.

White, Jonathan. *Terrorism and Homeland Security.* Boston: Cengage Learning, 2018.

Williams, Phil, and Roy Godson. *Anticipating Organized and Transnational Crime.* Netherlands: Kluwer Academic Publishers, 2002.

World Data. "Terrorism in Egypt." https://www.worlddata.info/africa/egypt/terro rism.php.

Zelin, Aaron. "Jihadist Groups in the Sahel Region Formalize Merger." *Jihadology.* https://jihadology.net/?s=jnim.

Zenn, J. "Boko Haram and Kidnapping of Chibok Schoolgirls." *Combating Terrorism Center* in Volume 7, Issue 5, (2014), pp. 1-8.

Zenn, J. "Leadership Analysis of Boko Haram and Ansaru in Nigeria." *CTC Sentinel* 7(2), (2014) pp. 23-29.

Zenn, J. "The Islamic State's Provinces on the Peripheries Juxtaposing the Pledges from Boko Haram in Nigeria and Abu Sayyaf and Maute Group in the Philippines." *Perspectives on Terrorism,* Vol. 13, No. 1 (February 2019), pp. 87-104.

International Journal on Criminology • *Volume 9, Number 1* • *Winter 2022*

Pandemic Covid-19: Lessons for Bioterrorism

Tewfik Hamel[1]

ABSTRACT

From the Spanish flu to the pulmonary plague epidemic (1924, Los Angeles) and then to the "parrot fever" pandemic of 1930, to the more recent epidemics of SARS, Ebola, and Zika: the last century has seen a succession of pandemic alarms reminding us of the limits of our scientific knowledge, the role of human behavior and technologies in the emergence and spread of infectious diseases. Moreover, research suggests that future pandemics are inevitable.

Keywords: Bioterrorism, Covid-19, Pandemic planning, National security, Globalization

Pandemia Covid-19: lecciones para el bioterrorismo

RESUMEN

De la gripe española a la epidemia de peste pulmonar (1924, Los Ángeles) y luego a la pandemia de la "fiebre del loro" de 1930, a las más recientes epidemias de SARS, Ébola y Zika: el último siglo ha visto una sucesión de alarmas pandémicas que nos recuerdan los límites de nuestro conocimiento científico, el papel del comportamiento humano y las tecnologías en la aparición y propagación de enfermedades infecciosas. Además, la investigación sugiere que futuras pandemias son inevitables.

Palabras clave: Bioterrorismo, Covid-19, Planificación pandémica, Seguridad nacional, Globalización

2019冠状病毒病大流行：为生物恐怖主义提供的经验

摘要

从西班牙流感、肺鼠疫流行病（1924年洛杉矶）、1930年"鹦鹉热"大流行再到近期非典、埃博拉病毒和塞卡病毒流行

---

1   Doctor in Military History and Defense Studies (University Paul-Valery, Montpellier 3) - Master in International Relations (Univ. of Strasbourg) - Interdisciplinary Diploma in European Studies (Institut des Hautes Etudes Européennes) – Bachelor's Degree in Political Science and International Relations (Univ. of Algiers)

                                    doi: 10.18278/ijc.9.1.6

病：上世纪已出现一系列大流行警报，提醒我们科学知识的限制、人类行为和技术在传染病出现和传播中发挥的作用。此外，研究暗示，未来大流行是不可避免的。

关键词：生物恐怖主义，2019冠状病毒病（Covid-19），大流行规划，国家安全，全球化

PART 1 - VIRUSES, WAR, BIOLOGICAL TERRORISM; HISTORY, PERSPECTIVES

Despite a century of medical progress, viral and bacterial disasters still surprise and frighten. In late 2019, alarming news from Wuhan, China, where an unknown virus was reported to cause pneumonia, started gaining international attention. Soon after, Wuhan was shut down in an attempt to contain the virus, only to discover it was already too late. As the new disease started spreading worldwide, in January 2020, Chinese researchers identified the virus: a new strain of deadly coronavirus. Covid-19 proves that we are still exposed to unknown and complex diseases.

From the Spanish flu to the pulmonary plague epidemic (1924, Los Angeles) and then to the "parrot fever" pandemic of 1930, to the more recent epidemics of SARS, Ebola, and Zika: the last century has seen a succession of pandemic alarms reminding us of the limits of our scientific knowledge, the role of human behavior and technologies in the emergence and spread of infectious diseases. Moreover, research suggests that future pandemics are inevitable.

Modernity has certainly increased the risk of pandemics, but has also generated a new risk, that of terrorism, and particularly bio-terrorism. Modernization multiplies interdependencies, increasing terrorism's methodological practicality and attractiveness. At all levels, the increased complexity of society and the economy creates opportunities and vulnerabilities. Sophisticated transportation and mobility networks provide terrorists with means of communication and advertising. However, terrorism is neither a recent nor a static phenomenon. It has evolved over time, even if it retains many of its historical[2] characteristics, alongside with global developments: imperialism, the strengths and weaknesses of the state and the structure of the world economy. Terrorist ideologies are usually based on religion, ethnicity, nationalism or the vision of a charismatic leader. Terrorists often believe they can achieve their goals, and hope that the state they face will be too weak to stop them or prevent their actions.

---

2   Daniel Benjamin, "Le terrorisme en perspective," *Politique étrangère*, no. 4, 2006, pp. 887-900.

Given the multiple discontents and frustrations of modernity, e.g., through the failures of the "market state,"[3] terrorism is able to seduce entities of various orientations, allowing them to popularize their causes, to provoke or intimidate the power or their enemies, to impress or intimidate the public, and to reinforce the adherence of the faithful.[4] But as terrorism has become more globalized, counter-terrorism has also evolved into a global geopolitical network. And because of the losses suffered by terrorist groups, biological weapons may become more attractive, especially with the spread of technologies that facilitate their conception and production.

Biological warfare agents are no longer limited to the battlefield, the military is no longer the only one at risk of biological attack. In some cases, these agents could be used on a new front: large metropolitan areas. To counteract the potentially devastating effects of an attack, it is necessary to understand the basic epidemiological concepts of biological agents used as weapons. As the Council of Europe explains:

> "The Covid-19 pandemic demonstrated the vulnerability of modern societies to viral infections and their potential for disruption. The intentional use of a pathogen or other biological agent for terrorism can be highly effective and cause damage—both human and economic—on a much larger scale than 'traditional' terrorist attacks, paralyzing societies for long periods of time, spreading fear and mistrust far beyond the communities immediately affected."[5]

Analyses of epidemic trends, their timing, forecasting, and reordering are crucial to design effective public health strategies. Historians may be surprised at the lack of preparedness for the Covid-19 crisis, as epidemics have shaped human history, including military conflicts, creating strategic challenges. Preparedness is necessary here because its absence in the event of an epidemic leads to impotence.

---

3   Bobbitt discusses the evolution of the modern state, and in particular, "the relationship between the art of war and the legal order insofar as this relationship conditioned and transformed the modern state and the society that states composed." Wars and the concomitant revolutions in the military field have been the driving forces behind the change in the constitutional order of states since the Renaissance: "Each of the important revolutions that have occurred in military affairs has brought about a political revolution in the fundamental constitutional order of the state." He traces the historical evolution of the state in model terms. Six constitutional orders have succeeded each other since the Renaissance, he says: 1) "Princely State," 2) "Royal State," 3) "Territorial State," 4) "Nation-State," 5) "Nation-State," and finally, 6) "Market-State" as a likely emerging model. The shift to "market-state" does not mean that the state will necessarily disappear for the simple reason that the market needs the state. Philip Bobbitt, *Terror and Consent: The Wars for the Twenty-First Century*, Knopf, New York, 2008, pp. 189-198. Philip Bobbitt, *The Shield of Achilles: War, Peace, and the Course of History*, Knopf, New York, 2002.

4   Martha Crenshaw, "The Causes of Terrorism," *Comparative Politics*, vol. 13, July 1981, pp. 379-399.

5   Council of Europe, "*The Council of Europe continues working to enhance international co-operation against terrorism, including bioterrorism*," Strasbourg, 25 May 2020.

True preparedness requires multiple commitments across geographic and organizational boundaries.

Pandemics create urgent demands and needs in the face of limited resources. To be effective in a real event requires skills and plans to be in place before the crisis itself. It is imperative to develop and implement clear measures, both at the individual and public level. The ultimate goal of pandemic planning is twofold:

(a) reduce the morbidity and mortality rates of the disease, and (b) reducing the recovery time so that economic and social activities can return to their usual level.

Vaccinations, if available, and behavioral practices are crucial to limit the spread of infection. Although diseases can cause moral panic in the absence of a cure, little attention has been paid to the psychological factors that influence pandemic spread, emotional distress and social chaos, factors that in turn affect public health. Scapegoating, violence and "class hatred in times of epidemic" are then a common response, as a means of expression for fears, hatreds and tensions. However, it is difficult to support the idea that "blame has always been the means of making mysterious and devastating diseases understandable, and therefore perhaps controllable."[6]

Psychological factors matter for a variety of reasons. They play a role in the failure to comply with vaccination and hygiene programs, and in the reaction of populations to infections and associated losses, as xenophobia has marked modern-day epidemics. In 1900, San Francisco suffered from a bubonic plague imported by sea, "public health efforts then suffered from limited scientific knowledge, and the twin demons of denial and discrimination." Instead of offering treatment, Mayor James D. Phelan stoked fear of the city's Chinese, calling them a "constant threat to public health," a prelude to the present "foreign virus" rhetoric: his policies actually made the epidemic worse. Similarly, Henry Gage, governor of California, denied the existence of the plague, fearing that the economy would suffer as his fellow citizens died.[7]

Psychological factors help to understand and manage the societal problems associated with pandemics: the spread of excessive fear in populations at risk of infection. In the event of a pandemic, planning must therefore include psychosocial reactions, including panic, emotions, and defensive reactions, which are psychosocial vulnerabilities that contribute to disease and distress.[8] An adapted response

---

6   Dorothy Nelkin & Sander L. Gilman, "Placing blame for devastating disease," in Arien Mack (ed.), *Time of Plague: The History and Social Consequences of Lethal Epidemic*, University Press, New York: 1991, p. 40.

7   Marilyn Chase, *The Barbary Plague: The Black Death in Victorian San Francisco*, Random House, New York, 2004, see Prologue.

8   Steven Taylor, *The Psychology of Pandemics: Preparing for the Next Global Outbreak of Infectious Disease*, Cambridge Scholars Publishing, 2019.

is crucial, because despite the underlying social-political controversies, circumstances, the severity of the symptoms, spreading quickly or not, the pandemics actually do not necessarily provoke violence and hatred.[9]

By their very nature, the characteristics and consequences of future pandemics, including Covid-19, are hardly predictable. However, this uncertainty should not be an excuse for a lack of planning, but rather underscore the need for comprehensive and flexible plans for inevitable future pandemics. Improving your organization's preparedness to function during a pandemic will help you anticipate future events.

Preparedness requires cooperation and collaboration on many levels, with individuals needing to protect themselves and their families; employers needing to devise strategy changes to prevent the spread of disease in the workplace and school; and health care providers and government agencies needing to test themselves and their environments.

Long before Covid-19, virologists were predicting other pandemics, perhaps from some kind of flu, with potentially devastating consequences. Epidemiologists and public health officials were calling for concrete plans to deal with the early months of a pandemic. In 2005, soon after the SARS outbreak, Michael Osterholm, director of the *Center for Infectious Disease Research and Policy*, wrote that influenza pandemics have occurred many times in history—10 in the last 300 years.

They cannot be avoided, but their impact may be reduced. A detailed operational plan should involve private sector food producers, medical suppliers, public health providers. law enforcement, and emergency managers. Most importantly, the plan should anticipate the disruption or even "collapse of global trade associated with

---

9   In striking cases, pandemics have done the opposite, as evidenced by the epidemics of unknown causes in antiquity, the great influenza of 1918-1919, and yellow fever in many cities and regions of America and Europe. These epidemic crises unified communities and healed wounds that had been deeply cut by previous social, political, religious, racial and ethnic tensions and anxieties. On other occasions, it is true, pandemics have divided societies through accusations and violence. Historians, physicians, and psychologists have yet to map when and where they occurred, to measure their intensities, or to examine the complex interplay of factors to explain why certain diseases were more or less exceptions. They have yet to raise the issues in a comparative framework of global epidemics. Studies of social violence, hatred, and disease have focused on a handful of pandemics—sometimes drawing parallels between the Black Death and cholera, in other places between syphilis and A.I.D.S., and sometimes two or three other diseases. Studies have not gone beyond these few pandemics to draw a comparative picture of disease and hate patterns. These studies have not compared levels of violence or intensity of hate with different pandemics in different places and times; instead, the hate potential of epidemics has been leveled. Existing studies have also failed to consider the extent to which certain characteristics of diseases—mortality rates, speed of death, novelty of a disease, mysterious causes, degrees of contagion, horror of signs and symptoms —determine whether a wave of collective hatred and violence is likely to ensue. Instead, in both popular imagination and scholarly literature, violent hatred is seen as the normal course of pandemics, supposedly rooted in timeless mental structures—certain mental structures, certain psychological constants. Cohn SK, "Pandemics: waves of disease, waves of hate from the Plague of Athens to A.I.D.S.," *Historical Journal* (Cambridge), vol. 85, no. 230, November 2012, pp. 535-555.

the pandemic," which would represent "the first real test of the resilience of the modern global distribution system."[10]

Pandemic/epidemic and national security

Pandemics are potentially destructive and therefore frightening. Because they are fraught with uncertainty, they often provoke contention and conflict, as we saw during the Covid-19 crisis. Thanks to vaccines, more reliable medical service delivery, more effective communication, and a more educated public, however, some argue that the occurrence of a new black plague is highly unlikely.

However, we are now faced with new risks, allowing diseases to reach pandemic levels and affecting our ability to find the right response: fragmentation of the media, tribalization of knowledge, the increasingly troubling status of scientific and political expertise, growing worldwide mobility, and the globalization and commercialization of pandemic response systems.[11]

Pandemics have reshaped societies for millennia. Similarly, the Covid-19 pandemic has shown us the importance of protecting ourselves from bacteria, germs and viruses. From tuberculosis to the avian flu and from HIV to coronavirus, these infectious factors share a common history: human interaction with animals. Known zoonotic (animal-to-human) diseases, these pathogens —both pre-existing and newly identified—have emerged and reemerged throughout history, causing epidemic-panic outbreaks and millions of deaths worldwide. These diseases must be considered from ecological, cultural, economic, and biological[12] perspectives.

Some countries have managed the recent crisis better than others, with few correlations with regime type. The factors for success in handling Covid-19 are the capacity of the state, the collective/social trust in government and effective leadership. Countries with these conditions have been able to limit the damage of pandemic.[13] Countries with dysfunctional states, polarized societies or poor leadership have responded poorly, leaving their citizens and economies exposed and vulnerable. Especially in times of crisis, leadership (civilian and military) is crucial. In countries that mismanaged the Covid-19 crisis, the pandemic simply exposed pre-existing governance failures. Historians have traditionally identified aversion to adaptation with ineffectiveness in practice.

---

10   Michael T. Osterholm, "Preparing for the Next Pandemic," *Foreign Affairs*. vol. 84, no. 4, July-August 2005.

11   Kristian Bjørkdahl & Benedicte Carlsen, *Pandemics, Publics, and Politics: Staging Responses to Public Health Crises*, Palgrave Macmillan, Basingstoke, UK, 2019.

12   David Waltner-Toews, *The Chickens Fight Back: Pandemic Panics and Deadly Diseases That Jump from Animals to Humans*, Greystone Books Ltd., 2007.

13   Francis Fukuyama, "The Pandemic and Political Order: It Takes a State," *Foreign Affairs*, vol. 99, no. 4, July-August 2020.

Often, these analyses involve institutions rather than individuals because, historically, organizations have often failed to learn from the mistakes of others and have failed to anticipate or adapt to new or unexpected situations. Although psychological factors influence this decision-making process,[14] President Donald Trump's personality and "tweeting politics" are not enough to explain the situation witnessed in the United States. In fact, "the obligation to adapt to unexpected circumstances tests both the organization and the system, revealing structural or functional weaknesses, the catastrophic potential of which may have been previously ignored."[15]

China has been effective. Its attempts to strengthen its position in the international arena during the Covid-19 crisis are simply a rehash of old methods, approaches and strategies, identical to those of other imperial powers. By definition, military and political control can be formal or informal. Driven by national interests, the Chinese are also motivated by strong ideological impulses or nationalist visions. Historians see science and medicine as a means of conveying imperialism and its applications.

Malaria and yellow fever suggested that blacks were immunized against these diseases, thus usable as slaves or convenient labor in unhealthy areas for whites. Watts examines the link between infectious diseases and imperialism and how imperialism used the fight against these diseases as a tool for intrusion and domination in underdeveloped regions and fragile states.[16] China's attitude will be no different in this regard.

Pandemic/epidemic: definition

For humanity, the history of viruses is one of fear, ignorance, grief, sacrifice, and bravery. Pandemics have caused mass deaths and immense social disruption. Other "virgin soil" epidemics struck populations alien to these newly introduced microbes. In *Encyclopedia of Pestilence, Pandemics, and Plagues*, Byrne offers an overview covering individual diseases (HIV/AIDS, malaria, Ebola, and SARS): Major epidemics (the Black Death, sixteenth-century syphilis, nineteenth-century cholera, and the 1918-1919 Spanish Flu), environmental factors (ecology, travel, poverty, wealth, slavery, and war); and historic and cultural ef-

---

14 Psychological factors influence political decision-making, and include leaders' personalities and beliefs, leadership style, emotions, images, cognitive coherence, and use of analogies. Their impact is seen especially in decisions made in times of crisis; in governments where there is a strong leader; and, in a country that is newly formed or undergoing regime change. Alex *Mintz* & Karl DeRouen Jr., *Understanding Foreign Policy Decision Making*, Cambridge University Press, Cambridge, 2010.

15 Eliot Cohen & John Gooch, *Military Misfortunes: The Anatomy of Failure in War*, The Free Press, New York, 1990, pp. 161-162.

16 Sheldon Watts, *Epidemics and History: Disease, Power and Imperialism*, Yale University Press, New Haven & London; 1999, p. 279, see also 207 and 241.

fects of disease (romantism-tuberculosis relationship, closing of London theaters during plagues, effect of venereal diseases on social reforms).[17]

Despite the multiplicity of causes and the diversity of modes of transmission of their effects throughout history, pandemics have circulated across national borders and continents causing great human suffering. From the Black Death in Asia and Europe to the smallpox and polio epidemics that decimated the Americas, to the contemporary crises of HIV/AIDS and avian influenza, epidemics are a permanent feature of the world's[18] societies.

"Pandemic" and "epidemic" have similar meanings. According to the *New Shorter Oxford English Dictionary*, an epidemic is a disease "customarily absent or rare in a population but causing outbreaks of high frequency and severity, or the temporary but widespread outbreak of a specific disease." Although it is a "widespread disease," there is no agreement on the extent or frequency of an epidemic. A pandemic is simply a worldwide or at least continent-wide epidemic. However, there is no quantitative measure of when an epidemic becomes a pandemic.[19]

Epidemics have been a concern since the 1990s: since then, the world has experienced a number of infectious diseases: SARS (severe acute respiratory syndrome); influenza A (H1N1); Middle East Respiratory Syndrome (MERS), a viral respiratory disease caused by a new coronavirus (MERS-CoV); Ebola virus; Zika virus; and Covid-19. Although more than 60% of the approximately 400 infectious diseases identified since 1940 are zoonotic, evidence suggests that the likelihood of pan-diseases has increased in the last century: travel, global integration, urbanization, and massive environmental exploitation.[20] New infectious agents may emerge wherever humans live, but studies suggest that the worst pandemics occur in tropical and subtropical regions.

The "hot spots" of (re)emerging infectious diseases are: Eastern China, Southeast Asia, East Pakistan, Northeast India, Bangladesh, Central America and in the tropical belt through Central Africa, from Guinea, Nigeria, DR Congo, Rwanda, and Burundi to Ethiopia.[21]

---

17   Joseph P. Byrne, *Encyclopedia of Pestilence, Pandemics, and Plagues, 2 Volumes*, Greenwood Press, Westport & London, 2008 (Preface by Anthony S. Fauci).

18   For a review of the major types of infectious agents and modes of transmission, including a historical overview of infectious diseases and attempts to control epidemics, see Barry Youngerman, *Pandemics and Global Health*, Facts On File, Inc, New York, 2008, pp. 3-27.

19   Niall Johnson, *Britain and the 1918-19 Influenza Pandemic*, Routledge, New York, 2006, pp. 25-26.

20   Stephen S Morse (et al.), "Prediction and prevention of the next pandemic zoonosis," *The Lancet*, no. 380, 2012, pp. 1956-1965.

21   Kate E. Jones, Nikkita G. Patel, Marc A. Levy, Adam Storeygard, Deborah Balk, John L. Gittleman, & Peter Daszak, "Global Trends in Emerging Infectious Diseases," *Nature* 451, February 2008, pp. 990-993.

Classification of the terms *"outbreak,"* "epidemic" and "pandemic"

Classification of terms		
Terms	Geographic distribution	Criteria
Outbreak	Localized (restricted)	Two or more cases (food or waterborne)
Epidemic (epidemic)	Community, State, Region	More cases observed than expected
Pandemic (pandemic)	Country, Continent, World	More cases observed than expected

Source: Eric J. Dietz & David R Black, *Pandemic Planning,* CRC Press, New York, 2012, p. xxviii.

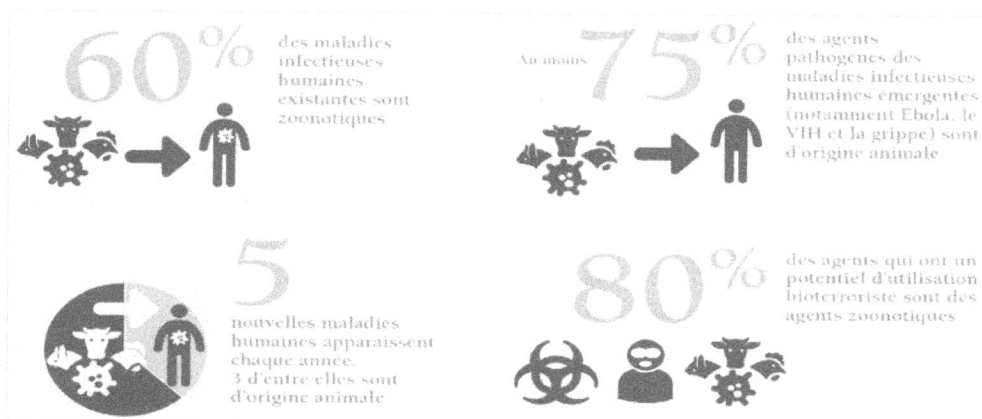

https://www.oie.int/fr/pour-les-medias/une-seule-sante/

Apart from the fatal consequences for the direct victims, epidemics have negative social, economic, political and security consequences; worse, when the pandemic has a new pathogen, a high mortality/hospitalization rate and circulates easily. Unlike natural disasters, which suddenly destroy a limited area, infectious diseases have the terrifying power to disrupt daily life globally, drying up public and private resources and paralyzing trade and transportation.

In our world, it is ever easier to move people, animals, and materials around the globe, but these same logistical advances, have made epidemics and pandemics nearly unpreventable. And as the Ebola, MERS, yellow fever, Zika, and Covid-19 epidemics have shown, we are ill-prepared to deal with their fallout. What can and should we do, to protect humanity in such cases?

The term "pandemic"—an epidemic affecting various countries or continents and a mass of people—refers not to the severity of a disease, but to its ability to quickly infect a large geographic area. Less deadly than expected, the Covid-19 virus is highly contagious and often transmitted asymptomatically. Ebola is deadly but difficult to track—victims die before they can transmit it. COVID-19, on the other hand, encourages people to neglect the disease, and so the virus has spread rapidly around the world, resulting in many deaths.

As a result, economies will recover slowly and in stages: the world will not return to its pre-COVID-19 state any time soon. Compared to the previous great plagues, this coronavirus pandemic is not as deadly as the Black Death (a term coined after 1800), which wiped out one third of the European population and drastically changed the lives of its survivors. This plague began to circulate across the European and Asian continents in 1347, causing immense devastation. The "Spanish Flu" epidemic of 1918 killed perhaps 50 million people worldwide. But the death rate relative to the total population was small compared to the impact of the Black Death, which killed 30% to 50% of the European population.[22]

Epidemics, modernity and the "global era"

Our globalized and hyper-connected world, where billions of people travel billions of kilometers each year, makes the spread of disease even easier. But it also offers scientists and health actors facilitated access to new technologies, new opportunities to collaborate and new ways of dealing with these diseases. The coronavirus outbreak has disrupted the world's daily life and led to increased levels of public surveillance and vigilance. What has made Covid-19 so dangerous is its combined with the fragility of the global economy after the post-2008 financial crisis.

Although lethal pathogens are usually quickly identified and controlled, the growth of high-speed transportation networks and the globalization of trade and travel have further accelerated the spread of disease. Indeed, many aspects of global society still make the world vulnerable to pandemic challenges. Already, the experiences of SARS and Ebola have shown how porous and fragile our public health systems are. The major characteristics of modernity—population growth, climate change, rapid transportation, the proliferation of mega-poles with inadequate infrastructure, war, persistent poverty, and growing social inequalities—contribute to persistently high-risk levels. None of these factors is likely to abate soon.

Covid-19 circulates faster in overcrowded urban concentrations lacking clean water and sanitation, which gives rise to new forms of urban,[23] political,

---

22 Norman F. Cantor, *In the Wake of the Plague: The Black Death and the World It Made*, Simon & Schuster, New York, 2001, pp. 6-7; see also John Kelly, The *Great Mortality: An Intimate History of the Black Death, the Most Devastating Plague of All Time*, Harper Perennial, New York, 2006.

23 The urban hierarchy has shifted from a place-based structure based on size to a relational structure based on urban networks. It reflects a distinction between somewhat idealized "flow spaces," where function derives from extra-regional linkages, and more familiar "place spaces," where most people live and function derives from linkages within a more or less bounded region. Whereas the city-regions of the past were self-contained markets that functioned as "functional hierarchies," the new global city system is based on a "relational hierarchy"—it is the relationships between key city-regions of the world that matter. Cities such as New York, London, Shanghai and Tokyo are much more closely related to each other than, for example, New York and Louisville or Toronto and Edmonton. Such findings should not be interpreted as an affirmation of the death of territory/place at the hands of digitization and globalization. The growing importance of a network-based

economic, and social organization. The extra-regional connections between cities are long-standing, but technological advances in transportation are expanding the distances they travel, the number of cities they connect, the areas they include, and the number of problems they generate. Our cities thus experience multiple cycles of degeneration and renewal, often chaotic.

Cycles that are sometimes interrupted by a sudden and unpredictable event such as Covid-19 or war, aggravating the risk of epidemics. What does it mean for city dwellers when their city's infrastructures—communication, transportation, electricity, water, and sanitation networks—collapse? How do political corruption and mafias undermine the built environment? How will pandemics affect social structures and relationships to authority? How do drug trafficking and crime reshape class, race, and gender? What impact do they have on vulnerable urban environments? For example, while the precise origin of the Covid-19 global pandemic is still unknown, the illegal wildlife trade in China may have encouraged its emergence.[24]

Urban populations are affected by violence, civil wars, drug trafficking, infrastructure collapse, and natural disasters, all of which weaken their immunity and resilience. Police forces may only have to respond to major incidents because of the loss of infected, quarantined personnel. Given the potential for social disruption, states may collude with organized crime to provide services and help maintain order. In Mexico, drug cartels provided food parcels to those in need during the pandemic;[25] in Brazil, gangs are countering a lack of control by imposing their own curfews.[26] Mexico City, New York, Beirut, Bangkok, Baghdad, and Saint-Denis are examples of cities that lack the quality of urban life that makes people vulnerable to an epidemic.

Epidemics and pandemics evolve for years, hidden behind massive ecological disruptions; they also take advantage of the erosion of public health infrastructures and public governance— amidst the failures of "millenarian capitalism."[27] The market cannot perform the functions of government. The links between de-

---

urban hierarchy does not exclude the influence of a city's hinterland. Some places will be more closely linked to their own hinterland than to exotic international cities, and in this case spatially close territories remain quite important. While significant, this interpretation of transition is not absolute. Richard Florida, *The Great Reset: How New Ways of Living and Working Drive Post-Crash Prosperity*, Harper, New York, 2010.

24 Graham Readfearn, "How did coronavirus start and where did it come from? Was it really Wuhan's animal market?" *The Guardian*, April 28, 2020.

25 "Mexican Drug Cartel Gives Out Food to the Poor Amid Pandemic," Organized Crime and Corruption Reporting Project (OCCRP), April 07, 2020.

26 Barretto Briso & Tom Phillips, "Brazil gangs impose strict curfews to slow coronavirus spread," *The Guardian,* 25 March 2020.

27 Walter Russell Mead, *Power, Terror, Peace, and War: America's Grand Strategy in a World at Risk*, Knopf, 2004.

mocratization and the market are empirically uncertain. From the beginning of Western economic development, there has been a (largely hidden) tension between market and democracy.

The present variant of capitalism lacks meaningful redistributive mechanisms. Contrary to the "Washington consensus," the market and the state are neither opposed nor alternative but linked by structural arrangements. Markets are always defined and governed by political and judicial institutions. The debate is about variation in institutional forms, not about domination of one over the other. The market presupposes a government that protects, directs, and controls. The foundations of the business world are political. Contrary to the globalist narrative, economic globalization was made possible by political change. But what politics has done, it can also undo.

Thus, since these trends will continue, let us look especially at policies to identify and contain emerging epidemics with pandemic potential, and investments to strengthen health preparedness and capacity. As a mirror of society, epidemics "are not random events that afflict societies in a capricious manner and without warning. On the contrary, each society produces its own specific vulnerabilities. To study them is to understand the structure of the society, its standard of living and its political priorities. In this sense, epidemic diseases have always been significant: the challenge of medical history is to decipher their meanings."[28]

Diseases are inherent to humanity, even if they do not all become epidemic. Sometimes, when the population is not immune, one of them becomes pandemic and affects human life for a long time. Other factors conducive to outbreaks of epidemics/pandemics are: poor hygiene, inadequate preventive methods, poor quality food, high population density, the increasing mobility of people, and also the way the disease itself is transmitted.

When Pericles died of the plague, Athens lost an important leader. His successors advocate another strategy, costly for the League of Delos. This episode of the Peloponnesian War shows the role of contagions and diseases in history; they have wiped out cultures and allowed others to prosper. Thus, disease has played a major role in wars of the past and could again in the present world—we must take steps now to be prepared.

National Security and Pandemic

National security is an amorphous and elastic concept that encompasses and relates to many issues and activities. Most definitions include the physical security of the individual and the state, and aim to preserve a certain pre-defined set of values and principles. Obviously, when these values are invoked, either directly (rights, laws) or indirectly (customs, habits), these defini-

---

28   Frank M. Snowden, *Epidemics and Society*, Yale University Press, New Haven & London, 2019, p. 7.

tions become subjective. Security is closely "linked to identity, and security policy to the construction of collective identity."[29] In the temporal dimension, immediate threats motivate national security more than distant ones. In the same way, human threats seem more alarming to national security than natural risks.[30]

These definitions explicitly separate "national security" from ordinary problems because of its urgent, existential or critical nature. Focusing on immediacy, coercion and the human factor, these definitions make "slow" issues (pandemics, climate change) difficult to access at the forefront of national security. For example, "the first plague pandemic, which lasted more than two hundred years," was a key factor in the decline of antiquity and the early Middle Ages. Its sporadic persistence from 541 to 750 had immense consequences. However, there are no systematic studies of this first plague main geopolitical, cultural and linguistic studies of the Mediterranean world. Eight centuries before the Black Death, a plague pandemic ravaged the shores of the Mediterranean, spreading from eastern Persia to as far as the northern British Isles.[31]

The Spanish flu, which German and British soldiers called *Blitzkatarrh* and *Flanders Flu*, killed 50 to 100 million people and was global in scope. It ravaged the entire world—the United States recorded 550,000 deaths (five times its total military deaths in World War I), with European deaths exceeding two million. Even though entire Allied battalions and Germans were decimated, the reasons for the deaths of many servicemen were concealed to protect public morale.

Philadelphia ran out of gravediggers and coffins as mass burial trenches were dug with construction equipment. The Spanish flu raised the specter of the Black Death of 1348 and the Great Plague of 1665; the medical profession, ravaged by five years of conflict, was unable to contain and defeat this new disaster.[32]

The Spanish flu struck 294,000 Allied soldiers in the fall of 1918 alone, causing major problems for both the Allies and the Germans. Historians and political scientists have argued that the flu helped defeat the Central Powers by striking German troops and devastating the Austro-Hungarian Empire.[33] For Spinney, the pandemic fueled the instability of the interwar period. It may also have changed

---

29 Bill McSweeney, "Identity and Security," *Review of International Studies*, vol. 22: no. 1, 1996, p. 82.

30 The "security label" implies "urgency," which identifies threats as sufficiently important to warrant emergency and exceptional measures, including the use of force. Barry Buzan, "New Patterns of Global Security in the Twenty-First Century," *International Affairs*, vol. 67, no. 3, 1991, pp. 432-433.

31 Lester K. Little, "Life and Afterlife of the First Plague Pandemic," in Lester K. Little (ed.), *Plague and the End of Antiquity: The Pandemic of 541-750*, Cambridge University Press, Cambridge, 2007, pp. 3-32.

32 Catharine Arnold, *Pandemic 1918: Eyewitness Accounts from the Greatest Medical Holocaust in Modern History*, St. Martin's Press, 2018.

33 David T. Zabecki, *The German 1918 Offensives: A Case Study in The Operational Level of War*, Routledge, 2006; Andrew T. Price-Smith, *Contagion and Chaos: Disease, Ecology, and National Security in the Era of Globalization*, The MIT Press, 2009.

the course of history by striking key leaders at important times—it worsened Woodrow Wilson's health at the Paris Peace Conference of 1919.

> They *[historians]* agree that he suffered a massive stroke the following October. His earlier bout with influenza was surely a contributing factor, they believe. He was unable to persuade the U.S. government to ratify the Treaty of Versailles or join the League of Nations. Germany was forced to pay punitive reparations, stoking the resentment of its people—something that could have been avoided if the United States had had a say. Making Wilson the major obstacle to its own goals, the Spanish flu could thus have contributed to World War II.[34]

However, despite its devastation, the terrible Spanish flu seems to have been forgotten. In the popular imagination, it was an incident of the First World War. In the United States, as the crisis diminished, the pandemic also faded from the collective memory. Their helpless despair over the pandemic bothered these optimistic and progressive Americans. But for the survivors, the trauma was endless, their end of life marked by grief and mourning.[35]

However, the association of "pandemic" and "threats" to national security re-emerged in the 1990s. Many leaders and publications warned of the danger of epidemics, called for a broad overhaul of traditional definitions of national and international security, and for a broadened vision of security that included infectious diseases, among others. The January 2000 Security Council meeting on AIDS was the first time in history that the UN addressed a health issue—a disease became a threat to international peace and security. The debate began with the *National Intelligence Council*'s assessment of the security risk posed by infectious diseases: "the continuing burden of infectious diseases may lead to economic decay, social fragmentation, and political destabilization in the most affected countries of the developing world.

The NIC warns that "over the next 20 years, new and re-emerging infectious diseases will threaten global health ever more." It points out that "these diseases will threaten U.S. citizens at home, U.S. military personnel deployed abroad, and will exacerbate social and political instability in key countries and regions where the United States has important interests."[36]

(Re)emerging infectious diseases continue to threaten national and international security, and the present globalization and ecological changes accelerate the

---

34   Laura Spinney, *Pale Rider: The Spanish Flu of 1918 and How it Changed the World*, Public Affairs, New York, 2017.

35   Nancy K. Bristow, *American Pandemic: The Lost Worlds of the 1918 Influenza Epidemic*, Oxford University Press, Oxford, 2012.

36   National Intelligence Council (NIC), *The Global Infectious Disease Threat and Its Implications for the United States*, NIE 99-17D, January 2000, p. 5.

danger. Their negative effects on states threaten international security. However, these infectious diseases receive little political attention because their effects are small. Only certain infectious pathogens threaten national security, based on their lethality, transmissibility, and ability to cause economic damage.

A specific disease thus becomes a safety issue when it imposes an intolerable burden on society through morbidity, mortality, and public concern. The 2013 WHO updated guidelines emphasize instead "national risk assessments," where each member state is urged to conduct its own.[37]

While the safety-health nexus has created a global commitment to pandemic policies, the institutional, technical, and political challenges to achieving this goal are immense. The promise of a systematic analysis of the pandemic-safety nexus remains illusory. At least the work exploring this linkage includes human security, extending the notion of security beyond the state to include basic human needs: education and health. The concepts of "human security" and "national security'" lead to competing views of security, as well as conflicting assessments of their importance which may threaten the lives of masses of people.

The security-defense community resists the arguments of the "globalisers," whose appeal to human security contradicts traditional approaches to national and international security that focus on physical threats to the state. Their analysis focuses on the threats these diseases pose to the territorial integrity and security of the state. Given the flaws in the management of the Covid-19 pandemic, this pandemic/biological weapons debate must therefore be framed by traditional standards.

Globalization and "Panic in the City"

The evolution of biological warfare and the modern use of biological weapons is difficult to separate from the deliberate use of natural diseases. However, the potential of biological weapons in attacks was demonstrated by the massive disruption caused by the use of anthrax in 2001 in the United States. The threat of biological weapons has never been more important than in recent years[38] Especially since the basic knowledge to create biological weapons is more accessible in our world than ever before.

These concerns mainly originate from the increased risk of such weapons to be acquired and used by terrorists. In response, anti- and counter-terrorism strategies have been developed and implemented. Counterterrorism encompasses defensive measures to reduce the vulnerability of individuals and property to ter-

---

37 World Health Organization, "Pandemic Influenza Risk Management: A WHO guide to inform and harmonize national and international pandemic preparedness and response," Geneva, May 2017, pp. 8-10.

38 William J. Broad & Judith Miller, "The threat of germ weapons is Rising. Fear, too," *New York Times*, December 27, 1998.

rorist acts, and counterterrorism refers to offensive measures that prevent, deter, and respond to terrorism.

Because of the terrorist threat, the risk posed by various microorganisms becoming bioweapons needs to be assessed and the evolution in the use of biological agents better understood. Yet even as political and military leaders prepare for urban military operations in the globalized era, the perception of the links between cities and war has not yet penetrated the sphere of mainstream political narratives on security. Policymakers think "narrowly about domestic urban counterterrorism and defending critical infrastructure where police forces and emergency services prevail."

They ignore "the fact that we face a future in which crises in global mega-poles will defy military resilience, demographic resources, and political will."[39] This theory links urban violence to the need for meta-strategy versus geo-strategy; for it, "war, like everything else, is urbanized," and conflict will occur first in "the strategic sites of our age: cities,"[40] with demographic and urbanization trends becoming so critical that urban activities will shape many of the critical security problems of the 21st century.[41]

As a framework for post-Cold War change, globalization gained prominence in the 1990s. For its defenders, this modern globalization paradigm is distinct from previous ones for it is "thicker and faster," broader in scope, but also "faster, cheaper and deeper."[42] The discourse dominating most of the political-ideological spectrum is conveyed by the hyper-globalists, for whom globalization implies liberalization, universalization, deterritorialization, internationalization, and the rise of global networks of interdependence.

The main differences from previous globalizations are the increased interconnectedness due to the information revolution, liberalization, the expansion of international trade, the diminishing role of governments, and the ease with which technology helps transfer funds, information, and ideas across borders. It has made borders more porous, but not unimportant. Another implication of globalization is the shrinking of distances and the "space-time compression" in various ways, depending on the situation.

The circulation of capital, goods, data, and people creates uninterrupted transnational flows and networks. This allows for accelerated interactions, but also the production of identities disconnected from a distinctive local belonging. This temporal political-spatial process in fact erases old borders and globalizes national

---

39   Michael Evans, "War and the City in the New Urban Century," *Quadrant*, no. 1-2, Jan-Feb 2009.

40   Stephen Graham, *Cities, War, and Terrorism: Towards an Urban Geopolitics*, Blackwell, Oxford, 2004, p. 4.

41   Tewfik Hamel, "La lutte contre le terrorisme et la criminalité: Un changement de paradigme?" *Global Security*, no. 5, 2016, pp. 45-79.

42   Joseph Nye, "Globalism Versus Globalization," *The Globalist*, April 15, 2002.

security. All these facets of the globalization—paradigm refer to four related processes: expansion (stretching of activities), intensity (intensification of the aforementioned), speed (acceleration of interactions), and impact (increasing importance of actions and decisions in distant places).

When it comes to security, globalists (referring to the growing connection of the international system: the increasing flow of money, goods, information, and people) focus on globalization itself. "They see a world in which threats to the security of people," which are inherently transnational, complement, if not replace, threats to the security of nations. Most see this process, not as the product of an invisible hand or unseen forces. "In addition to addressing the dark side of globalization, globalists argue for the need to exploit the opportunities it offers— by securing open markets."[43]

These globalists usually see a decline in wars between major powers and the rise of new security problems, including pandemics. For them, globalization causes serious social fragility, creates critical vulnerabilities and spreads violence and identity conflicts. Its various aspects potentiate other transnational dangers (first, in fragile states): proliferation of weapons, including weapons of mass destruction (WMD), cyber-attacks, nationalism, religious antagonism, ethnic violence, criminality, drug trafficking, the spread of infectious diseases, environmental degradation, and competition over resources.[44]

They advocate for the theory of "world chaos," according to which the armed forces are now being drawn into a guerrilla warfare affecting the national territory itself. A "panic in the city" scenario, stimulated by the possible use of chemical or biological weapons in urban areas, would involve an evolution of the missions of militaries. Warfare has left the battlefield and is infiltrating society. These "globalists" are worried about "chaotic conditions" created by asymmetric attacks on national territory. Historically, one of many tasks of the armed forces was to defend the population against the armies of other states.

A "catastrophic" attack (with WMD) is only the worst-case scenario. Even a "dirty bomb" would result in enormous losses, with widespread panic and disruption. Hence the inclusion in the threat spectrum of the risk to the population of previously unthinkable casualties caused by few foreign or/and domestic individuals. Civilians will not be able to bear the physical and psychological aspects of a "cataclysmic attack": preparing for it and responding to it is clearly a military matter.

---

43   Ivo H. Daalder & James M. Lindsay, "Power and Cooperation: An American Foreign Policy for the Age of Global Politics," in Henry J. Aaron, James M. Lindsay, & Pietro S. Nivola, *Agenda for the Nation*, Brookings Institution Press, 2003, pp. 299 and 303-304.

44   "In the field of international security, globalization has most often been associated with ecological degradation, refugee flows, international crime, uncontrolled proliferation, and religious fundamentalism. These are represented as 'new threats' that may ultimately lead to 'global chaos' or even 'world war,'" writes Laurent Goetschel, "Globalisation and Security: The Challenge of Collective Action in a Politically Fragmented World," *Global Society*, vol.14, no.2, 2000, p. 264.

Many original strategic theories have thus called for increased military involvement in homeland security, with its role limited to supporting the civil authorities. Proponents of the "panic in the city" scenario envisioned internal security as the preliminary, or even primary, mission of the armed forces. They argue that if the perception of a sanctuary national territory disappears during an attack, the population will panic and flee to safer areas.

To avoid this scenario, the military must consider the most plausible, transnational, and asymmetric threats to national territory including the use of panic as a weapon, not the least probable, as a classic response to external aggression. Important, but not dominant, strategists have embraced this vision of globalization, the orientation of which can be summarized as "chaos on the coast, panic in the city."[45]

Traditionalists dominate security and defense expertise, and believe that ethnic conflicts, the collapse of peripheral states, pandemics or environmental problems are not existential risks. The role of the strategist and theorist is to distinguish the ephemeral from the structural, and the focus on global chaos is typical of this drift. Although many humanitarian and environmental problems cross borders, nation-states—their governments, armies, laws and legitimacy—are and will remain the dominant force in world affairs. A world of interdependent states may differ from a world of highly independent states—which never existed—it is still a world of states. For these strategists favoring a State-centered analysis, the major threat comes from hostile nation-states.

That said, globalist theories are outside the mainstream of national security and foreign policy. At least for national security, these currents, including the idea of human security, have not dominated. " prevails in economics, realists and their belief in the primacy of states as arbiters of the security of the international system dominate in strategy: to what extent will the Covid-19 pandemic bring about a fundamental change?

Impact of pandemics on international peace and security

Epidemics and pandemics can undermine the prosperity, legitimacy, structural cohesion, and of course, the security of states. The unpredictability of a serious infectious disease outbreak, its speed of spread, and public fears can lead to widespread disruption and prevent states from maximizing their economic power and governing as well as possible. At least 47 countries and territories around the world have already had to postpone local and national elections because of Covid-19.[46] This can lead to increased poverty, intrastate violence and

---

45   Sam J. Tangredi, "The Future Security Environment, 2001-2025: Toward a Consensus View," in Paul J Bolt, Damon V. Coletta, Collins G. Shackelford, Jr. (eds.), *American Defense Policy*, Johns Hopkins University Press, 2005, p. 57.

46   Global overview of COVID-19: Impact on elections, *International IDEA*, Stockholm, Sweden,

political instability, with negative effects on regional economic and political stability, international relations and development. These inequalities lead to instability, and thus to tragedy.

What would make the situation even worse? The likelihood of war. Apparently, the option of war is different from the measures taken to fight Covid-19. By its very nature, war requires national mobilization, including manpower and soldiers in training camps, military bases, factories, mobilization zones, ships at sea, etc.: the opposite of what leaders are doing at home— the opposite of what the leaders are doing now, imposing social distancing. The worsening of Sino-American relations has little to do with Covid-19. Long before the pandemic, there were few official U.S. texts that did not mention China as an enemy, a challenge, or a rival.

Pandemics can foster political and economic discord between countries but are unlikely to generate major armed conflict. Examining the likely impact of Covid-19 on the risk of war, Posen believes that this pandemic is more peace-promoting. It impacts all major powers and restricts all opportunities for war. Conversely, it makes all governments more pessimistic about their short/medium-term prospects. Since states often go to war in the grip of excessive confidence, pessimism induced by a pandemic should promote peace. In *The Causes of War*, historian Geoffrey Blainey argues that

> At their outset, most wars share a common characteristic: optimism; belligerents are usually optimistic about their chances of military success. When the elites on both or all sides are confident, they are more likely to take the plunge—and less likely to negotiate, believing that they will fare better by fighting. Peace is served by pessimism.[47]

Wars (intra and inter-state) amplify problems caused by disease. They contribute to the spread of diseases and aggravate ensuing socio-economic consequences. They also disrupt traditional means of communication. Indeed, pandemics are exacerbated by conflicts. The UN Security Council notes that the reverse is also true: pandemics can cause or exacerbate instability. Its September 2014 resolution 2177 on Ebola in West Africa recognizes that "in the most affected countries, peacebuilding and development are at risk of being undermined by the Ebola epidemic."

Furthermore, "the epidemic undermines the stability of the most affected countries and, if not contained, may lead to further civil unrest and social tensions, a deteriorating political climate and increased insecurity." For the Council,

---

March 18, 2020, https://www.idea.int/news-media/multimedia-reports/global-overview-covid-19-impact-elections

47   Barry R. Posen "Do Pandemics Promote Peace? Why Sickness Slows the March to War," *Foreign Affairs*, April 2020.

"the unprecedented scale of the Ebola epidemic in Africa constitutes a threat to international peace and security."

The Ebola outbreak in West Africa has revealed weaknesses in the global strategy for pandemic control in geographical areas with reduced public health capacity. In human history, armed conflicts have been a major cause of death. They cause death and injury on the battlefield, but also displacement of populations, collapse of health and social services, and increased risks of disease transmission. Countries in conflict are potential areas for the emergence of new diseases (Ebola in Uganda) or the resurgence of old or rare diseases. Detection of new pathogens may be delayed and diseases may spread before control measures are in place—making it nonsense to "declare war" on Covid-19.

Resolution 1308 on HIV/AIDS recognized in 2000 "that HIV poses one of the most formidable challenges to the development, progress and stability of societies and requires an exceptional and comprehensive global response." While both resolutions emphasized that these health crises can disrupt countries in society. With the current COVID-19, accusations about the source and spread of the virus have already intensified international tensions. The battle over Chinese masks is one example.

President Trump's announcement of a travel ban on Europe was poorly received by trans-Atlantic allies. As friction between Washington and Beijing increases, Covid-19 has fueled conspiracy theories both in China and the United States. Some members of the U.S. Congress have called the disease the "Chinese coronavirus." Senator Tom Cotton has even claimed that Covid-19 could be a Chinese biological weapon.[48]

These attitudes are not new, as "there is a long history of 'tainting' the world. This has largely consisted of blaming outsiders, either those outside the majority population, outsiders residing in the community, or outsiders in general. "These are all forms of 'the geography of blame,' because we attach danger to places that we think can hurt us or cause us harm. As syphilis spread across Europe in the 15th century, for example, people looked for scapegoats. The Germans called it the "French disease" while the French called it the "Italian disease." The historian Johnson wrote that some people described the disease as *foreignness*:

> This externalization or projection of blame or guilt may be related
> to religious conceptions of illness as sinful or to the simple desire to
> find an explanation or scapegoat for a plague afflicting a commu-
> nity [...] this projection is natural ... there is a link between imag-
> ining the disease and imagining the stranger. It may lie in the very
> concept of evil, which is archetypally identical to the non-us, 'the

---

48   Alexandra Stevenson, "Senator Tom Cotton Repeats Fringe Theory of Coronavirus Origins," *New York Times*, Feb. 17, 2020.

stranger.' What is wrong or unnatural cannot be of us, but must be of the 'other.' One of the clearest expressions of such an exteriorization of blame is when a geographical name is attached to a disease. The name suggests the origin and blame of the disease. It often refers to countries inhabited by people of a different race or to countries with a history of conflict.[49]

This provoked a chaotic global response. A similar trend can be seen at the international level: a global rush to close borders, turning inward and scapegoating rather than multilateralism. Most countries turned inward, implementing travel bans, export controls, withholding or hiding information and marginalizing the World Health Organization (WHO) and other multilateral institutions. A major economic challenge facing humanity is the loss of production, which can never be recovered.

Hence the current situation is much more dangerous, and its potential impact may last much longer than the 2008 global financial crisis. The interconnectedness of economies means that the loss of production in one region can lead to the shutdown of production elsewhere. Production losses also affect the banking networks that provide loans to vulnerable companies. The combination of the banks' exposure and the uncertainty about the duration of the crisis leads the banks to be very cautious. At work is the interaction of three networks: disease, production, and finance. Minimizing the damage requires an analogous combination of policies:

- better coordinate disease containment to minimize production losses,

- identify critical links in production chains and ensure that they do not break down and cause cascading failures of companies,

- and step in to fill the lending gap caused by the growing credit freeze.

But politicians overwhelmed by the crisis are trying to deflect attention abroad, citing the belief that the real culprit in the crisis is globalization and suggesting that the only way to reduce vulnerability is to isolate ourselves from the world. Conversely, managing the pandemic requires a global and coordinated response among states, or the crisis will worsen with increasing costs to the global economy and public health.[50]

---

49 Niall Johnson, *Britain and the 1918-19 Influenza Pandemic: A Dark Epilogue*, Routledge, London & New York, 2006, p. 152.

50 Jackson examines disease contagion, production networks, as well as financial propagation (the spread of economic crises between regions) and systemic risk. The pandemic shows how each of these areas is central and intimately connected. In an era of global networks, addressing the epidemic requires a proactive response that takes into account these distinct and dependent domains. Matthew O. Jackson, *The Human Network: How Your Social Position Determines Your Power, Beliefs, And Behaviors*, Pantheon Books New York, 2019.

The danger lies in the uncooperative connection rather than in the connection itself. In contrast, doctors and scientists around the world have preferred to share information and resources.[51] Because just as you can't treat a termite infestation by smoking one room in your house, focusing on a specific geographical may temporarily hinder the spread of the pandemic, but will not enable to control it.[52]

Can the epidemic decide the outcome of the war?

Prevention, detection, and countermeasures allow for the control of pandemic risks. However, these measures cannot be ensured in conflict areas. In World War II, at the beginning of the Allied occupation of Naples, the perturbation of civil affairs almost prohibited the collection of accurate epidemiological data. The medical services were disorganized and the public health service was chaotic. Thus, no precise data existed on the virulence of infectious diseases.

More broadly, a vast historical literature describes the impact of infectious diseases on military campaigns. Epidemics not only reshape society, but also influence the outcome of wars. In various conflicts, they have won battles, altered campaigns, and modified strategies. War and disease have been linked throughout history, as soldiers, weapons, and pathogens cross paths on the battlefield. Battles are then engaged only by the remnants of armies, survivors of the epidemics of the camp. An analysis of the main conflicts before the twentieth century reveals many cases where disease has influenced the outcome of events.

The Athenian experience of the plague reminds us of this. Thucydides describes how, during the Peloponnesian wars, the disease demoralized the Athenians, undermined political power and weakened the army, then unable to achieve its military objectives. Entrenched behind their walls, the Athenians waited for the Spartan army, their strategy consisting in avoiding a frontal clash. Food abounded—Athens can count on its maritime imports.

At the same time, the Athenian fleet attacked the ports of Sparta. Pericles abandoned his rural areas to defend Athens behind its walls. His maritime strategy consisted of raids of his fleet against Sparta and support of the siege by trade ships. But when the second year of war began, the plague stroke and surprised everybody, reports Thucydides. It swept Athens, killing men, women, and children. It devastated Athens and anarchy broke out, morale was affected, and Athenians cast doubt on Pericles' strategy, eventually forcing him to make peace with Sparta.

In 1344, a conflict broke out between Genoese and Mongols. In 1346, the plague devastated the Mongol army besieging the city of Kaffa, which ended up

---

51   Kelly Crowe – "'We're opening everything': Scientists share coronavirus data in unprecedented way to contain, treat disease Social Sharing," *CBC News*, 1 February 2020, https://www.cbc.ca/news/health/coronavirus-2019-ncov-science-virus-genome-who-research-collaboration-1.5446948

52   Tedros Adhanom Ghebreyesus, *Covid19—Strategy Update*, World Heath Organization, Geneva 14/04/20, p. 12.

having to lift the siege. A horrendous detail—the Mongols catapulted the corpses of their plague-stricken soldiers into the city. Is the story true? It is still unsure whether Mongols wanted to spread the disease or not; however, some inhabitants of Kaffa were infected by the plague.[53]

Bubonic plague in Jaffa, yellow fever in Haiti and typhus in Russia show how diseases influence war. During the Haitian Revolution of 1802, Napoleon sent 50,000 men to retake the French colony, but his expeditionary force shrank due to the yellow fever. A year later, he gave up and sold Louisiana to the United States.[54] Napoleon had previously stopped advancing east of the Mediterranean because of the plague in Jaffa.

Long before Napoleon, the plague politically and economically weakened the Byzantine Empire. Its capacity of resistance decreased, whereas the disease spread in the Mediterranean world. The weakness of the Byzantine army, its powerlessness in the face of the foreign attacks, was due to its inability to recruit and train new soldiers, because of the illnesses and deaths. In fact, before 542, Justinian's generals had reconquered a large part of the Western Roman Empire from the Goths, the Vandals, etc.

But after 542, the emperor had difficulty recruiting and paying troops. The territories submitted by his generals revolted. The plague reached Rome in 543, and probably Britain in 544. This "Justinian" plague did not die out until 750, when a new order emerged. A new powerful religion, Islam, was born, and its followers controlled a territory that included the former empire of Justinian and the Arabian Peninsula. Meanwhile, much of Western Europe came under French control. Was the plague responsible for this? If so, history is written not only by men but also by microbes. The decline in population impacted the army and defenses of Byzantium, while the imperial administration and economy faltered.[55]

Rome did not escape the ravages of epidemics either. The moral decline, corruption, and divisions had certainly weakened a Roman empire vulnerable to foreign invasion, but significant climate changes and diseases also facilitated its fall. In 161 AD, the Roman general Lucius V Rus defeated the Parthians (1 originating from modern-day Iran) after 5 years of battles. But the Roman army brought back a terrible germ ("Antonine plague" according to the Roman dynasty of the Antonines) which raged for 15 years in Rome and killed about 5 million people, including Lucius Verus.

Through trade routes, the plague spread from Persia to Spain and from Britain to Egypt. At the height of the epidemic, it caused up to 2,000 deaths per day,

---

53   William J. Bernstein, *A Splendid Exchange: How Trade Shaped the World*, Atlantic Monthly Press, New York, 2008, pp. 140-141.

54   Elizabeth Kolbert, "Pandemics and the Shape of Human History," *New Yorker*, March 30, 2020.

55   Colin Barras, "The Year of Darkness," *New Scientist*, vol. 221, 2014, pp. 34-38.

according to Roman sources. The plague disrupted businesses and enterprises, wiped out cities and towns, decimated 10% to 20% of the population and a staggering 90% of Roman forces, thereby hastening the decline of the empire.[56]

In American history, the disease prevented the conquest of Canada in 1812; disrupted its war strategy in Mexico; paralyzed General Robert E. Lee's offensive in 1862; and influenced the outcome of World War II. Epidemic contagion also influenced the colonization of North America: smallpox and other malaria diseases depopulated the areas around the colonies, allowing settlers to move in. The disease benefited the United States in its wars against the Amerindians, but also affected them when their troops were engaged abroad.[57]

A smallpox epidemic swept the Americas at the beginning of the American Revolution. In 1776, the military action and the political agitation increased the movement of populations, thus those of the microbes and the epidemic worsens. The epidemic therefore strongly affected the outcome of the war in each colony and the life of everyone in North America.[58]

Throughout the ages, epidemics have decimated armies, suspended, and cancelled military actions, and ravaged the populations of states, belligerent or not.[59] In 568 AD, the ruler of Aksum of Ethiopia laid siege to Mecca with hundreds of war elephants. The invasion failed because a deadly disease—smallpox, according to accounts of the time—decimated the troops. Along the way, the army infected Arab and Egyptian ports. Later, these ports were besieged by African tribes and the epidemic spread to Nubia through the traffic and trade routes.[60]

Historians believe that the U.S. military spread the "Spanish flu" pandemic. The war favored it by overcrowding military camps in the United States and trenches in Europe. The flu struck in three waves (spring 1918, fall 1918, and winter 1919); the second wave was the deadliest. "The Spanish flu passed through the United States like the pioneers; it followed their footsteps, which became railroads."[61]

---

56 Kyle Harper, *The Fate of Rome: Climate, Disease, and the End of an Empire*, Princeton University Press, Princeton, 2017, pp. 20, 115.

57 David Petriello, *Bacteria and Bayonets: The Impact of Disease in American Military History*, Casemate, Oxford, 2016; Roger E. Thomas, Diane L. Lorenzetti, & Wendy Spragins, "Mortality and Morbidity Among Military Personnel and Civilians During the 1930s and World War II From Transmission of Hepatitis During Yellow Fever Vaccination: Systematic Review," *American Journal of Public Health*, vol. 103, no. 3, March 2013, pp. 16-29.

58 Elizabeth A Fenn, *Pox Americana: The Great Smallpox Epidemic of 1775-82*, Hill & Wang, New York, 2002.

59 Smallman-Raynor Matthew & Cliff Andrew, War *Epidemics: An Historical Geography of Infectious Diseases in Military Conflict and Civil Strife, 1850-2000*, Oxford University Press, Oxford, 2004.

60 Kaushik Roy & Sougat Ray, "War and epidemics: A chronicle of infectious diseases," *Journal of Marine Medical Society*, vol. 20, no. 1, January-June 2018, pp. 50-54.

61 Alfred W. Crosby, *America's Forgotten Pandemic: The Influenza of 1918*, Cambridge University

The virus traveled with the military, from camp to camp and then across the Atlantic. At the height of the military effort (September-November 1918) influenza and pneumonia struck 20% to 40% of American soldiers and sailors. This high morbidity disrupted training and operations and disabled hundreds of thousands of soldiers.

The flu broke out in a military camp in Kansas and spread eastward with American troops, killing 50 to 100 million people worldwide, including some 500,000 Americans. It killed more people in 24 months than AIDS did in 24 years.[62] In the American campaign in Meuse-Argonne (September-November 2018) during the second wave of the Spanish flu, the epidemic diverted resources needed for combat, transportation, and services to the sick and dead.[63]

During World War II, typhus posed major challenges. During the American army's North African campaign, there were more than 102,000 cases of typhus[64], not to mention 90 cases of dengue fever and 470,000 cases of malaria. During the Guadalcanal offensive, which had major stakes, tropical diseases handicapped two-thirds of the 1st Marine Division: it had to be withdrawn, which blocked the offensive.[65]

During the fighting around Sansapor (in by-then Dutch New Guinea), bush typhus proved to be as threatening as Japanese attacks. Shortly after the first soldier showed symptoms, alerting the medical staff, 135 soldiers were already ill. In some areas, the disease was so devastating those outposts were abandoned. The disease put the 1st Infantry Regiment out of action, hampering operations and strategy.[66] Today, Covid also worries strategists: could the virus really hinder military training?

Press, Cambridge, 2003, pp. 63-64.

62 John M. Barry, *The Great Influenza: The Story of the Deadliest Pandemic in History*, Alfred W. Crosby, *America's Forgotten Pandemic: The Influenza of 1918*, 2nd ed. Cambridge University Press, Cambridge, 2003.

63 Carol R. Byerly, "The U.S. Military and the Influenza Pandemic of 1918-1919," *Public Health Reports*, vol. 125, 2010, pp. 82-91; Peter C. Wever & Leo van Bergen, "Death from 1918 pandemic influenza during the First World War: a perspective from personal and anecdotal evidence," *Influenza and Other Respiratory Viruses*, vol. 8, no. 5, 2014, pp. 538-546.

64 J. C. Snyder, "Typhus Fever in the Second World War," *California Medicine*, vol. 66-1, Jan. 1947, pp. 3-10.

65 John L. Zimmerman, *Marines in World War II: The Guadalcanal Campaign*, U.S. Marine Corps, 1949, pp. 156-164. The Battle of Guadalcanal, which lasted from August 1942 to February 1943, was the first major U.S. counteroffensive against the Japanese in the Pacific, it also marked the culmination of Japanese expansion and can rightly be considered one of the major turning points of the Pacific War. Mark Stille & Howard Gerrard, *The Naval Battles for Guadalcanal 1942: Clash for supremacy in the Pacific*, Osprey, 2013.

66 Robert K. D. Peterson, "The Real Enemy: Scrub Typhus and the Invasion of Sansapor," *American Entomologist*, vol. 55, no. 2, Summer 2009, pp. 91-94.

The risk of "securitization"

The increased role of the state in people's lives, due to Covid-19, also widens the social divide. Governments that used to be resistant to public spending are suddenly handing out billions. This is not necessarily bad but alienating Covid-19 from national security can give a country a siege mentality, when this approach is futile in the face of a disease that defies geographic or political barriers.

Making infectious diseases a safety issue attracts attention, increases the perception of the global effects of the pandemic, helps to fund public health, establishes national practices and boosts funding for international initiatives. But it may also hinder the cooperation that public health practitioners seek.

As the virus spreads, President Trump is shifting from denial to blaming China, with U.S. officials insisting in various forums that Covid-19 be named the "Wuhan virus." This rhetoric does not affect China's management of the crisis, but it can undermine global cooperation. This is because health strategies do not mesh well with the theme of national security, as global health is seen as a common 'good" of and between states; whereas national security places the needs of the state above others.

Vaccine nationalism "is incompatible with the fight against Covid-19," warns WHO Director-General Tedros Adhanom Ghebreye, who calls for sharing the tools to fight Covid-19. The damage caused by Covid-19 could be drastically reduced if rich countries are committed and contribute to a solid response: they should therefore share treatments and vaccines globally. Ghebreyesus insists. "For the world to recover faster, it must act together, because it is globalized: economies are intertwined. One part of the world or a few countries cannot be a safe haven and recover."[67]

Prevention (quality vaccination programs and efforts to reduce the risk of animal-human transmission), detection (reliable surveillance structures to collect and test samples), and response are the keys to controlling pandemic risk. It is impossible for these mechanisms to spread to conflict zones, as wars usually disrupt the means of communication. The Ebola pandemic in West Africa had already revealed the chronic weaknesses of the global strategy for fighting pandemics in areas with reduced public health capacity. In lawless war zones, detection capacity is lacking and response is often slow and difficult.[68]

The tightening of U.S. sanctions against Iran and the polio outbreak in Syria are reminders that health interventions, while technical, can become political weapons. Blocking or suspending a health policy can make the opponent obey you,

---

67   Georgina Hayes, "'Vaccine nationalism' will not help fight the virus, says WHO chief," *The Telegraph*, August 6, 2020.

68   Paul H. Wise & Michele Barry, "Civil War & the Global Threat of Pandemics," *Dædalus: American Academy of Arts & Sciences,* Fall 2017, pp. 71-84.

or even submit completely. In war zones, belligerents may insist on vaccinating pro-opposition sectors. This shows how intrusive targeted health policies can be.

Making infectious diseases a security issue may move health up the political agenda, but it is not without risk. Defining a public health problem as a security issue distances responses to disease from civil society and brings them closer to the necessarily less transparent military-security model. As an indicator of a field of practice around the state, the concept of "security" usually refers to a range of issues: power, urgency, threat/defense dynamics, legitimate use of extraordinary means, and infringement of sovereignty.

Defining a health problem as a threat to security could lead to a legalistic rather than a public health approach. However, various technologies can prevent local epidemics from developing into global pandemics. They require organized and effective governance—and political will. Paradoxically, here, the rhetoric of war does not lead to the desired cooperation.

"War on a Virus": The Role of War Discourse

The use of warlike language by various leaders against the Covid-19 pandemic—formerly against poverty, against drugs—signals a possible shift of many sectors of daily life into a security logic. Here, the representation of dangers becomes a tool of the state to maintain its legitimacy and justify its existence. The discourse on security can and must be understood as the constant reporting of danger by the state, rather than as the state's response to a danger. This adaptation of concepts and events to security-related debates and discursive postures does not actually always proves to be a source of security.[69] This war language leads leaders to caricature threats, concentrate power and deploy armed and security forces, even if they are ill-equipped to defeat poverty, drugs, or a virus.

With his theories on war, peace and politics, Clausewitz opened a perspective, still relevant today, according to which war is a tool of state policy, "the womb in which war develops." His *On War* is one of those great books—like religious texts or classics of political theory—in which soldiers, statesmen, and scholars find inspiration and legitimacy for what they are trying to accomplish.

But he warns, politicians should not attempt to use war to achieve irrelevant goals. As in the past, the mobilizing power of war remains indispensable, but should be handled with extra caution. War is "an act of violence to compel its

---

69 Barry Buzan, Ole Waever, & Jaap Wilde, Security: *A New Framework for Analysis, Lynne* Rienner Publishers, London, 1998, p. 32; Ole Wæver, "Securitization and Desecuritization," in Ronnie Lipschutz (ed.), *On Security,* Columbia University Press, New York, 1995, pp. 45-86. David Campbell, *Writing Security: United States Foreign Policy and the Politics of Identity,* University of Minnesota Press, Minneapolis, 1998, pp. 50-51.

adversary to respect our will. Its nature is above all violent, interactive and political."[70] Outside this context, we no longer speak of war but of something else.

Historically, the emergence of the modern state and professional troops gave rise to bureaucratic armies with official doctrines. In the same way, a cultural understanding of war has emerged, codified in oppositions, classic in strategic and political discourse, between "war" and "peace," which concern distinct situations. Countries at peace go to war, then war ends and peace returns.

These basic data imply, among other things, that armed conflict is defined sand, wars have a beginning and an end; and there are enemy, allied, and neutral states. "Rousseau explained that war is not a relationship between man and man, but between state and state. In principle, war presupposes defined adversaries, a beginning and an end."[71] This is a crucial distinction, because actions that are lawful in war are not lawful in peacetime: society has developed an acceptable code of belligerence: the laws of war. But since reality rarely conforms to these black-and-white concepts, political discourse attempts to reconcile them with a complex reality. In the end, the discourse of war distorts Covid-19's real-life situation, endangers the soundness of the public debate, distracts leaders and public opinions, and squanders international goodwill.

"Waging war" on a virus is the deceptive analogy of mobilizing scarce resources to confront a civil peril. Such rhetoric cultivates nationalism and facilitates the abuse of political power as agents of the state gain new power. The UN Special Rapporteur on Counter-Terrorism and Human Rights, Fionnuala Ni Aolain, warns of the risk of "a parallel epidemic of authoritarian and repressive measures" in addition to the "health epidemic."[72]

Of the many ways to fight the pandemic, waging war on it does not seem the most appropriate. Addressing civilian problems and their possible solutions is not the military's strong suit: in the military, the initial question is often about what to do rather than what the problem is. Thus, the distinction between "peace" and "war" leads to the distinction between combat operations and "military operations other than war." This distinction shows that the original function of the military is combat,[73] which distinguishes it from the police, for example. Knowing how to conduct a war or "operations other than war" thus defines—politically, even ideologically—what the military must do.

Politicians and academics make a different use of metaphors and terms

---

70   Von Clausewitz, *On War*, pp. 5-7.

71   Pierre Hassner, "Guerre et paix à l'âge de la mondialisation," in Yves Michaud (ed.), Qu'est-ce que la globalisation? Odile Jacob, Paris, 2004, pp. 79-95 (80).

72   Selam Gebrekidan, "For Autocrats, and Others, Coronavirus Is a Chance to Grab Even More Power," *New York Times*, March 30, 2020.

73   See for example Harry Summers, *On Strategy. A Critical Analysis of the Vietnam War*, Random House Pub, New York, 1995, p. 184.

when referring to the Covid-19 pandemic and other issues on which a violent vocabulary and rhetoric is imposed on (e.g., "war," "cold war," "war on poverty"). Scientists have different discourses from historians, etc. Each profession has its own prism—including the military. Each profession has its own prism—including the military, of course. The approach of political leaders and senior state officials is above all practical: it must orient action and strategies. Already subject to time-resource constraints, political discourse must act on events and shape reality. Argumentation and practical deliberation, this discourse influences how to respond to circumstances and events.

Thus, the originality of political discourses is to "provide motives for action." They provide actors with premises (beliefs about the circumstances of the action, instrumental beliefs, values and objectives) to justify, criticize and, thus, decide on the action.[74] The "performative statement" of declaring war thus goes beyond the description, interpretation, or contestation of reality. When an individual or collective subject has the authority and the means to carry out his "act of language," he does not describe, but creates a new reality.[75] "Waging war on a virus" is seductive, specified because many chosen political leaders feel their wars and also what they want us to remember about them. Because of the link between content, context and intent of a communication, the terms defining war are necessarily "fighting words" and when they are "adopted by the state itself, they can be transformed—via state institutional arrangements and by law—into violence."[76]

There are also marked differences between a war economy and a coronavirus economy. Historically, war has fueled autocracy, secrecy, and xenophobia. None of this mitigates the severity of a pandemic, nor does it help to build societal resilience, streamline public health structures, or stimulate the responsible citizenship that is so crucial during a pandemic.

War economies require increased mobilization of labor and accelerated production. Conversely, the Covid-19 economy demobilizes labor and stalls production. Whether "war" is invoked literally or metaphorically is less important than the material consequences of its repeated use. Especially since George W. Bush launched his "global war on terror," it is everywhere, and seemingly unlimited: no one knows how to defeat an ideology (or a virus for that matter). Result: in the age of endless wars, "wartime is the only time we have": this "wartime" is not an exception to normal peacetime: it is a reality, suggesting that we are living in a continuous wartime.

---

74 Isabela Fairclough & Norman Fairclough, *Political Discourse Analysis,* Routledge, New York, 2012, p. 95.

75 John Austin, *How to do things with Words*, Harvard University Press, Cambridge, 1992.

76 Rosa Brooks, *How Everything Became War and the Military Became Everything: Tales from the Pentagon*, Simon & Schuster Paperbacks, New York, 2016, p. 22.

Hence, the "presence of war as a permanent feature" of our institutions, given its invasion of daily life. As such, the "power of war cannot really be eradicated" by signing an agreement to end hostilities. Even after the conflict, the draft continues, since the legal state of war (legalizing the use of government war powers) "may last for several years. Thus, while hostilities have their own precise time frame, "wartime" has no "temporal boundaries of its own."[77]

Politicians and rulers design specific narratives, linking the policies they propose to the needs of citizens and to their own concerns for legitimacy. They are tempted to (and can) shape citizens' preferences. However, if society no longer knows how to define a specific situation as "war," its members forget which rules apply. Hence, society loses its collective ability to restrain violence. Because no democracy emerges from a state of permanent war without harm, we are experiencing the "irruption of the penal state" accompanied by a discourse tailored to legitimize the refocusing of the state's missions on the maintenance of order and the control of populations seen as deviant and dangerous.[78]

The conceptual limitation of a national strategy is that its priorities must address both the threats and the remedies, and the threats are many and the resources are few. Hence the importance of an accurate diagnosis: pandemics first condemn the elderly and the vulnerable, and debt increases. Even if they disrupt the economy, these pandemics do not create a lasting vacuum: criminal entities quickly fill it. For the virus is not the only peril in this socio-economic crisis. Transnational criminality uses it to weaken institutions and to enrich itself; this will last as long as the high profit/low risk paradigm.

Organized crime threatens economic recovery. Lockdowns financially burden small and medium-sized businesses. motivated primarily by money, criminal groups can expect to extend their control over entire sectors, offering enticing, cheap and unofficial loans, thereby solving their money laundering problems.

While the control of public tenders is intended to prevent these illicit practices, the scale of investment during this pandemic, and official pressure to support companies quickly, could precipitate these processes, thereby encouraging criminal infiltration. With their annual illegal revenues of between $1.6tn and $2.2tn, these groups not only make money but can also finance violence, corruption, etc., undermining legal economies, health, and public welfare, while destroying the environment.[79]

---

77   Mary L. Dudziak, *War Time: An Idea, Its History, Its Consequences*, Oxford University Press, New York, 2012, pp. 4, 8, 36, 91.

78   Loic Wacquant, *Punir les pauvres. Le nouveau gouvernement de l'insécurité sociale*, Agone, Marseilles, 2004, p. 13 and 167.

79   Channing Mavrellis, "Transnational Crime and the Developing World," Global Financial Integrity, Washington, DC. in March 2017, p. xi.

and those on welfare programs, or other precarious jobs. African Americans suffer the worst morbidity and mortality rates. Some students struggle to participate in online courses because they lack the necessary resources. Such inequities are long-standing but are now hitting harder than usual.[86]

Thus, diseases have caused shocks in Europe, such as the reformation of Martin Luther and the European expansion in the New World. For example, at the beginning of the 16th century, because of demic epi, Hernando Cortez (who did not have 600 soldiers) conquered an Aztec empire with millions of inhabitants. Less than 50 years later, the population of central Mexico has decreased by 90%. This demographic collapse impacts the religion, defense, and culture of Mexico, allowing the European conquest of the region.[87]

Epidemics thus impact politics and revolutions, entrench discrimination and strike the societies where they spread, affecting personal relationships, the work of artists and intellectuals[88] and the human and natural environment. Above all, they impact history by forcing human beings to return to the big questions, such as man's relationship to God. The bubonic plague killed half of the inhabitants of entire continents and thus had a major impact on the advent of the industrial revolution, on slavery and serfdom. As Ebola and Covid-19 still show, epidemics have a major impact on social and political stability.

Return of civil unrest: a question of when, not if

Pandemics disregard borders, and together can weaken societies, political systems, economies, and armies. Humanity is focused on the challenges of the day, more than on the distant implications of the coronavirus crisis, but great changes are coming. Major crises have unforeseen but profound consequences. How will the Covid-19 pandemic affect the risk of violent conflict and hopes for world peace? There is no easy answer to this question as the crisis is constantly evolving and mutating.

That its impact has varied across different regions and conflict zones further complicates the picture. Moreover, the relevant criteria for assessing the risk of Covid-19 provoking power confrontation differ from the factors that aggravate unrest in vulnerable states. This uncertainty complicates current and future attempts to control violent conflict.

---

86 Melissa De Witte, "Past pandemics redistributed income between the rich and poor, according to Stanford historian," *Stanford New*, April 30, 2020.

87 David Petriello, *Bacteria and Bayonets: The Impact of Disease in American Military History*, Casemate, Oxford & Philadelphia, 2015, pp. 35-41; William H. McNeill, *Plagues and Peoples, Anchor Books*, New York, 1976, pp. 1-3 and 162-165.

88 Jonathan Jones, "Brush with the Black Death: how artists painted through the plague," *The Guardian*, Feb. 15, 2012; Hisham Matar, "Hisham Matar on how the Black Death changed art forever," *The Guardian*, June 6, 2020.

Developed and developing countries are combining public health, fiscal, and monetary policy actions to at least slow Covid-19, protect lives and limit the multiple effects of containment. Even less than public safety and health, the geopolitical implications of the crisis will dominate in the long run. For perturbed economies, the political, commercial, and macroeconomic implications of Co vid-19 will be profound. The pace and extent of the virus' spread will determine which industries are most at risk. The divergent responses of governments and major commodity producers will also disrupt supply chains.

While crises have always accelerated the course of history, this one is not likely to disrupt global security. Rather, it will intensify existing trends. The geopolitical consequences of Covid-19 could disrupt traditional alliances and push states toward populism in a growing nationalist and protectionist climate. Most countries have gone into lockdown, banning travel, controlling exports, hiding data, and disdaining multilateral entities such as the WTO and UN.

Despite the worrying consequences of less global cooperation, private countries will put their internal problems ahead of global ones. Under pressure, rich countries will be tempted to close their borders, worsening the plight of migrants, which the UN says has risen from 150 million worldwide in 2000 to 272 million in 2019.[89] Restrictions on travel and movement do not prevent migration; closing land, sea and air borders increases the use of cross-border smugglers. Similarly, victims of human trafficking are more vulnerable to Covid-19: a lack of basic ser vices will worsen their plight.[90]

Efforts to counter the COVID-19 pandemic have resulted in an unprecedented retraction of the movement of people, both across borders and within countries. Some leaders have adopted hostile attitudes toward migrants, whom they perceive as a risk of contagion. While these measures may reduce migration and smuggling, they can increase the profits of smugglers and the vulnerability of migrants, militarize borders and limit safe routes. As the political atmosphere becomes hostile to migration, the risks of the route and the prices of remittances are likely to increase.

This can deter careful operators and attract organized crime, which is more likely to exploit migrants for profit. To avoid the emergence of a post-pandemic landscape of a worse grant crisis and more lucrative smuggling by organized crime, it is crucial to monitor and mitigate the impact of Covid-19 on migrants and refugees during the pandemic. For example, in the mid-19th century and in

---

89 Department of Economic and Social Affairs, "The number of international migrants reaches 272 million, continuing an upward trend in all world regions, says UN," UN, 17 September 2019. https://www.un.org/development/desa/en/news/population/international-migrant-stock-2019.html

90 Jean-Luc Lemahieu & Angela Me, "How Covid-19 Restrictions and The Economic Consequences Are Likely To Impact Migrant Smuggling And Cross-Border Trafficking In Persons To Europe And North America," United Nations Office on Drugs and Crime, Vienna, 14 May 2020.

Tunisia, "smuggling, quarantine, and cholera worked together."[91]

The current pandemic has left its mark on everyone: isolation, uncertainty, anger, anxiety; this, coupled with the economic shock, is causing psychological distress. The full political and social impact of the pandemic has yet to be felt. Even if this impact is not yet fully included in the current estimates, Covid-19 will cause vast suffering and often unbearable burdens for states. Initially economic, its effects will undoubtedly worsen food insecurity in the world.

Its rapid spread has had a staggering domino effect on the global economy, nothing indicates an improvement in the short-term. The pandemic has severely impacted the Asian garment industry and millions of people may lose their resources. Measures to contain Covid-19 have exacerbated the health problems affecting major African economies. Fears about Covid-19 continue to affect the global commodities market, including an already fragile oil market. The pandemic is enabling new illegal transactions. Those who have lost their resources or are fleeing conflict, violence and danger are defenseless against smugglers and traffickers.

Measures to curb the spread of Covid-19 create opportunities for criminal networks. Reduced social and public services leave the forgotten without support. Organized crime has quickly learned to manipulate and take advantage of these restrictions, as the Covid-19 virus presents global society with unprecedented challenges:

> The first factor is the way organized crime uses political and so-cial crises caused by the virus to strengthen its legitimacy and its hold on populations and governments. This cynical opportunism in times of crisis is nothing new—mafia groups have long used humanitarian agencies to influence people and governments. The Yakuza were the first to respond to earthquakes and tsunamis in Japan; the Jalisco bus distributed aid to hurricane victims in western Mexico last year; similarly, al-Shabaab provides food aid and supplies during the cyclical droughts in Somalia.[92]

Travel restrictions due to the coronavirus are disrupting business supply chains. Farmers are short of migrant workers (in countries such as Spain, Canada, etc.); reduced air traffic is affecting the flow of goods and aid; and expats work from home, putting a damper on ongoing projects. Income losses due to anti-COVID

---

91   "Likewise, regulations enjoining compliance with quarantine were promulgated. As the Sanitary Board expanded its operations to combat the scourge of cholera morbus and other epidemics, the ever-stricter enforcement of quarantine may have encouraged smuggling; thus smuggling, quarantine, and cholera work together." Julia A. Clancy-Smith, *Mediterraneans: North Africa and Europe in an Age of Migration, C. 1800-1900*, University of California Press, Los Angeles, 2012, p. 180.

92   Mark Shaw & Tuesday Reitano, "COVID-19: Strengthen civil society in a time of unprecedented change and undermine criminal governance," Global Initiative against Transnational Organized Crime, Geneva, 31 March 2020.

measures and the overall recession will increase food insecurity.[93] The environment is increasing the cost of international trade—even of basic commodities. For example, the pandemic has had a major impact on European economies. The European Commission estimates that the Eurozone's GDP will fall by 8.7% in 2020.[94]

The fragility of states is long-standing, but the strain of the pandemic will make some even weaker or defaulting, adding to their debt burden. The world's public and private debt is already massive, but Covid-19 will require huge public expenditures to fund health care and support the unemployed, making it even worse. As the economic perils of Covid-19 pile up, unrest could spread to poor countries, threatening their domestic stability. One likely scenario is "increased protests; the next decade will see unprecedented unrest. The majority of these 37 "high-risk" states are in Africa and Latin America."[95]

The developing world will indeed face enormous demands that it may not be able to meet. The Covid-19 pandemic could push 500 million people into poverty if the global community does not intervene. The IMF and World Bank estimate that failure to address the pandemic could push half the world's population (7.8 billion people) into poverty.[96] It remains to be seen whether developed countries will provide the necessary assistance, given their national requirements.

This assistance is questionable, as *ActionAid* suggests that only one-third of G7 official aid in 2003 is "real." The rest is "fanciful" aid for various purposes, but not poverty. Only 10 cents of every dollar of U.S. aid is "real" and almost 1/3 of aid from the UK—seen as the most serious in this area—is considered phantom. A large portion of this "aid" is used to hire private consulting firms working on privatization programs, *ActionAid* reveals.[97]

The Athenian experience with the plague should convince us of the power of the invisible. In the Peloponnesian wars, Thucydides describes how the plague panicked the Athenians, weakened the government and the army, and left them unable to achieve their key military objectives. The worst thing about the pandemic-Covid 19-was the general unpreparedness of governments, with emergency public health measures proving modest compared to those for national security.

---

93 Food and Agriculture Organization (FAO) "Crop Prospects and Food Situation," *Quarterly Global Report*, no. 2, of the United Nations, Rome, Italy, July 2020.

94 European Commission, "Summer 2020 Economic Forecast: An even deeper recession with wider divergences," Press release, Brussels, 7 July 2020. https://ec.europa.eu/commission/presscorner/de tail/en/ip_20_1269

95 Miha Hribernik & Tim Campbell, "Emerging markets face acute instability as pandemic fuels unrest," Verisk Maplecroft, July 16, 2020.

96 Larry Elliott, "Coronavirus could push half a billion people into poverty, Oxfam warns," *The Guardian*, April 9, 2020.

97 Firoze Manji, "Make looting history," *Pambazuka News*, no. 214, July 2005; *Pambazuka News* 197: Special Report on "Debt and Africa," *Pambazuka News*, Special Report, no. 197, 10 March 2005.

The military conception of the global challenges has led the leaders to neglect such vital issues as public health and revealed the powerlessness of the leaders of many countries, heavily equipped with sophisticated weapons, drones, missiles, etc. (United States, France, Great Britain, etc.) in the face of microscopic perils. As in previous crises, Covid-19 revealed the blind spots in state preparations for pandemics. Covid-19 flaws are all the stranger because biosecurity and biodefense were at the heart of recent Western plans to deal with the peril of biological weapons.

PART II - THE BIOTERRORISM PERSPECTIVE

Epidemiologists Malik Peiris and Yi Guan write that "nature remains the worst bio-terrorist threat of all."[98] Yet despite their potential consequences, pandemics and biological weapons have not received the attention they deserve. Although "biowarfare" and "bioterrorism"" are often used interchangeably, bioterrorism specifically refers to the actions of a subnational entity, rather than a state. With this uncomfortable reality in mind, this article aims to highlight the importance of a new paradigm, one in which non-military security issues become paramount. However, designing effective policies requires knowing the history of biological weapons and their uses. This second part now shows how technological advances change our approach to the biological weapon, for combating it also helps containing pandemics.

Technoscientific progress and terrorism

Globalization involves interdependent trends that impacts security challenges and issues:

1) Growth (number and capacity) of actors (state and non-state) impacting events.

2) Increased border porosity.

3) Progress of democratic governance and market economies, which have failed to become the only forms of government or economic organization.

4) Growth in regional and global integration processes.

5) "Annihilation of space by time," a concept that suggests a 21st century marked by anarchy, failed states, and prolonged irregular conflicts.

---

98   Mark Honigsbaum, *The Pandemic Century: One Hundred Years of Panic, Hysteria, and Hubris*, W. W. Norton Company, 2019.

The combination of such political, technological, geopolitical, demographic, and environmental changes leads to conflict, especially intra-state conflict, promotes state disintegration, stimulates extremism, and facilitates the recruitment of non-state actors. The growing urbanization and demographics of developing countries and the competition for resources are causing these changes, which are sources of conflict. Added to this is the spread of civilian and military technology, which is increasingly available. In addition, the persistence and emergence of "safe havens" will create a security environment conducive to extremism, terrorist, criminal and insurgent groups, and protracted identity-based conflicts.[99]

Technological and scientific advances have major upheavals in sectors such as trade, finance, social relations, and the military, to name but a few. The transformation is accelerating, seemingly without any available brakes. The evolution of the techno-scientific environment profoundly affects the international framework. New technologies are changing the production and distribution of wealth, leading to rapid and potentially dangerous social, economic and political changes. Global economic competition is intensifying, driven by the emergence of multinational groups with no national commitments and with a powerful influence on world trade.

The same tools that empower people are used by terrorists to increase their power to harm and their global reach:[100] technologies that enhance the ability to cooperate, collaborate and communicate also limit military and security effectiveness.[101] Technology offers the enemy unprecedented access to the tools of globalization: the Internet, cellular telephones, money transfers, ease of movement, international trade, etc.

More broadly, technological and scientific progress contributes to the proliferation of major international players, both in number and in capacity:

1) expanded role played by non-state actors on the international, regional, and national scenes, including in the security field.

2) a numerical increase of actors, which are able, thanks to techno-scientific progress, spread their projection capacities and, thereby, their power.

This increases the likelihood that a growing group of actors will challenge states.

---

99 Tewfik Hamel, "*La Stratégie d'engagement des Etats-Unis dans le Sud à l'ère de la mondialisation,*" PhD thesis in Military History, under the direction of Jacques ABEN, Centre de Recherches Interdisciplinaires en Sciences humaines et Sociales de Montpellier, Université Paul-Valéry, Montpellier, 2020.

100 Terror is a means of controlling populations through fear. Gough uses the expression "the machine of terror." Hugh Gough, *The Terror in the French Revolution*, 2nd Ed., Macmillan, London, 2010, pp. 29-30.

101 Paul T. Mitchell, *Network Centric Warfare and Coalition Operations*, Routledge, New York, 2009, pp. 2-3.

International terrorism alone is one of the most virulent examples of these changes in the privatization of violence. "The ever-increasing ability of individuals and groups to collect, analyze, disseminate, and act quickly on information signals the elimination of traditional barriers between national and international affairs and the decline of the nation state." Thus, the coming decades will see the expansion of non-state actors in international crises, "exerting a disturbing influence on all sectors of society without reference to national borders."[102] Weaver warns of the expansion of "an informal network of small, loosely organized underground cells with worldwide support centers: in the United States, around the Persian Gulf, in Germany, Switzerland, Scandinavia, Sudan, Pakistan and Afghanistan." The nature of terrorism has changed: "e-mail and faxes are driving the jihad."[103]

Undeniably, the techno-scientific environment is shaping peoples and societies faster and more profoundly than what even informed observers could imagine. Technology is the only major modern process that has reduced the power of demography, providing less populous countries with advanced weapons systems that guarantee better control of migration flows. This process also empowers individuals and small groups.

The social implications of the techno-scientific revolution are omnipresent and far-reaching; first of all, on our political systems and values, forcing each nation to reconsider its vulnerabilities and its sovereignty. The main driving force behind the global connection between individuals and societies at all levels is information technology, which is proliferating at an exponential rate. From almost zero in 1990, the number of users worldwide has soared in the last 20 years, with on average more than 40% annual increase. Today, more than 1.6 billion people[104] on all continents are connected, stimulating globalization, productivity, and information sharing.

Here, the challenge is not to limit who can come online, but to:

1) understand the economic, legal, political, and security paradigms of geo-cyber, and

2) learn to manage them in the age of synthetic biology and nanoscience. The most pressing question is not how technology and science will change, but how this process of change and evolution will itself be managed.

The end of the twentieth century saw the gradual breakdown of the Weberian monopoly of organized violence. Techno-scientific advances have allowed groups of young people, angry, defiant and frustrated, to undermine the stability

---

102 Henry H. Shelton, "A Word from the Chairman," *JFQ*, Summer 1999, pp. 4-5.

103 Mary Anne Weaver, "Blowback," *The Atlantic*, May 1996.

104 Ian Goldin, "Globalization and risks for business: Implications of an increasingly interconnected world," Lloyd's 360° Risk Insight, James Martin 21st Century School, University of Oxford, London, 2010, p. 12.

of the societies in which they live. Activities facilitated by porous borders, access to weapons and technologies and the diffusion of ideas and images that promote envy, anger, hatred, greed, etc. In an interdependent world, a few malicious individuals with a modest budget can paralyze the economy in specific locations. If some actors are willing to engage in such actions, a few fanatics with a "dirty bomb" or a bio-weapon can cause death on an unimaginable scale.[105]

So let us look at these non-state actors who can transform the international system and destroy the economy of a modern nation, undermining the authority and legitimacy of the state or corrupting social cohesion. They must be treated, not as mere outlaws, but as a new threat, as seriously as inter-states wars of the past.[106] They can disrupt the system and paralyze the rules in use, at least on a national scale; perhaps on a global scale.

The *vertical* shock that they generate generates *horizontal* waves, crossing national and sectoral borders, to the point of disrupting almost all the rules. Globalization transmits shock waves ever faster and stronger, and the war of powers, which has become suicidal, can no longer provide them with a strategic organizing principle and resource acquisition. Interdependence means that the failure of a single network can cause the failure of others: transport, water, electricity, etc. The Covid-19 pandemic revealed this.

Bioterrorism

The emergence of new diseases; the "tinkering" with pathogens and their deliberate addition to the arsenals of the powers that be have changed our perception of infectious diseases. After nearly eight decades of success with vaccines and antibiotics against infectious diseases, the pathogen is back in the picture. Infectious diseases are once again the leading cause of human mortality worldwide. Worse: deliberately spreading disease has gone from possibility to fact.

Often, these diseases circulate through human ignorance—war, travel, trade, social or dietary changes; various natural epidemics show their destructive potential on the economy and social life. In addition, of the risk now exists of a deliberate spread of a disease through bioterrorism.[107] For example, in recent decades, the United States alone has experienced biological attacks or incidents targeting civilians, such as anthrax (*Anthrax Bacillus*, 2001).

Although the threat of bioterrorism is a major challenge in the 21st century,

---

105 Fred Charles Ikle, *Annihilation from Within*, Columbia University press, New York (USA), 2006, p. 84.

106 "International affairs will increasingly be determined by large and powerful organizations rather than by governments." Moreover, "terrorist tactics will become increasingly sophisticated and designed to achieve mass casualties," predicted the NIC in 2000, *Global Trends 2015, op. cit.*, p. 50.

107 Alfred Jay Bollet, *Plagues and Poxes: The Impact of Human History on Epidemic Disease*, Demos, NY, 2004.

the potential of infectious agents as weapons has been known for centuries: the history of warfare is replete with attempts to trigger disease. Thanks to medical advances in recent decades, disease was no longer a major national security concern; but that is changing. In 2016, at the Future of War conference, George Poste spoke of the risk of emerging infectious diseases; a bleak future where disease would once again play a central role in world affairs.

For example, the H5N1 virus (mortality rate: 60%) has been proven to have been transmitted by infected birds, before mutating to human-to-human transmission. It is estimated that H5N1 has caused more than 150 million deaths worldwide. Mr. Poste lists as current biological threats: pandemic influenza; antibiotic-resistant infections; bioterrorism; and new technologies altering the current disease landscape.[108]

Of great concern is the potential for bioterrorism to cause illness, death, and panic, suffocating available resources. Bioterrorism was identified as a concern by political and military leaders in the late 1980s, after the fall of the Soviet block and the Gulf War. There was concern that state biological weapons programs were losing control, providing weapons and scientific expertise to terrorists.

Bioterrorism is the intentional use, or threat of use for terrorist purposes, of microorganisms (bacteria, viruses, fungi, parasites, or toxins) to induce disease, death, or any biological disorder in humans, animals, plants, or any living organism, to influence a government or to intimidate and coerce a population. Bioterrorism consists of deliberate acts such as the introduction of pests that destroy food crops; the spread of a virulent disease between animal husbandry facilities; and the poisoning of water, food, and blood supplies. The act of bioterrorism ranges from a simple hoax to the actual use of biological weapons.

In practice, biological terrorist attacks are difficult. Their success is unlikely, given the technical difficulties and constraints. The ability to manipulate pathogens, toxins, and chemicals requires sophisticated scientific knowledge of epidemiology, biology, chemistry, and advanced delivery systems. Making a biological weapon is an arduous and complex process, depending on the pathogen to be "weaponized." But of course, technological, scientific and transportation advances limit these difficulties.

In a world of rapid technical and scientific progress,[109] bioterrorism has its advantages and limits. The highly effective biological weapon must always cause death or disease; it must be highly contagious with a short incubation period, in-

---

108 https://www.youtube.com/watch?v=QJ1lhaVSR-U&feature=youtu.be&list=PLNoVefpaPtVOjn28
piSMBnMv6D6ldaV43

109 Secretariat of Defense and National Security (SGDSN), *Future Shocks: Prospective Study to 2030: Impacts of Technological Transformations and Disruptions on our Strategic and Security Environment*, Paris, May 2017, http://www.sgdsn.gouv.fr/uploads/2017/04/sgdsn-document-prospectives-v5-bd.pdf

fectious at low doses and stable during its dissemination. The weapon must be storable and mass-produced. The disease must be undetectable as a bioterrorist agent; the target population must have little or no immunity or access to treatment; the terrorist must be able to protect or treat his own forces and/or supporters against the infectious agents or toxins.[110]

Too small for the human eye, impossible to smell or taste, biological agents are attractive to potential terrorists: less costly than nuclear; difficult to detect dissemination, even over large areas; those involved can protect themselves and flee before the effects emerge: panic, especially in health care facilities and the economy. Detecting and diagnosing the diseases they cause requires sophisticated techniques and equipment. All of these agents are natural and easily retrievable. In ancient times, arrows were poisoned with venom. In 2016, the WHO-animal listed 118 animal diseases and infections that could be used as biological weapons.[111]

Of all recorded diseases affecting humans, over 60% are zoonotic; 75% of emerging diseases are also zoonotic. Bioterrorism uses all zoonotic infectious agents, circulating easily from animals to humans and vice versa. Bioterrorism can thus affect the lives of millions of people, without alarm, starting from biological agents more powerful than conventional and chemical weapons. Advances in biochemistry and biotechnology simplify the development and production of these weapons, while genetics and neuroscience may hold even greater potential.[112] Easy to produce, widely available agents, and technical know-how have led to a new spread of bioweapons and an increased desire for them.[113]

Biowarfare agents are among the most extreme forms of random violence. Even with limited casualties, the impact of a bioterrorist attack is high. Bioterrorism and biowarfare employ live agents or toxins to be disseminated-delivered by infected individuals, insects, aerosols, and by contamination of water and foodstuffs. Thus, biological threats and risks are mostly low probability, but high impact in nature.

Thus, governments need to incorporate a possible increase in extremism into their emergency crisis plans. Even though a biological attack by terrorists or a hostile nation is unlikely, it still requires public health planning. This is a major lesson from the Covid-19 crisis, which also revealed weaknesses in systems that must respond to biological emergencies.

---

110 Nicholas J. Beeching, David A.B. Dance, Alastair R.O. Miller, & Robert C. Spencer, "Biological warfare and bioterrorism," *Clinical Review,* vol. 324, February 2002, pp. 336-339.

111 Vladan Radosavljevic, Ines Banjari, & Goran Belojevic, *Defense Against Bioterrorism: Methods for Prevention and Control,* Springer, 2018, p. 4.

112 Malcolm Dando, *Neuroscience and the Future of Chemical-Biological Weapons*, Palgrave Macmillan, 2015.

113 Ryan, C Patrick, "Zoonoses likely to be used in bioterrorism," Public Health Reports, Washington, D.C., vol. 123, no. 3, 2008, pp. 276-81.

This crisis should accelerate contingency planning for biological attacks that overwhelm medical capabilities, cause illness and death, and disrupt the economy and society. For while potential pathogens are plentiful worldwide, resources for research, development and countermeasures remain scarce. Ensuring that such a master plan is focused and productive begins with prioritizing diseases and agents in the event of a public health emergency.

Classification and prioritization

How to plan for uncertainty? The crucial classification of biological agents for prioritization is a very complex process. Established in 2005 to strengthen Europe's defenses against infectious diseases, the European Centre for Disease Prevention and Control envisions the methodology for prioritizing diseases in a report addressing best practices for prioritizing infectious disease threats.

To identify, assess, and communicate current and emerging public health threats from communicable diseases, the center reviewed 17 studies and compared five communicable disease risk ranking methodologies: bibliometric index, Delphi technique, multi-criteria decision analysis, qualitative algorithms, and questionnaires. Without being able to "recommend a single definitive approach," it presents a disease prioritization tool that operates by weighting. It provides an assessment of the strengths and limitations of the available methods, with suggestions for good practice to inform decision-makers' choice of risk ranking methods.[114]

The judgment of public policymakers, planners, health and safety professionals is a key element. Based on a list drawn up on historical facts, NATO has identified 14 agents presenting "unequal dangers." In this list, four are considered to be of primary concern because of the risk of terrorism: smallpox, anthrax, plague and botulinum toxin.[115] The agents of the bioterrorist threat are classified into three groups:

- Group A: the most dangerous microorganisms. Easily spread or transmitted by contagion, they can cause public panic and social disruption and require special public health preparation: anthrax, botulism, plague, smallpox, tularemia, viral hemorrhagic fever.

- Group B: microorganisms and toxins causing less serious illnesses, which are mediated or spread. With moderate or low morbidity-mortality rates, they

114 European Centre for Disease Prevention and Control, "Best Practices in Ranking Emerging Infectious Disease Threats: A Literature Review," Technical Report, Stockholm, February 2015, pp. 1 and 20.

115 Délégation aux affaires stratégiques, *Prospective géostratégique à l'horizon des trente prochaines années*, Délégation à l'information et à la communication de la défense, Ministère de la Défense, Paris, 2008, p. 169.

require progress in diagnosis and increased surveillance: Brucellosis, Rhine, Typhoid fever, Psittacosis, Q fever, Typhus, etc.

- Group C: Emerging diseases; genetically modified microorganisms that may belong to this last category; readily available, produced and disseminated; high potential for morbidity and mortality, major health impact: Nipah virus and hantavirus.

The *U.S. Center for Disease Control and Prevention* (CDC) has classified biological agents into three distinct groups, based on their public health impact (severity of illness and death), potential for dissemination, public perception, and ease of prevention. This classification into categories A, B and C is a complex decision-making process based on:[116]

- The agent's ability to disseminate,

- Mortality rate,

- Preparatory public health process.

- Ability to cause public panic.[117]

Biological agents		
Bacteria	**Virus**	**Toxins**
Plague	Smallpox	Botulinum toxin
Anthrax	Viral hemorrhagic fever	Ricin
Tularemia	Viral encephalitis	Marine toxins
Q fever		Venoms
Brucellosis		Lococcal staphylococcal enterotoxin B

Prioritization of diseases and pathogens requires a set of qualitative, intangible, or subjective criteria that vary among stakeholders. These criteria can also be interdependent, which complicates the evaluation. For example, the case fatality rate of a disease has both a social and an economic effect. Given the complexity of the disease classification process, it is important to ensure transparency and accountability.

---

116 Lisa Rotz, Ali Khan, Scott Lillibridge, Stephen M. Ostroff, & James M. Hughes, "Public health assessment of potential biological terrorism agents," Emerging Infectious Diseases, *vol. 8, no. 2,* February 2002, pp. 225-230.

117 Ellison D. Hank, *Handbook of Chemical and Biological Warfare Agents*, CRC Press, NY, 2008, pp. xxviiii-xxx.

At the government level, prioritizing diseases is primarily a matter of allocating financial and human resources to safeguard human health; this is a crucial step in rationalizing public policy: achieving the maximum objectives with the minimum effort.[118]

In the broad perspective of public health, prioritizing infectious diseases is a long and complex process; leaders face multiple pressures before any public policy is implemented. For example, the "Vigipirate" emergency plans and their variations, in particular "Piratox" and "Biotox," cannot be limited to describing the responsibilities of the various levels of actors and their interactions.

The imperative of decision-makers is not only academic, but also and above all practical: it is to precisely identify the problem, and optimally blend theory and practice, planning and action, strategy and tactics, to achieve the best results. However, the vast and complex state apparatus does not facilitate the formulation of a coherent and rational national or even sectoral policy; moreover, formulating a strategy is one thing, executing it is another.

Strategic assessment is a crucial element of a state's ability to adapt its strategy to changing conditions. The assessment of the physical and social environment is a crucial stage in the implementation of a national strategy. In the art of governing, national security mechanisms and institutions simply issue presidential decisions. It includes:

- policy formulation,

- the development of planning strategies and guidelines,

- allocation and alignment of resources,

- tracking and monitoring implementations,

- and performance evaluation based on feedback loops.

Although biothreats have been widely discussed in recent years, policies targeting such potential dangers failed to secure public support and adequate funding.

Particularity of a biological attack

"Terrorist attack" suggests bombs, suicide bombers or similar acts; almost no one thinks of the more sophisticated means: gases or toxic agents transmitted through contaminated food, water, and air. Citizens are aware of many forms of terrorism, but rarely consider the deadliest, ignoring the

---

118 Massinissa Si Mehand, Piers Millett, Farah Al-Shorbaji, Cathy Roth, Marie Paule Kieny, & Bernadette Murgue, "World Health Organization methodology to prioritize emerging infectious diseases in need of research and development," *Emerging Infectious Diseases*, vol. 24, no. 9, September 2018.

idea of terrorists detonating a nuclear device in a metropolis, even though policy-makers and security experts always assume such an act is possible on national soil.

Under the rubric of "asymmetric," many scenarios have been envisaged since the mid-1990s. The most worrisome of these is the heavy attack involving weapons of mass destruction (WMD). In addition to manipulating the political environment, the attacker could infiltrate irregular forces carrying chemical agents into the national territory; the strategic strikes would then come from within. Even a "dirty bomb" would cause widespread death, panic, and major disruption. Thus, a strategy that provides for a wide range of biothreat/bioterrorism scenarios is needed. for many biological agents are far more deadly per unit than the worst chemical warfare agents.

The most worrisome aspect here is the prospect of a biochemical attack. Unlike chemical terrorism, biological terrorism is insidious: its agents strike populations without any visible reaction before incubation (several days or even weeks). Among the chemical, biological, radiological, and nuclear threats, bioterrorism most urgently calls for new strategic thinking on:

- the status of evaluation intelligence,

- characterization of emerging threats,

- prevention, response, deterrence,

- planning for preparedness, detection, countermeasures, recovery and mitigation, knowing that nowadays disease surveillance, and control systems rely on post-symptomatic notification.

The threat of deliberate release of biological agents is the most complex and problematic WMD threat to humanity. Having (as far as is known) political, religious, ideological, or criminal motivations, such bioterrorist acts, could be planned by groups (or single individuals), or even be state-sponsored, as part of an asymmetric strategy.

Theoretically, the bioterrorist attack can be overt or covert. But it is likely that these attacks will remain covert. Thus, the bio-terrorism warning system must be able to identify a signal early, without any claim to it. An effective surveillance system is one of proactive information and requires intercepting the health signal and assessing it early, in order to raise the alarm immediately.

There is no rule of thumb for how many people can be infected by a single patient. Meanwhile, the nature of the contagion and the complexity of the bio-threats clearly compound the problem. In this case, the first victims of the intentional epidemic become weapons for the aggressor, spreading the disease at every step. Food can also undermine bioterrorist attacks. Hence, the importance of food security—first of all of the large food supply chains: air caterers, collective kitchens, etc. —and secondly, the need to ensure the safety of the food supply.

rather easy to obtain and distribute—produce a terrorist effect, spreading chaos and terror among populations.[123] Such a weapons system consists of four elements.

- The payload, the biological agent itself.

- The ammunition protecting and transporting this load to maintain its strength during delivery.

- The delivery system: missile, vehicle (plane, boat, vehicle), shell, human being, food.

- The dispersal system spreading the charge over the target. Potential dispersants are aerosols, explosives, and food or water contamination. Aerosols are the most effective means of generalized dispersal.

Today, bioterrorism is an obvious crime, but "back then [in 2001] it was not at all. Bioterrorism was not criminalized in most countries." More than a criminal tool, the biological weapon was seen as a violation of an arms control treaty: a political issue, therefore. "Hence a huge problem when it comes to non-state actors: terrorists don't care about arms control agreements."[124]

At the international level, biological and toxin weapons are prohibited by the *Convention on the Prohibition of the Development, Production and Stockpiling of Bacteriological (Biological) and Toxin Weapons and on their Destruction*, which entered into force in 1975 and has been hailed as a cornerstone of the international architecture for WMD control. But biological weapons issues are the least regulated of the WMD and it is unlikely that terrorist groups will feel bound by international agreements.

The scope of bioterrorism is broad: no single department or agency can respond to emerging atypical threats, terrorism, WMD proliferation, organized crime and other transnational perils. These threats require coordinated policy, planning, and execution by national security agencies, but additionally, cooperation with local governments. No single military, police or security agency can provide security against bioterrorism. Biodefense touches on many aspects of society and is a matter of national and homeland security, public health and economic security. Its success requires: awareness, surveillance, and preparation.

Here, the responses are cross-cutting as shown in Covid-19. For the government, this creates problems of ownership and resource allocation. Bioterrorism brings together three elements (terrorist, biological agent, living target) from different professions and expertise. Hence, the need to find ways of cooperating

---

123 See, e.g., Alexander Freund, "Ricin - An Easy-to-Obtain Bio-Weapon From the Internet," *Deutsche Welle*, 15 June 2018, https://www.dw.com/en/ricin-an-easy-to-obtain-bio-weapon-from-the-intern et/a-44242451

124 Gigi Kwik Gronvall, *Preparing for Bioterrorism: The Alfred P. Sloan Foundation's Leadership in Biosecurity*, Center for Biosecurity of UPMC, Baltimore & Maryland, 2012, pp. 65-66.

to achieve their objectives. Thus, veterinary expertise and the exchange of veterinary-medical skills are beneficial to the citizen and to the government.[125]

Hence, the call for coordinated efforts to detect biological agents and infectious diseases: hospital preparedness, intelligence gathering and planning. Whether bio-measures or pandemics, preparedness plans must include business and public health officials and leaders—civil society. In 2003, the "Biotox-Piratox" laboratory network was created in France, a specialized component of the antiterrorist plan dedicated to the analysis of folds, packages and substances that may contain dangerous biological or chemical agents. Since 2011, the network has extended its missions to all suspicious substances in the environment, drinking water and/or the food chain, due to deliberate and intended harm or negligence.

The network must act quickly, in effective collaboration with the health services, the police and the army, to avert the threat to the public. In the event of exposure to a biological agent, victims are cared for by the ORSAN-REB system (formerly ORSAN-BIO).[126] These measures, which are designed to cover risks with civil security plans, are complemented by the control of threats, particularly terrorist threats, through VIGIPIRATE and other government plans. The Army Health Service and the General Delegation for Armaments are mobilized, along with the Pasteur Institute, the CEA, and some laboratories of the CNRS and Inserm.

On November 19, 2019, Patrice Binder, Director of Inserm said, "[l]ooking at the archives, since its inception in 2003, the network has processed 1,300 alerts. In 2003, 207 separate incidents were recorded, but since 2010, this number has dropped to 150 per year. Thanks in part to a better understanding of what we look at and the organization of the network, the number of analyses of suspected bio-terrorism agents has dropped from 77.8% to less than 2% in 2011."[127]

---

125 Prime Minister, *"Interministerial Instruction: Relative to the structure and operation of the national network of 'BIOTOX- PIRATO" laboratories,"* No. 278/SGDSN/PSE/DTS, Paris, May 4, 2018. http://circulaires.legifrance.gouv.fr/pdf/2018/06/cir_43600.pdf

126 The national planning doctrine has evolved in the event of an "exceptional health situation" (EHS), which refers to "the occurrence of an emerging, unusual or unknown event that goes beyond the framework of routine alert management due to its scale, severity or media character, and which may lead to a crisis." Initially based on specific plans, it has evolved towards the definition of global response strategies, adapted to the various levels of territorial intervention. This planning framework is based on the organization of the health system response (ORSAN) to HSE. The ORSAN plan is a care organization device, thought up by the Regional Health Agencies in 2014. It was first partially applied during the summer of 2014 when Ebola entered the French territory, then in full in February 2015 during the seasonal flu epidemic. The ORSAN plan was reactivated on November 13, 2015, following the terrorist attacks in Paris, then on July 14, 2016, during the Nice attacks. This plan includes 5 components used to organize care when one of the 5 situations likely to impact the health system occurs.

127 "French bio-terrorism network of labs," *Health In Europe,* November 19, 2013, https://healthcare-in-europe.com/en/home/index.html?src=scrollto

What is the probability of a biological attack? Psychosis or real danger

Human pathogens and toxins pose a real risk to human health and safety from potential release, either accidentally (biosafety) or intentionally (biosecurity). What is the likelihood that terrorists will use biological weapons? With so many unknowns, it is difficult to assess these risks and threats. But advances in technology and science are significantly expanding the range, scope, severity and probability of biothreats. For Interpol, the threat is "real,"[128] "given the potential benefit that could be derived from biological weapons, it is surprising that there are so few recorded instances of their use."[129]

The idea of using biological agents in warfare is not new. Turning natural ingredients into weapons was practiced in pre-modern times, much more than is commonly thought.[130] But, like the uses of poisons and chemicals, records of the use of disease as a weapon are rare. Even when the practice is recognized, modern historians lack the evidence to conclude that "historical documentation of the use of biological warfare has always been scarce."[131] Historians of biochemical warfare accept the common assumption that there is little early evidence of biochemical strategies. The obscurity of the historical record may discourage academic pursuit of the subject.[132]

Poisoned arrows, poisonous honey, contaminated wine, poisoning of water wells, etc., have long been used as secret weapons. The anthrax attacks of the fall of 2001 have sparked interest in the history of biological warfare. The siege of Kaffa (present-day Feodosija, Ukraine) is often cited as a reminder of the effects of using disease as a biological weapon,[133] however, the only account of the Mongols deliberately spreading the plague comes from a single source from the 14th century Genoese writer Gabriele de Mussis, *Historia de Morbo*.

---

128 "Interpol chief says threat of bioterrorism is real," *Irish Examiner*, March 27, 2006, https://www.irishexaminer.com/world/arid-30251202.html

129 Mark Wheelis, "Biological warfare before 1914," in Erhard Geissler & John Ellis van Courtland Moon (eds.), *Biological and toxin weapons: research, development and use from the Middle Ages to 1945,* Oxford University Press, London, 1999, pp. 8-34.

130 Among the important studies that addressed biological weapons before 1945 (until 1970), see *The Problem of Chemical and Biological Warfare*, published in six volumes by SIPRI in 2000 and available via the following link https://www.sipri.org/publications/2000/problem-chemical-and-biological-warfare

131 James A. Poupard & Linda A. Miller, "History of Biological Warfare: Catapults to Capsomeres," *Annals of the New York Academy of Sciences*, vol. 666, no. 1, December 1992, pp. 9-20.

132 The adjective "biochemical" is often used as a catch-all term for biological and chemical agents in general. Mark Wheelis, "Biological warfare before 1914," in Erhard Geissler and John Ellis van Courtland Moon (eds.), *Biological and toxin weapons: research, development and use from the Middle Ages to 1945*, Oxford University Press, London, 1999, pp. 8-34.

133 Mark Wheelis, "Biological Warfare at the 1346 Siege of Caffa," *Emerging Infectious Diseases*, vol. 8, no. 9, September 2002, pp. 971-975.

The epidemic would have been provoked voluntarily by the Mongolian army, sending the corpses of its plague victims over the walls of the city. His account, long cited as the first known act of biological warfare, is certainly of great historical interest, but also relevant today in assessing the threat of military or terrorist use of biological weapons.[134]

Interest in biological agents is not limited to sectarian, religious or environmental groups. Most individuals and groups that have used biological agents have had traditional criminal motives. Available data suggest that the vast majority of cases have criminal motives, although there is a lack of documented cases of a terrorist group using biological agents just to extort money.

Indeed, the extortion commonly employed by terrorists is often combined with other acts that induce the victim to change his or her behavior. It is therefore crucial to separate the clearly criminal perpetrators from those with political agendas. Bio-crime involves the use of a biological agent to kill, terrorize, or incapacitate one or a few individuals for revenge; or for the desire to extort financial gain.[135]

The ancient strategy of poisoning the enemy with corpses or fecal matter is still of use today. Examples go back to the 6th century BC, when the Assyrians are said to have poisoned enemy wells with rye ergot. During the early 18th century Franco-Indian War, the British are said to have provided blankets of smallpox victims to Native Americans, resulting in their decimation. The history of warfare with biological weapons goes back to mythology, but apart from poisoning wells, poisoned arrows, the use of the plague as a weapon, etc., no one really waged deliberate biological warfare until the modern era.[136]

A biological agent is usually defined as a genetically modified organism that is resistant to all known drugs, highly contagious, and capable of harming thousands of people. However, many suspected attacks do not take place in this way: the experience of bioterrorism concerns mainly small-scale attacks. This implies that vigilance in identifying a biological attack and its countermeasures must be high, as it may diverge from the expected pattern. Having failed to contaminate the local water supply, in 1984 a religious sect in the United States deliberately contaminated restaurant salad bars with *Salmonella typhimurium* to disrupt local elections.

Food is easier to contaminate than water. Terrorists can attack the food chain at several stages: targeting livestock and crops during production, harvest-

---

134 Rosemay Horrox, *The Black Death*, Manchester University Press, Manchester & New York, 1994, pp. 16-17.

135 Seth W. Carus, *Bioterrorism and Biocrimes. The illicit use of biological agents since 1900*, Center for Counterproliferation Research, National Defense University, Washington, D.C., February 2001.

136 Adrienne Mayor, *Greek Fire, Poison Arrows, and Scorpion Bombs: Biological and Chemical Warfare in the Ancient World*, Overlook Duckworth, New York, 2009; Judith Miller, "Biological Weapons, Literally Older Than Methuselah," *New York Times*, September 19, 1998.

ing, storage, or transportation; and processed foods during processing, manufacturing, storage, transportation, or distribution. Foodborne outbreaks can be a precursor to a bioterrorist attack; but contaminating drinking water requires the addition of unrealistic amounts of biological agents to a city's food supply.[137]

Another example is that of the 2001 anthrax letters case, in which five people died in the United States. In 1993, a cult in Japan carried out an anthrax spore attack with no physical casualties, and white supremacists talk about the coronavirus as a biological weapon.[138] The Timothy Wilson case shows that "world events influence the time and place of an attack. He says he wants to attack a hospital because of the Covid-19 pandemic and its increased impact through media attention on the health sector. He admits that if he contracts the virus, he will conduct a "lone wolf attack" and try to kill as many as possible."[139]

On March 24, 2020, the U.S. Department of Justice expanded its definition of terrorism to include the deliberate spread of Covid-19, so that the terrorism charge would apply to any individual who wanted to spread the virus; if it was proven that she/he had acted deliberately, she/he would be charged with terrorism for "intentional exposure and infection of others." Since the virus appears to meet the definition of a 'biological agent,' such acts could potentially implicate the nation's terrorism laws.

This pandemic—like many past crises and emergencies—has been exploited by extremists. Following disturbing reports of how extremist groups are attempting to exploit the Covid-19 crisis, the department warns that "threats or attempts to use Covid-19 as a weapon against Americans will not be tolerated." The directive calls "attention to the categories of offenses, relevant to the types of pandemic-related crimes we are witnessing. 1 - we know that individuals and businesses are taking advantage of the Covid-19 crisis to use fraudulent or illegal schemes. 2 - you may encounter criminal activity, from malicious hoaxes to threats targeting specific individuals or the public; to intentionally exposing and infecting others with Covid-19," etc.[140]

---

137 Food terrorism is "an act or threat of deliberate contamination of food for human consumption with chemical, biological, or radionuclear agents for the purpose of injuring or killing civilian populations and/or disrupting economic or political stability." Institute of Medicine of the National Academy, *Addressing Foodborne Threats to Health: Policies, Practices, and Global Coordination*, National Academy Press, Washington, D.C., 2006, p. 60.

138 For a historical overview see; see Stefan Riedel, "Biological Warfare and Bioterrorism: A Historical Review," In *Baylor University Medical Center Proceedings*, vol. 17, no. 4, 2004, pp. 400-406.

139 Bridget Johnson, White Supremacist in COVID-19 Hospital Bomb Plot Allegedly Wanted to Attack Power Grid," *Homeland Security Today*, March 31, 2020.

140 Deputy Attorney General, "*Department of Justice Enforcement Actions Related to Covid-19: Memorandum For All Heads Of Law Enforcement Components, Heads Of Litigating Divisions. And United States Attorneys*," Office of the Deputy Attorney General, U.S. Department of Justice, Washington, D.C., March 24, 2020, p. 2.

A quick scan of neo-Nazi forums and white supremacist channels, using jihadist tactics to enrich their strategies[141] shows how these individuals use misinformation and conspiracy theories to fuel extremist narratives and fuel their mobilization. These local or international extremists encourage their followers to attack during the panic to create panic, target minorities and immigrants, and celebrate the death of their enemies.

According to a Department of Homeland Security memo, white supremacists and neo-Nazis advocate "the obligation" to spread the virus, if one contracts it. "NGOs such as *The Anti-Defamation League* report that forums such as "What to do if you get Corona 19" advocate "going to your local mosque or synagogue, public transportation, or local multi-ethnic neighborhood."[142] Neo-Nazi blogs advocate for "exterminating" immigrants and excluding ethnic minorities from the health care system, claiming that the "swastika is the best cure for Covid-19." Their propaganda blames the "inferior" races for Covid-19 and advocates the permanent closure of borders.

The Islamic State, on the other hand, encourages jihadists to play on the fear and chaos caused by the pandemic to attack vulnerable populations in Europe and the United States. Supporters of the Islamic State make the coronavirus a "soldier of Allah" and urge followers to praise the pandemic, which is hurting the U.S. and European economies. They also make COVID-19 a divine punishment against atheists, Shiites, Christians, and minority peoples in China, Iran, and Italy. Islamist websites and blogs consulted by the author also call for the spread of Covid-19 among infidels, as a "jihad coronavirus."

Biological weapons can also provide an attractive option for a nation or group unable defend itself in any other way and threatened with massive casualties. Terrorists who have previously suffered such casualties may find biological agents an attractive alternative to conventional weapons because of their relatively low cost, relative accessibility, and ease of production, delivery, and deployment.

Their use, or even a simple threat, can cause serious social chaos, as biological weapons cause much greater destruction and loss of life than nuclear, chemical or conventional weapons, in relation to their mass, manufacturing and storage costs. Thus, these biological agents can be used for strategic deterrence, in addition to their offensive utility on the battlefield. In view of the serious consequences of such an attack, governments must be able to react as soon as possible—even if the variety of bioterrorism pathogens greatly exceeds the means to combat them all.

---

141 New Jersey Office of Homeland Security and Preparedness, "*White Supremacist Extremists Exploit Jihadist Tactics,*" State of New Jersey, December 16, 2019.

142 Sonam Sheth, "White supremacists discussed using the coronavirus as a bioweapon, explosive internal document reveals," *Business Insider*, March 22, 2020; Aris Folley, "FBI warns white supremacists encouraging members to spread coronavirus to law enforcement, Jews: report," *The Hill*, March 22, 2020.

The real social and economic cost of an infectious episode could therefore be far greater than the number of human casualties.

Estimating these costs poses many problems: defining damage and avoiding double counting in various statistics, measuring direct losses. The indirect costs of bioterrorist attacks vary according to their distribution across activities, sectors, countries, and time. Covid-19 has shown that some sectors and activities are more vulnerable than others. The indirect intertemporal implications depend on the nature and scale of the attacks, the type of policies adopted by the state in response to the attacks, etc.

Bioterrorism in the age of the biotechnology revolution

Covid-19 proves it: biological threats increasingly deserve the attention of policymakers and security and public health professionals.[143] Biotechnology in the age of synthetic biology expands the range of defense risks. Referring to concepts, approaches, and tools that can modify or create biological organisms, synthetic biology aims primarily to reduce the burden of disease, improve agricultural productivity, or solve pollution problems.

Synthetic biologists are at the forefront of engineering living cells and helping to treat diseases, detect toxic compounds in the environment and produce rare drugs. Chemists, biologists, and engineers engaged in this multi-disciplinary field involved in creating and regulating genetic circuits, manipulating biochemical pathways, editing and modifying the genome, notably through molecular assembly. Although the contributions of synthetic biology are very promising, they can also have malicious uses, threatening citizens.[144]

Modern technology is seen as a solution to many problems. Enormous savings are being realized through ICT, allowing companies to accurately assess, minimize risk and quickly adapt to change. Operationally, it provides the same results with fewer resources. Armies are increasingly using it to gain a sizeable advantage on the battlefield and to increase the conceptualization of operations. For the military, the technology compresses operational cycles, allows precise strikes at great distances, based on real-time data; also, improved cooperation. But this weapon is double-edged. Fascinated but reluctant, many military thinkers fear the prospects of technology's impact on war.

---

143 "The time has come to recognize the glaring fact that despite enormous blood/gold expenditures to 'kill, capture, stop' our way to strategic success in counterterrorism, there are more terrorists in the world today than there were on September 11, 2001, and Covid-19 is likely to lead to the creation of more," warns Michael Nagata in a special issue titled "COVID-19 & Counterterrorism," CTC *Sentinel*, vol. 11, Combating Terrorism Center, U.S. Military Academy, West Point, June-July 2018, p. 5.

144 Christina Smolke (ed.), *Synthetic Biology: Parts, Devices and Applications*, Wiley-Blackwell, Weinheim, Germany, 2018.

Thus, the threat of the use of biological agents against the military and civilians seems worse today than it ever was. At least ten countries have biological weapons programs, the full extent of which is unknown.[145] Technological advances are necessarily changing the threat spectrum, making it more difficult to inspect and monitor biological and toxin weapons because of the proliferation of dual-use facilities[146] and the growth of industrial biotechnology.[147]

The potential for misuse of dual-use technology is illustrated in genomics research. While this knowledge has improved the ability of governments to detect, prevent and treat infections caused by biowarfare agents, experts point to the possibility of "personalizing" classical biological agents, making them more difficult to detect, diagnose and treat.[148] In addition, biological hazards can arise from a variety of disasters, laboratory accidents and pandemics. For example, an FBI investigation blames the ""anthrax envelopes" discovered in the United States on a microbiologist working in a military laboratory.[149]

A two-levels analysis enables to assess the effect of a new technology: efficiency and social system. Historically, at the inception of a new technology, actors and populations emphasize its "efficiency" and underestimate or overlook potential effects on the social system. The new technology is embraced for its efficiency; its ability to change the way people entertain themselves, work slowly, etc. The full range of spillovers and impacts is not clear. The full range of spillover effects and dilemmas are related to how these technologies affect thought and work: effects at different levels. The full range of impacts and dilemmas is in the way these technologies affect thinking, working, selective effects, and the transformative power of the new technology is to change old ways of thinking and operating, and to provide new capacities for action.[150]

The biotechnological revolution has generated many new methodologies in diagnoses, antimicrobials, and vaccines. The possibility of using biotechnology to

---

145 Michael K Jacobs, "The history of biologic warfare and bioterrorism," *Dermatologic Clinics*, vol. 22, no. 3 - July 2004, pp. 231-337.

146 Jonathan B. Tucker, *Innovation, Dual Use, and Security: Managing the Risks of Emerging Biological and Chemical Technologies*, MIT Press, Cambridge & London, 2012.

147 National Research Council, *Industrialization of Biology: A Roadmap to Accelerate the Advanced Manufacturing of Chemicals*, The National Academies Press, Washington, D.C., 2015.

148 Claire M. Fraser & Malcolm R. Dando, "Genomics and Future Biological Weapons," *Nature Genetics*, vol. 29, no. 3, December 2001, pp. 253-256; John Logan Black, "Genome Projects and Gene Therapy: Gateways to Next Generation Biological Weapons," *Military Medicine*, vol. 168, no. 11, 2003, pp. 864-871.

149 Office of Public Affairs, "*Justice Department and FBI Announce Formal Conclusion of Investigation into 2001 Anthrax Attacks*," U.S. Department of Justice, February 19, 2010. https://www.justice.gov/opa/pr/justice-department-and-fbi-announce-formal-conclusion-investigation-2001-anthrax-attacks

150 John Arquilla & David Ronfeldt, "Cyberwar is Coming!" *Comparative Strategy*, vol. 12, 1993, pp. 141-165.

design new "advanced biological warfare agents" must be considered. Biotechnology can also provide applications for weaponizing, disseminating, and delivering biological agents, with new agents targeting specific human biological systems: cardiovascular, gastrointestinal, neurological, or immunological.[151]

Of course, as biotechnology advances, so do these risks of militarization by governments or non-state actors. For example, the DNA equipment required to synthesize some deadly contagious germs is cheaper and easier to purchase than others.[152] According to experts, "the biotechnology underlying the advanced biological agents can advance very quickly, causing a diverse and elusive spectrum of threats."[153]

Transgenic plants and animals could be modified to mass produce bioregulatory proteins or toxins. Transgenic insects, such as bees or mosquitoes, could produce and deliver biological toxins. A genetically engineered mosquito would produce and secrete a biological toxin in its saliva, delivering the toxin while feeding. These transgenic insects would probably not go unnoticed; because, developed for "traditional agents," most countermeasures will be ineffective for advanced biologically based agents such as protein-based transgenics.

Five major attributes of these advanced biological agents have been described: high virulence associated with high specificity; absence of countermeasures for the attacked population; possibility of easily camouflaging the agent; high resistance to adverse situations; and controllability.[154] Thus, assessing the potential vulnerabilities linked to advances in biology and biotechnology seems necessary to answer the following:

- What kind of biology security risks are currently emerging?
- What is their rate of evolution?
- What are the options to mitigate them?

This implies a paradigm shift, with the Covid-19 pandemic creating a climate for this shift. The complexity and global reach of contemporary economies make us more vulnerable to sudden disruptions: this is perhaps the most lasting effect of this pandemic. Societies everywhere are far more attentive to resilience.

---

151 James B. Petro, Theodore R. Plasse, & Jack A. McNulty, "Biotechnology: impact on biological warfare and biodefense," *Biosecurity and bioterrorism: biodefense strategy, practice and science*, vol. 1, 2003, pp. 161-168.

152 Ian Goldin & Chris Kutarna, *Age of Discovery: Navigating the Risks and Rewards of our New Renaissance*, St. Martin's Press, New York, 2016.

153 Central Intelligence Agency, "*The Darker Bioweapons Future*," Washington, D.C., November 2003, p. 2. https://fas.org/irp/cia/product/bw1103.pdf

154 Michael Daly, "The Emerging Impact of Genomics on The Development of Biological Weapons-Threats and Benefits Posed by Engineered Extremophiles," *Clinics in Laboratory Medicine*, vol. 21, no. 3, September 2001, pp. 619-629; Malcolm Dando, *The New Biological Weapons*, Lynne Rienner Publishers, London, 2001, pp. 10-12.

New disruptions are probably inevitable, and now that we know the adverse consequences, individuals, businesses and governments will work to reduce their exposure to such disruptions.

The need for a paradigm shift

The paradigm defines the type of problems to be studied, the criteria by which a solution is evaluated, and the experiments that are acceptable. In this way, it helps to allocate resources: a ""national security paradigm" provides decision-makers with a compass that defines strategies and sets medium- and long-term priorities for military forces, aid programs, diplomacy, and intelligence. It also helps prepare the public for what lies.

The ultimate challenge for a decision maker is to set priorities. A conceptual framework—linking events—is an essential tool. Security and defense failures often result from "the inability to define objectives, choose the appropriate means to achieve those objectives, and shape a public opinion willing to pay the necessary price in a timely manner."[155] Neither automatic nor mechanical, the intellectual framework allows for the development of specific policies.

For a decision-maker facing a pressing or ambiguous situation, this framework is preferable to improvisation. Paradigms gather the processes by which actors act and influence the vision of reality of various publics. Paradigms are interpretive schemes that organize experiences and guide action, providing coherence to seemingly disparate elements, programs, and ideas. Thus, a paradigm guides policy and helps establish priorities.

Including the decision-making process in the game structure helps to confront conflicting options and reveals order in chaotic-looking interactions. While no conceptual framework captures reality in all its complexity, "without a theory, facts remain silent."[156] Theories are simplified images of reality; starting from the essential factors, they try to make our complex world accessible.

For national security, the paradigm helps set priorities and allocate resources; it sends signals to other governments, the public and parliamentarians about what the government wants to do. Crucial in times of crisis and instability, the strategic paradigm provides perspectives to decision makers. In a chaotic episode, it inspires relevant decisions and actions. The paradigm is thus a kind of "beacon" guiding decision making.

Historically, France has neglected biodefense research, development, acquisition, and doctrine. Terrorist attacks in recent years have drawn more attention

---

155 Henry Kissinger, "Limits to What the U.S. Can Do in Bosnia," *The Washington Post*, September 22, 1997.

156 John Keegan, *History of War Volume 1: War in History*, L'esprit Frappeur, Paris, 2000, p. 23.

and resources to medical countermeasures and biological detection systems. Most biodefense initiatives originate in the military, but civilian government agencies are contributing to these efforts.

This field of biodefense lacks strategic direction and remains fragmented: a gap that needs to be filled by instituting a high-level, politically accountable coordination of official and/or societal approaches, conducting regular multi-sectoral simulations, for effective preparedness. This coordination would involve the various sectors concerned in these preparations; build trust and engage stakeholders (legislators, human and animal health, security and foreign affairs actors; private sector; local leaders; and youth).

This strategy aims at unifying the objectives of the policy with the means to achieve them: it is indeed crucial that the policy corresponds to the means to achieve it. For unlike the private sector, governments cannot freely allocate factors of production or define their own objectives. "Control over revenues, inputs and agency objectives is entirely vested in entities outside the agency: legislatures, courts, politicians and interest groups. The constitution or legislation that creates these public bodies assigns them vague objectives, lists broad concerns and leaves it to later political forums to determine their precise meaning. In particular, Parliament has considerable influence in setting their budgets."[157]

Yet these administrations are traditionally resilient: few renew themselves without strong external pressures. Innovative and energetic leadership is crucial to launching any major change. Indeed, implementing change is a complex task for these organizations because of the particular constraints within which they operate. In contrast, "business management focused on the 'bottom line' (profits), government management is focused on the 'top line' (constraints)," which impacts the state's ability to act.

Indeed, one difficulty in developing a national strategy is that the priorities are both threats and remedies, and there are many threats and few resources. The decision-making process differs from country to country,[158] and the appointment of a national coordinator helps to address a problem specific to the senior public service: its need for political support because of its lack of control over resources.

Covid-19 has disrupted every aspect of daily life: citizens, businesses, and governments have all felt its impact, which will undoubtedly lead to significant societal changes in risk management. Similarly, gauging the impact of the pandemic has been a major challenge. The unpredictability of a serious infectious epidemic, its speed of spread and the fears of public opinion can be very destabilizing. There is also uncertainty about the ability of global health agencies to take into account the complex political realities on the ground.

---

157 James Q. Wilson, *Bureaucracy*, Basic Books, New York (USA), 1989, p. 115.
158 James Q. Wilson, *Bureaucracy*, *op.cit.*, pp. 115, 299-300.

The future is being prepared and cannot be predicted. The enormous cost of Covid-19, the multiplication of epidemics in recent years (Ebola, SARS, etc.), techno-scientific progress, the emergence of non-state actors as a strategic threat, etc. All of this justifies a change in the national security paradigm. The growing biological threat may emerge from nature, from a deliberate attack or from an accidental release. The state must foster a culture of preparedness in the field of biothreats; and homeland security agencies must be especially attentive to safety, security, and regulatory requirements.

In the area of counterterrorism, the global pandemic and its aftermath will provide an opportunity to focus on biological agents, which will likely enhance detection and preparedness capabilities:

1) Spend prudently to prevent before an epidemic or biological attack strikes, rather than thinking too much, too late.

2) Ensure rapid, open and accurate communication between nations and aid agencies, instead of secrecy and territorial disputes.

3) Combat disease and prevent panic.

Conclusion

Biological attacks and infectious diseases can cause catastrophic waves of mortality, social disruption, and foment dissent and distrust in government. Nothing is more crucial than quick and decisive action for emergency response. Thus, France cannot sort out what it is preparing for. It must think the unthinkable and learn to deal with bio-threats. Biological risks are becoming a common element of the geopolitical landscape. History has proven that biological pathogens and toxins can be used as weapons.

Thus, a review of preparedness is needed to improve the national biodefense posture. The current situation requires strong government action to optimize national resilience, coordinated efforts in bio-logical detection, hospital preparedness, data collection and bio-defense planning. The state must develop contingency plans, including projected needs and our technological gaps in protection, detection, decontamination, and medical biodefense.

The challenge of new protection systems is their load, cost, length of performance and effectiveness on a wide range of agents. They require devices that capture, block, or destroy agents better than the current ones. For risk analysis, the problem is the wear and tear of time and the cost and price of developing biosecurity and biodefense programs.

The most damaging psychological bias is the "recession effect"[159] (focusing

---

159 Hermann Ebbinghaus, *On memory: A contribution to experimental psychology*, Teachers College, New York, 2013.

on the most recent), which prevents a thorough examination of the past and a broad view of the future. Recently, other threats have predominated: terrorism, cyber security, drones. But any post-coronavirus strategy will need to integrate bio-threats and infectious diseases. The Covid-19 pandemic did not radically change the security environment. It has not changed the course of history, but accelerated it.

International Journal on Criminology • Volume 9, Number 1 • Winter 2022

BIBLIOGRAPHIC WATCH

The History of Terrorism: A State of Knowledge and Debate

Daniel Dory*

John Lynn II, *Another Kind of War. The Nature and History of Terrorism*, Yale University Press, New Haven - London, 2019, 507 pp.

ABSTRACT

Lynn's book can be seen as one of the most ambitious elaborations, or even the culmination of half a century of work on the history of terrorism. Understanding the nature and importance of this historiography, requires recalling two elements. First, the fact that in the understanding of terrorism, and therefore also in its definition, three reference strata, each with its own particular history, intervene in varying proportions.

Keywords: Terrorism studies, Historiography, Wave theory, Theoretical perspectives, John Lynn

La historia del terrorismo: un estado de conocimiento y debate

RESUMEN

El libro de Lynn puede verse como una de las elaboraciones más ambiciosas, o incluso como la culminación de medio siglo de trabajo sobre la historia del terrorismo. Comprender la naturaleza y la importancia de esta historiografía requiere recordar dos elementos. En primer lugar, el hecho de que en la comprensión del terrorismo, y por tanto también en su definición, intervienen en proporciones variables tres estratos de referencia, cada uno con su historia particular.

Palabras clave: Estudios del terrorismo, Historiografía, Teoría ondulatoria, Perspectivas teóricas, John Lynn

doi: 10.18278/ijc.9.1.7

恐怖主义史：相关知识和辩论进展

摘要

Lynn的著作可被视为半世纪以来关于恐怖主义史的著作中最负有企图心、甚至是最出色的著作之一。理解这部历史编纂学的本质和重要性，需要回顾两个要素。第一，就理解恐怖主义及其定义而言，三个参考阶层（各自拥有特定的历史）发挥不同比例的影响。

关键词：恐怖主义研究，历史编纂学，浪潮理论（Wave theory），理论视角，约翰·林恩

The recent publication of his book by the American military historian John Lynn provides a remarkable opportunity to assess the achievements and debates in the history of terrorism. It is easily understandable that such an approach mobilizes issues that go far beyond those of a single specialized branch (or discipline) of terrorism studies, for only a serious study of the terrorist phenomenon in all its temporal (and spatial) depth can produce an adequate knowledge of it. The paucity of comments by too many "specialists," for whom terrorism only begins with the contemporary forms of jihadist Islamism (or even with the acts of Mohamed Merah), is enough to prove this. This is why, unlike the previous Bibliographic Watch, the focus here will be on Lynn's work alone, situating it first in the specialized historiography. Then, we will focus on his contribution to the two debates that have run through the discipline since its implicit beginnings in the mid-1960s; namely, the debate on the origins of (modern?) terrorism, and that on the most relevant periodization for understanding its successive transformations.

Half a century of historiography

Lynn's book can be seen as one of the most ambitious elaborations, or even the culmination of half a century of work on the history of terrorism. Understanding the nature and importance of this historiography, requires recalling two elements. First, the fact that in the understanding of terrorism, and therefore also in its definition, three reference strata, each with its own particular history, intervene in varying proportions. A *polemical stratum* (the most effective and invasive), through which the "terrorist" designates the infamous and absolute enemy, whose "cowardly and barbaric" acts put "the whole world" and "civilization" in danger. Of course, from this infamous construction of "terrorism," the designation of concrete "terrorists" varies according to the times, the geopolitical situations and the actors engaged in semantic and practical wars. The *legal stratum* aims at defining, qualifying and repressing acts (and/or thoughts and feelings such as "hatred"); it therefore requires a certain precision that anti-terrorist legislations (strongly dependent on the polemical stratum) have the greatest difficulty to achieve. The *scientific stratum* on the other hand, is conceived as an effort to analyze and understand the terrorist act, considered as a technique belonging to the repertoire of political violence. It must constantly be borne in mind that this intellectual enterprise can only be achieved on the condition that the terrorist fact is removed from the grip of the polemical stratum.[1]

The second element that must be remembered when looking at the history of terrorism as a whole, concerns the very modalities of production of this knowledge. In fact, unlike other branches of university historical research, the history of terrorism emerged and remains to this day the business of journalists or researchers with little or no specialization in terrorism studies (i.e., in the *terrorism studies* that developed in the Anglo-Israeli-American world in the early 1970s).[2] The result was a series of works of very uneven value, not very cumulative, rarely based on primary sources (archives, surveys, databases) and, obviously, too often dependent on the needs of actors managing the conjunctural imperatives of the polemical stratum. It is thus a very heterogeneous historiographic corpus that we are dealing with here, where some solid scientific works rub shoulders with various propagandist hoaxes, only interesting as illustrations of the innumerable manipulations to which terrorism lends itself to due to its nature as a (mainly) psychological weapon.

In view of the above-mentioned particularities, a very quick overview of the historiography of terrorism can be made, without which the contribution of Lynn's book cannot be properly assessed. Without in any way aiming at exhaustiveness, we can consider the 1965 book by French journalist Roland Gaucher[3] as the first essay to consider terrorism from the perspective of its history, covering the period from the *Catechism of Netchaev* (1869) to the end of the OAS (1962). It was followed, more than ten years later, by the first English-language synthesis by Albert Parry, a Russian-American historian, and it still remains a source of interesting data.[4]

A year later, in 1977, the influential historian Walter Laqueur published *Terrorism*, which, despite its obvious flaws in data treatment and lack of chronological coherence,[5] was to have a definite influence on future work.[6] Prior to 2001, L. Bonante's brief popular synthesis, especially interesting for its rich iconography,[7] and Martha Crenshaw's large, edited volume, *Terrorism in Context*,[8] containing some solid case studies with historical depth, deserve attention.

The two decades following the attacks of September 11, 2001, have seen a tremendous quantitative expansion in studies of terrorism (but much less qualitative improvement...), and leaving aside for now the works that participate directly in the historiographical debates that will be discussed later, we can retain the following references. First of all, the good journalistic synthesis by Dominique Venner[9] constitutes in a way the extension of Roland Gaucher's work until 2001. At the same time, a compilation of extracts from hastily assembled texts appeared in the United States, which completes Laqueur's anthology in certain respects.[10]

We remain in the domain of amateurism and pseudo-encyclopedic confusion with the book of the English polygrapher Andrew Sinclair,[11] who offers a vast moralistic fresco without much scientific interest. A similar comment can be made about the book by the British journalist Matthew Carr,[12] whose 2006 volume is riddled with ideological bias, while benefiting from the achievements of some serious works that are beginning to appear around particular periods, groups and causes. Moreover, Carr rightly considers terrorism as a cultural fact, giving rise to novels, films, etc., which constitute important sources for studying the terrorist fact in all its complexity.

Despite the very pertinent plea of historian Isabelle Duyvesteyn in 2007 in favor of the development of the history of terrorism as a major theoretical and practical issue,[13] the quality of synthetic works remained generally mediocre in the following years. We owe to Michael Burleigh, a historian not specialized in terrorism, a volume whose political influence (due to the uncritical repetition of the major themes of the "Western" propaganda) was undoubtedly greater than its scientific impact.[14]

The persistent gap between the often-remarkable sectoral advances and the theoretical deficiencies that too often affect the synthesis works that deal with the whole of the history of terrorism,[15] is clearly seen with the publication in 2013 of the collective work directed by J. Hanhimäki and B. Blumenau, which offers a series of high-quality monographic chapters on well-defined periods or episodes.[16]

A much more ambitious project gave rise, in 2015, to the publication of *The Routledge History of Terrorism*. This large collective volume, edited by Randall Law, aims to synthesize knowledge from antiquity to the present day.[17] Unfortunately, both conceptual imprecisions and the very uneven value of the chapters (ranging from excellent to deplorable) prevent this work from becoming the expected reference work.

As for recent works in French that offer a general approach to the history of terrorism, Gilles Ferragu's book,[18] without great theoretical pretensions, provides useful data, despite explicit ideological biases that the informed reader has no trouble detecting. Similar remarks can be made about Jenny Raflik's[19] book, which, without being a history of terrorism, is directly relevant to our subject and therefore deserves to be mentioned here. For, despite an often-confused presentation and a large number of factual errors (of dates (p. 25) or factual ones such as the "assassination of Nasser" (p. 281)), this work makes it possible to sketch out a reflection on the conditions of the elaboration of a history of terrorism. Finally, in 2016, the latest edition of the collective volume edited by Gérard Chaliand

and Arnaud Blin[20] was published (first published in 2006). The volume includes a small anthology of indispensable texts, even in fragmentary form, for the novice researcher. The mass of data gathered in this volume, however, contrasts with the poverty of the theoretical contribution concerning the historiographic debates that will be discussed later.

In the course of 2019, three large collective textbooks on terrorism and counterterrorism have been published. Concerning the Routledge textbook, we have already indicated (see note 2) the deplorable treatment given to the history of terrorism. The second volume,[21] explicitly focused on events after September 11, 2001, logically makes no room for history. On the other hand, the third manual[22] devotes its second part to "the history of terrorist violence," containing three chapters dealing respectively with the Middle Ages, the 19th and the 20th centuries (pp. 85-129), to which is added a (rather weak) chapter on the historical approach to terrorism (pp.194-206). Here again, a reflection on the status, the objectives and the conditions of elaboration of the history of terrorism is largely missing.

It is therefore in this context of sectoral advances and persistent difficulties in truly founding the field of the history of terrorism as a discipline in its own right that John Lynn's book is published. As such, it can be read both as a kind of state of the art and as an attempt to structure a rapidly expanding scientific field. In order to assess the extent to which the author has achieved these ambitious goals, we examine his contribution to the discussion of the two major historiographical problems surrounding the origin of terrorism and (thus) its operational definition on the one hand, and the periodization of the history of terrorism on the other. As we shall see, in both cases, Lynn suggests, if not definitive solutions, at least some extremely stimulating ideas.

The definitional problem and the origins of terrorism

The question of knowing when terrorism emerges in the repertoire of political violence depends on its definition. And we know of the endless debates about the definition of terrorism, which lead practically every researcher to suggest, if not an original definition, at least adjustments to the formulations in use at a given time. With this in mind, rather than giving yet another definitional proposal, Lynn identifies a set of descriptive features or elements of "terrorism" (pp. 5-6), including the use or threat of violence against noncombatant (or defenseless) victims; provoking fear and outrage among larger audiences; and among whom, through the mediatization effect, psychological reactions may engender behaviors consistent with the terrorists' political, social, and cultural goals.

It does not matter, at this stage of the analysis, whether this characterization is absolutely satisfactory or not. Indeed, many comments can be made about the nature (and especially the identity) of the victims, or the necessarily political motivations of the terrorist act (a question that is usefully discussed in Chapter 13, which deals with narcoterrorism). What is important to remember, however, is the overall relevance of these features, which offers a framework both flexible and sufficiently precise to delimit the field of the history of terrorism. In particular, we retain the important idea according to which the terrorist act does not only aim at provoking fear (with its inhibiting effects), but also, and sometimes even particularly, outrage, i.e., an emotion which pushes to action and to revenge, and which can thus provoke reactions which can help the terrorists' cause.[23]

Perhaps less convincing and unwieldy is the author's subsequent distinction between six levels of terrorism, differentiated according to the capability resources of the actors, ranging from states to individuals (inaccurately equated with "lone wolves"), armed forces, social groups, criminal entities, and sub-state groups engaged in "radical" terrorism (pp. 7-13). Solid ground is found later in the paper when Lynn differentiates the strategic intentions associated with the use of terrorist techniques (pp. 22-27), namely, intimidation, initiation (the first phase of an insurgency), attrition (of the enemy's will), evolution (based on a gradual shift to regular confrontation, following the Maoist pattern in particular). Here Lynn, whose specialty is, let us recall, military history, revives a current of thought on the strategic dimension of terrorism, whose antecedents even precede the birth of *terrorism studies*.[24] With these clarifications, the reader has a clear framework, sometimes debatable, but sufficiently coherent to be able to engage in the teeming subject of the history of terrorism.

From then on, the question of the inaugural moment of this form of violence also arises. In this respect, Lynn's contribution is extremely interesting, because he identifies the decisive moment around the middle of the 19th century when terrorism, integrated into a revolutionary and/or insurrectionary dynamic, becomes an "ism." That is to say, a specific technique of political violence with its own theory, modus operandi and history (p. 108). Two conditions shape this preliminary moment, which begins with Heinzen's theoretical writings and ends with the first truly terrorist attacks, around 1893. The first condition, according to Lynn and many other authors, is the French Revolution, which, beyond the episode of the Terror (1793-1794), inaugurates an era in which the ideas of popular sovereignty and democracy radically challenge the legitimacy of previous rulers and political systems, while giving the right to govern to more or less violent individuals and groups of citizens claiming to represent popular will, legitimacy or any other cause.[25] The second condition, outlined by Lynn in his remarkable fifth chapter (pp. 105-150), consists of the gradual realization of the tactical futility of mass urban insurrectionary warfare based on the construction of barricades, following the failure of the revolutions of 1848. The disaster of the Paris Commune in 1871 definitively confirmed the unsuitability of this form of combat in the face of regular military formations equipped with increasingly powerful weapons.

In this context, Lynn, in the wake of previous works on the issue,[26] identifies "The Murder," a text first published by Karl Heinzen in 1849, as the starting point for the intellectual construction of terrorism.

It is thus by the articulation of political conditions, theoretical reflections and technical innovations (dynamite, handguns, popular press with great circulation, etc.) that terrorism appears at the end of the 19th century, differentiating itself from political assassinations (like the murder of Tsar Alexander II in 1881), even if the actors of the attack designate themselves as "terrorists." This point is important, because if it is true that there is a certain fuzzy zone of intersection between the political assassination and the terrorist act, it is advisable to underline their difference which holds with the identity of the victims; personal in the first case and vectorial in the second.[27]

On the basis of the above considerations, it is possible to distinguish a long "prehistory"[28] (in which the Zealots, the Assassins and many other actors take their place) from the inaugural moment of terrorism, conceived as an exclusively modern phenomenon. And we are talking here about an inaugural *moment*, rather than risking a precise date,[29] even if the year 1893, especially because of the attack on the Liceu theater in Barcelona, seems to us a good option.[30]

Once the question of the beginning has been resolved, it remains to be seen whether there are identifiable periods in the history of terrorism, and if so, how many, and above all, according to what criteria. This is the subject of the second major historiographical debate, in which Lynn also engages creatively.

The "waves" and "novelty" in the history of terrorism

To understand the value (and limitations) of Lynn's book's contribution to periodization in the history of terrorism, we must grasp the complexity of that issue in 2019.

The first (and still dominant) attempt in this area is the work of the political scientist David Rapoport, which was carried out, perhaps somewhat hastily, under the impact of 9/11 and then developed and adjusted in a series of consecutive publications.[31]

In essence, Rapoport distinguishes four successive waves of terrorism from the 1880s, when the phenomenon began, according to him, in Russia. These "waves" are differentiated mainly according to a specific "energy" that is linked to the nature of the causes (understood here as motivations) that give them their originality. These four waves are:

1 - *The anarchist wave* (1880-1920)

2 - *The anti-colonial wave* (1920s-1960s)

3 - The *wave of the "New Left"* (1960s- late 1980s?)

4 - *The religious wave* (1979- ?)

The duration of each wave is variable, for while the first two lasted about forty years, the third lasted about twenty years, and the end of the fourth (current) wave is difficult to predict. Moreover, the overlapping of the different moments makes this periodization sufficiently flexible to make it an excellent pedagogical tool, even if its factual and conceptual bases quickly prove to be very fragile. Still, the main efforts to construct a periodization in the history of terrorism so far start from (and depart from) the general framework elaborated by Rapoport.

In 2007, British historian Marc Sedgwick presented an organization of data based on the effects of inspiration (and therefore also of contagion) that configured sequences of recourse to terrorism.[32] In this perspective, he distinguishes four waves (like Rapoport...) designated according to their country of origin: Italian (beginning around 1820 with the Carbonari and extending until the end of the Zionist campaign in 1948); German (between 1919 and 1945, mainly "fascist"); Chinese (beginning in 1937 and continuing today in the form of anti-colonial struggles); and Afghan (since 1979, with a mainly Islamist tonality). Beyond obvious errors and conceptual shortcomings, this approach has the advantage of showing the possibility of organizing the corpus of historical data by emphasizing the impact of a few founding episodes in the genesis of more or less prolonged terrorist campaigns. However, by focusing on the causes/motivations of the actors, Segdwick ends up focusing more on the political and contextual history of terrorist acts than on the transformations of terrorism as a specific technique belonging to the repertoire of political violence.

Two years later, political scientists Rasler and Thompson attempted a quantitative empirical validation of Rapoport's wave theory using the ITERATE database for the years 1968-2004.[33] The conceptual problems are considerable here as well, especially the confusion between strategies and modus operandi, as well as the uncertainties about the ideological motivations of the actors. But on the basis of the frequency of attacks linked to the causes that the actors claim, Rapoport's scheme seems largely validated, at least for the last two waves. This same article was republished two years later in the collective work directed by Jean Rosenfeld, entirely devoted to the discussion of the "wave theory."[34] Among the very uneven texts in this confused and heterogeneous volume, we retain the chapter by Marc Sageman,[35] who formulates, from the sole case of Al Qaeda, the hypothesis of a kind of progressive degradation of motivating ideas that corresponds to a correlative transformation of the acts they inspire. Thus, the generation of "founders" of this social movement is composed of educated men belonging to the upper and middle wealthy classes of several Arab countries, who in addition to a solid academic education possess considerable financial means (e.g., Osama Bin Laden).

This is followed by a second generation of upper-middle class students who are sent to Europe to complete their studies and who become involved in Islamism as a consequence of their rejection of the Western way of life, their isolation, and the contacts they make in mosques. This generation (which is that of the perpetrators of September 11ᵗʰ) is followed after the destruction of the Afghan sanctuary by a third, whose actors are the sons and grandsons of unskilled immigrants populating the "working class" neighborhoods of large Western cities. These young people are fascinated by the heroic acts of previous jihadists, but themselves poorly or not at all educated and generally involved in delinquency (or even criminality) at a very early age. They form unstable groups of "friends" who are the basis of the "*leaderless jihad*" that Sageman has studied elsewhere. In this particular case, we have the hypothesis of a generational succession within the same terrorist wave (here "religious") which would account for its internal transformations and the reasons for its decline. This hypothesis, which enriches Rapoport's theory, has not yet been tested (to our knowledge) on any other body of data.

In 2016, Parker and Sitter published an article on "The Four Horsemen of Terrorism,"[36] which provides a new critique of the wave theory, while remaining, once again, within the framework of motivational (or "causal") criteria. In this case, we are not dealing with successive waves, but with the permanence of four "strains" which, following an analogy borrowed from virology, each go back to a "patient zero" dating from the middle of the 19th century. In this perspective, the authors insist above all on the permanence of terrorist "lineages" that are perpetuated in various historical contexts by imitation and influence.

John Lynn ultimately follows Rapoport's approach, also basing it on ideological "causes," but modifying it by merging the second and third waves. The result is the following periodization (p. 13):

- *First wave*. From the aftermath of the revolutions of 1848 to around 1920. Corresponds to the era of "propaganda by deed" and to the emergence of a "self-conscious" terrorism, with specific modes of operation and an international diffusion of counterterrorist practices and responses (Chapter 5, pp. 105-150). The violent anarchists and the Russian revolutionaries best represent this trend.

- *Second wave*. From 1945 to 1980. It brings together ethno-nationalist movements (such as the Irgun, the FLN and the Tamil Tigers) and Marxist groups such as the Tupamaros, the RAF, and the Weathermen.

- *Third wave*. From 1980 to the present. It begins in the wake of the Iranian Revolution, and the Soviet invasion of Afghanistan, not forgetting the enormous impact of the Israeli invasion of Lebanon in 1982 (which Lynn opportunely recalls on p. 297). This wave is essentially "religious" and overwhelmingly Islamist (Chapter 9, pp. 253-266), and the author distinguishes regional jihads (Hezbollah, Hamas; Chapter 10, pp. 267-288) from global jihads such as those waged by Al Qaeda and the Islamic State (Chapter 11, pp. 289-331). Suicide attacks are part of the modus operandi that distinguish this period, although non-religious groups (such as the Tamil Tigers) also resort to them.

We therefore see that Lynn, while adopting Rapoport's "causal" criterion, achieves a slightly different periodization, giving (rightly) greater historical depth to terrorism, while proposing a more coherent approach to its successive waves, which nevertheless does not integrate the years 1920-1945 into a truly comprehensive picture.

On the other hand, the inherent limitations of focusing on motivational and contextual aspects of ideology obscure the essential problem of why, in a given geopolitical situation and while claiming the same cause, some individuals and groups resort to terrorism, while others choose different modalities of action (violent or non-violent).

It should also be noted that the weakness of identifying solely a motivational criteria became clear during a debate that occupied a large part of specialized researchers between the mid-1990s and the early 2000s, concerning the existence of a "new" terrorism. Although rarely explicitly linked to the theme of the overall periodization of the terrorist fact, this question emerges around 1995, notably under the impact of the sarin gas attack in the Tokyo subway by the Aum Shinrikyo sect on March 20, 1995,[37] and the Oklahoma explosion (April 19, 1995). Later, of course, the insistence on the willingness of religiously inspired networks to commit attacks, apparently without clear political claims or achievable goals, found some semblance of confirmation on September 11, 2001. This debate, which manifested above all a dismaying ignorance of history on the part of many "specialists" in terrorism, took a rather confused and repetitive turn before going out of fashion towards the end of the 2000s; it nonetheless constitutes an interesting milestone in the recent historiography of terrorism that should not be overlooked.[38] And if it is still of interest today, it is undoubtedly because it suggested the possibility of using other facts and criteria than those of ideology to differentiate particular moments of terrorism. Thus, to take only a few examples about which there are already promising sketches of reflection, we can cite the transformations linked to the techniques of mediatization of the terrorist act;[39] the changes concerning the modes of operation;[40] the evolution of counter-terrorist devices;[41] or the avatars of the literary representation of terrorism.[42]

A welcome synthesis that leads to interesting perspectives

If Lynn's book undoubtedly marks an important milestone in the historiography of terrorism, while contributing to a possible "historical turn" in terrorism studies,[43] it is probably because of its theoretical ambition. The result is an organization of the volume according to two complementary criteria, producing a periodization on the one hand (the three waves of "radical" sub-state terrorism discussed above), and a typology on the other (according to decreasing capability variables).

Thus, a presentation of the theoretical framework of the book (Chapter 1, pp. 1-30), is followed by a good synthesis on terrorism or, more exactly, state terror (Chapter 2, pp. 31-50); then by a very interesting and timely evocation of "military terrorism," directed by regular armed forces against civilian populations, and of which the criminal bombing of Dresden (February 13-15, 1945) is an emblematic example (Chapter 3, pp. 51-75). Chapter 4 (pp. 76-104) concerns racial violence (although exclusively white...) in the United States between 1865 and 1965, that is, between the end of the Civil War and the triumph of the civil rights movement, with interesting information on the three moments that mark the history of the Ku Klux Klan (KKK). This chapter, which according to Lynn illustrates a form of terrorism exercised by social groups, often in the majority and according to eth-no-racial criteria, also serves as an antecedent to the developments contained in Chapter 12 (pp. 332-358), devoted to the "violence" of the Radical Right, still in the United States, a subject to which we shall return later.

This rather complete panorama of the history of terrorism envisaged by Lynn according to the two criteria just mentioned (periodization and typology), also leads to working hypotheses concerning the future of this phenomenon. In this respect, the history of terrorism, insofar as it falls within the general frame-work of studies on terrorism, cannot be limited to the pursuit of an exclusively academic knowledge, however necessary it may be. And if the history of terrorism, rigorously undertaken, must allow for a better analysis and understanding of this manifestation of political violence, it cannot fail to be used to envisage—with all the necessary precautions—its future evolution.

In order to do this, the "wave theory" appears as a sound basis for explor-ing, as Lynn also does in the last chapter of his book (pp. 416-432), the more or less weak signals that make it possible to foresee either the possible end of the fourth wave (of Rapoport),[44] or the appearance of a fifth wave, the characteristics of which are still the subject of controversy. Thus, in 2007, J. Kaplan proposed a quite confused and unspecific theory concerning a fifth wave, made up of trib-alism and mass violence inspired by millenarian beliefs. Its actors would come from the previous waves following internal transformations that lead them to want to realize the "new world" immediately by extermination and/or replace-ment of populations (hence the role of rape). As examples of these movements, Kaplan cites the Khmer Rouge before they came to power, the Ugandan *Lord's Resistance Army*, or the Janjaweed militias in Darfur.[45] Despite its inaccuracies, this essay opens up some avenues for reflection on the potential use of terrorism by groups and networks (globalist or not) committed to messianic projects for the transformation of humanity in the shortest possible time, the study of which is beyond the scope of this text.

A few years later, Jeffrey Simon formulated a hypothesis no less confused, but totally different, concerning the "fifth wave."[46] Indeed, for this author, it is technological innovations (notably the Internet) much more than particular ideological motivations that are shaping a "new terrorism," implemented mainly by solitary actors or small more or less autonomous groups. This perspective also allows Simon to recycle the theme of the threat of the use of CBRN (chemical, biological, radiological and nuclear) weapons, recalling the potential danger of "rogue states," enemies of the West and particularly of Israel.

Much more concrete but limited in their theoretical scope due to the adoption of criteria based on the motivations presiding over the choice to resort to terrorist acts, several hypotheses have been formulated in recent years. Thus, according to Benoît Gagnon, the fifth wave could be structured (at least in North America) by ecoterrorism,[47] because of the increasing violence of the actions of radical environmentalist groups. On the other hand, and without it being strictly speaking a wave, many authors mention, if not the emergence, at least the aggravation of terrorist actions committed for mainly criminal reasons.[48] This variant is the subject of a chapter in Lynn's book (Chapter 13, "Narcoterrorism," pp. 359-388) where various processes of hybridization and criminal drift are examined, as well as the use of terrorism by Colombian and Mexican cartels as a means of intimidating the population and the authorities in order to influence political decisions, particularly in the area of extradition to the United States.

Finally, for the last ten years or so, there has been a massive diffusion in academic circles and "Western" governmental institutions of the theme of the threat (obviously very serious) of "extreme right-wing" terrorism, to which Lynn devotes Chapter 12 (pp. 332-358) of his book on the basis of almost exclusively North American data. Without being able to discuss this theme in depth as it deserves, let us note that all the conditions are met for transferring the counter-terrorist system from jihadist terrorism (which is possibly in decline) to terrorism originating from the "extreme right." Indeed, the combination of "supremacism" and "racism" (exclusively by whites), as well as "conspiracy," "populism," "anti-Semitism," and a few other repulsive "isms," synthesized in the vague category of "extremism" polemically associated with terrorism, means that the ingredients are available to envisage the emergence of a fifth wave of terrorism, which has apparently been developing since around 2011 (Breivik case).[49]

Thus, while the future of terrorism remains controversial, its past is becoming much better known. Certainly, enormous strides remain to be made in order to achieve an empirically and theoretically coherent and cumulative history of terrorism. Lynn's book is undoubtedly an important milestone on the road to consolidating this field of research, which is essential to understanding terrorism and for public and private action to confront it effectively. It is therefore predictable that it will become an essential basic reference on the subject for the next few years.[50] This is a book to be read and studied in depth, without hesitation.

Notes

1 Daniel Dory, **Senior** Lecturer at the University of La Rochelle, specialized in the geopolitical analysis of terrorism.

2 See, for example: Edna Reid, "Evolution of a Body of Knowledge. An Analysis of Terrorism Research," *Information Processing and Management*, Vol. 33, N° 1, 1997, 91-106; Daniel Dory, "Les *Terrorism studies* à l'heure du bilan," *Sécurité Globale*, N° 22, 2020, 123-142. Concerning specifically research in the history of terrorism, its indispensable character and the little interest it arouses on the part of researchers subjected to the grip of the immediate, is already pointed out by Andrew Silke "The Road Less Travelled. Recent Trends in Terrorism Research," in: A. Silke, (Ed.), *Research on Terrorism. Trends, Achievements and Failures*, Frank Cass, London - Portland, 2004, 186-213. This does not prevent this same author from giving a very small and scientifically deficient place to history in the reference manual he recently edited: Leonard Weinberg, "A history of terrorism," in: A. Silke (Ed.), *Routledge Handbook of Terrorism and Counterterrorism*, Routledge, London-New York, 34-56. For a confused but useful discussion of the difficulties of understanding terrorism in the social sciences, particularly in France, see: Michel Wieviorka, "Terrorism in the Context of Academic Research," in: Martha Crenshaw (Ed.), *Terrorism in Context*, Pennsylvania State University Press, Pennsylvania, 1995, 597-606.

3 Roland Gaucher, *Les Terroristes*, Albin Michel, Paris, 1965. Translated and published in English in 1968 by Sacker and Warburg, London.

4 Albert Parry, *Terrorism. From Robespierre to Arafat*, The Vanguard Press, New York, 1976. Despite its title, which obviously obeys the imperatives of the Israeli propaganda of the time, and numerous conceptual inaccuracies, this book remains a stimulating attempt to put together a mass of often relevant data.

5 See, for example, David Rapoport's highly critical account in *The American Political Science Review*, Vol. 73, No. 1, 1979, 393-4.

6 Walter Laqueur, *Terrorism*, Weidenfeld and Nicolson, London, 1977. Translated into French: *Terrorisme*, PUF, Paris, 1979. Interesting point: following this author's habit of publishing the same text several times under different titles, this book appears in 2001 as: *A History of Terrorism*, Transaction Publishers, New Brunswick-London, 2001, with a new seven-page introduction, theoretically indigent but warning about the danger of weapons of mass destruction (WMD) falling into the hands of terrorists (thus anticipating the disinformation campaign that preceded the invasion of Iraq in 2003). On the other hand, in two respects Laqueur did a useful job. First, by extending the field of the history of terrorism to cultural and especially literary facts, for example in: W. Laqueur, "Interpretations of Terrorism: Facts, Fiction and Political Science," *Journal of Contemporary History*, Vol. 12, N° 1, 1977, 1-42. On the other hand, in 1978 he published *The Terrorism Reader*, an anthology of selected texts that filled an obvious gap in sources. Later republished with Yonah Alexander (Meridian Books, 1987) and included and updated in *The Voices of Terror*, Reed, New York, 2004.

7   Luigi Bonante, *Le terrorisme international*, Casterman-Giunti, Paris-Florence, 1994.

8   Martha Crenshaw, *Terrorism in Context*, Pennsylvania State University press, Pennsylvania, 1995. It should also be recalled that Dr. Crenshaw co-edited with John Pimlott the *Encyclopedia of World Terrorism* (3 Vols.), Sharpe, Armonk, 1997, which contains abundant material of historical interest.

9   Dominique Venner, *Histoire du Terrorisme*, Pygmalion, Paris, 2002.

10 Isaac Cronin (Ed.), *Confronting Fear. A History of Terrorism*, Thunder's Mouth Press, New York, 2002.

11 Andrew Sinclair, *An Anatomy of Terror. A History of Terrorism*, Pan Books, London, 2003.

12 Matthew Carr, *La mécanique infernale. The History of the 20th Century through Terrorism* [2006], Éditions Héloise d'Ormesson, Paris, 2008.

13 Isabelle Duyvesteyn, "The Role of History and Continuity in Terrorism Research," in: Magnus Ranstorp, (Ed.), *Mapping Terrorism Research*, Routledge, London-New York, 2007, 51-75.

14 Michael Burleigh, *Blood and Rage. A Cultural History of Terrorism*, Harper Perennial, London, 2008.

15 For an example, among others, but very significant, see: Henry Laurens, "Le terrorisme comme personnage historique," in: H. Laurens; M. Delmas-Marty, *Terrorismes. Histoire et Droit*, CNRS Éditions, Paris, 2010, 9-66. This text, sometimes interesting, shows the limits of the treatment of the question by educated non-specialists, who situate the Sandinistas in Guatemala (p. 47), or assimilate Al-Qaeda to the *focos guévaristes*.

16 Jussi M. Hanhimäkli; Bernhard Blumenau, (Eds.), *An International History of Terrorism*, Routledge, London-New York, 2013. See the book's Introduction (pp. 1-13) to appreciate its scope and limitations.

17 Randall D. Law (Ed.), *The Routledge History of Terrorism*, Routledge, London-New York, 2015. The Introduction (pp. 1-11) offers interesting reflections on the history and historiography of terrorism. By the same Randall Law one can also consult (with similar problems concerning the specificity of the terrorist fact): *Terrorism. A History* [2009], 2nd Ed. by Polity, Cambridge, 2016.

18 Gilles Ferragu, *Histoire du Terrorisme*, Perrin, Paris, 2014. Two years before, Michaël Prazan's book, *Une Histoire du terrorisme*, Flammarion, Paris, 2012, was published, which tells us more about the author's obsessions than about the subject of the book, although it is sometimes interesting for the interviews with various protagonists it contains.

19 Jenny Raflik, *Terrorism and Globalization. Approches historiques*, Gallimard, Paris, 2016.

20 Gérard Chaliand; Arnaud Blin, (Dirs.), *Histoire du Terrorisme. From Antiquity to Daech*, Arthème Fayard/Pluriel, Paris, 2016.

21 David Martin et al. (Eds.), *Terrorism and Counter Terrorism Post 9/11*, Edward Elgar, Cheltenham/Northampton, 2019.

22 Erica Chenoweth et al. (Eds.), *The Oxford Handbook of Terrorism*, Oxford University Press, Oxford, 2019. This book was reported in the Literature Watch cited in note 2.

23 This idea was previously developed by the author in: John Lynn II, "Fear and Outrage as Terrorists' Goals," *Parameters*, Vol. 42, No. 1, 2012, 51-62.

24 See, for example: Thomas P. Thornton, "Terror as Weapon of Political Agitation," in: Harry Eckstein (Ed.), *Internal War. Problems and Approaches*, Free Press, New York, 1964, 71-99; Edward Price, "The Strategy and Tactics of Revolutionary Terrorism," *Comparative Studies in Society and History*, Vol. 19, No. 1, 1977; and especially: Andrew Kidd; Barbara Walter, "The Strategies of Terrorism," *International Security*, Vol. 31, No. 1, 2006, 49-80.

25 The relationship between the French Revolution and the emergence of terrorism has been explored further in: Martin A. Miller, *The Foundations of Modern Terrorism*, Cambridge University Press, Cambridge, 2013. See the summary of his argument on p. 2.

26 Daniel Bessner; Michael Stauch, "Karl Heinzen and the Intellectual Origins of Modern Terrorism," *Terrorism and Political Violence*, Vol. 22, No. 2, 2010, 143-176.

27 A good overview of this issue can be found in: David George, "Distinguishing Classical Tyranicide from Modern Terrorism," *The Review of Politics*, Vol. 50, No. 3, 1988, 390-419.

28 It is this "prehistory" that is, for example, and at the cost of many conceptual acrobatics, the subject of the first part of: Randall Law (Ed.), *The Routledge History of Terrorism*, Routledge, London-New York, 2015, 13-59.

29 This moment is well evoked by Gilles Ferragu, "L'écho des bombes: L'invention du terrorisme "à l'aveugle" (1893-1895)," *Ethnologie Française*, Vol. 49, N° 1, 2019, 21-31.

30 On the context of this remarkable attack: Angel Herrerín López, "1893: año clave del terrorismo en la España de la Restauración, " *Espacio, Tiempo y Forma*, Serie V, T. 20, 2008, 71-91.

31 See especially: David C. Rapoport, "The Fourth Wave: September 11 in the History of Terrorism," *Current History*, Vol. 100, 2001, 419-424; David C. Rapoport, "The Four Waves of Modern Terrorism," in: Audrey Kurth Cronin; James M. Ludes (Eds.), *Attacking Terrorism*, Georgetown University Press, Washington, 2004, 46-73; David C. Rapoport, "The Four Waves of Modern Terrorism. International Dimensions and Consequences," in: Jussi M. Hanhimäkli; Bernhard Blumenau (Eds.), *An International History of Terrorism*, Routledge, London-New York, 2013, 282-310. Note that the idea of a "terrorist wave" is an old one, as it is already found in Roland Gaucher's book ref-

erenced in note 3. For a convenient presentation of Rapoport's theory, see: Jeffrey Kaplan, "Waves of Political Terrorism," in: William R. Thompson (Ed.), *Oxford Research Encyclopedias. Politics*, 2016 (online).

32 Marc Sedgwick, "Inspiration and the Origin of Global Waves of Terrorism," *Studies in Conflict and Terrorism*, Vol. 30, No. 2, 2007, 97-112.

33 Karen Rasler; William R. Thompson, "Looking for Waves of Terrorism," *Terrorism and Political Violence*, Vol. 21, No. 1, 2009, 28-41.

34 Jean E. Rosenfeld (Ed.), *Terrorism, Identity and Legitimacy. The Four Waves theory and political violence*, Routledge, London-New York, 2011.

35 Marc Sageman, "Ripples in the waves. Fantasies and fashions," in: Jean E. Rosenfeld (Ed.), *Terrorism, Identity and Legitimacy. The Four Waves theory and political violence*, Routledge, London-New York, 2011, 87-92.

36 Tom Parker; Nick Sitter, "The Four Horsemen of Terrorism: It's Not Waves, It's Strains," *Terrorism and Political Violence*, Vol. 28, No. 2, 2016, 197-216. This article was followed by a discussion, including by Rappoport on pp. 217-235 of the same issue. From a different perspective, we also have the testing of "wave theory" in relation to ecoterrorism, a phenomenon hardly considered by Rapoport. See: João Raphael da Silva, "The Eco-Terrorist Wave," *Behavioral Sciences of Terrorism and Political Aggression*, Vol. 12, N° 3, 2020, 203-216.

37 On the (disastrous) impact of the Aum affair on the process of constructing the "new terrorism" theme related to the use of weapons of mass destruction (WMD), see Ian Reader's excellent article, "Globally Aum. The Aum Affair, Counterterrorism and Religion," *Japanese Journal of Religious Studies*, Vol. 39, No. 1, 2012, 179-198.

38 For a good overview of the debate, see: Steven Simon; Daniel Benjamin, "America and the New Terrorism," *Survival*, Vol. 42, No. 1, 2000, 59-75; as well as historian Isabelle Duyvesteyn's very relevant focus, "How New is the New Terrorism?" *Studies in Conflict and Terrorism*, Vol. 27, No. 5, 2004, 439-453. For an updated view of the issue: Stuart Gottlieb (Ed.), *Debating Terrorism and Counterterrorism*, Sage-Cq Press, Los Angeles-London, 2014, Chapter 1: "Is the 'New Terrorism' Really New?" 1-34.

39 See the interesting periodization proposed by Catherine Bertho Lavenir, "Bombes, protes & pistolets. Les âges médiologiques de l'attentat," *Cahiers de Médiologie*, N° 13, 2002, 17-35.

40 On this issue, historical research could, for example, be inspired by the theoretical and methodological achievements of the following article: Brian Jackson; David Frelinger, "Riffling Through the Terrorist's Arsenal: Exploring Groups' Weapon Choices and Technology Strategies," *Studies in Conflict and Terrorism*, Vol. 31, No. 7, 2008, 583-604.

41 A true history of counterterrorism, which seeks to identify its invariants, local differences and temporal transformations, is still largely untried. For an overview of the interest of the question: Robert J. Art; Louise Richardson, "Introduction," in: Robert J. Art; Louise Richardson (Eds.), *Democracy and Counterterrorism. Lessons from the Past,*

United States Institute of Peace Press, Washington, 2007, 1-23. Perhaps the best introduction to this issue to date is Beatrice de Graaf, "Counter-Terrorism and Conspiracy. Historicizing the struggle against terrorism," in: Randall Law (Ed.), *The Routledge History of Terrorism*, Routledge, London-New York, 2015, 411-427. In contrast, Lynn's chapter on counterterrorism (Ch. 14, "Homeland security," pp. 389-415) only deals—superficially—with the case of the U.S.

42 On the fruitfulness of this area of research, see especially Lynn Patyk's excellent chapter, "The age of terrorism in the age of literature," in: Randall Law (Ed.), *The Routledge History of Terrorism*, Routledge, London-New York, 2015, 470-483.

43 See: Giovanni Mario Ceci, "A 'Historical Turn' in Terrorism Studies?" *Journal of Contemporary History*, Vol. 51, No. 4, 2016, 888-896.

44 On this point, see Leonard Weinberg; William Eubank, "An End to the Fourth Wave of Terrorism?" *Studies in Conflict and Terrorism*, Vol. 33, N° 7, 2010, 594-602. This article, which suggests the decline of Rapoport's fourth wave (Islamist, largely equated with Al Qaeda) testifies both to the problematic nature of the "wave theory" and, more importantly, to the difficulty of incorporating into it the emergence of the Islamic State in 2014. In this regard, see also the following note by Xavier Raufer, "Une dégénérescence des djihadistes et peut-être du djihad," *Sécurité Globale*, N° 20 NS, 2019, 143-145; a text which, moreover, resonates with the hypothesis that Marc Sageman formulates in the work mentioned in note 35.

45 Jeffrey Kaplan, "The Fifth Wave: The New Tribalism," *Terrorism and Political Violence*, Vol. 19, No. 4, 2007, 545-570. See also: Jeffrey Kaplan, "Terrorism's Fifth Wave: A Theory, a Conundrum and a Dilemma," *Perspectives on Terrorism*, Vol. 2, No. 2, 2008, 12-25.

46 Jeffrey Simon, "Technological and lone operator terrorism. Prospects for a fifth wave of global terrorism," in: Jean E. Rosenfeld (Ed.), *Terrorism, Identity and Legitimacy. The Four Waves theory and political violence*, Routledge, London-New York, 2011, 44-65.

47 Benoît Gagnon, "L'Écoterrorisme: Vers une cinquième vague terroriste nord-américaine?" *Security & Strategy*, N° 3, 2010, 15-25.

48 See Riikka Puttonen's recent development; Flavia Romiti, "The Linkage Between Organized Crime and Terrorism," *Studies in Conflict and Terrorism* (Preprint), 2020.

49 For a good, up-to-date summary: Vincent A. Auger, "Right-Wing Terror: A Fifth Global Wave?" *Perspectives on Terrorism*, Vol. 14, No. 3, 2020, 87-97.

50 And this, despite its few deficiencies and the obstacle represented by the difficulty of accessing the supplements announced by the author on the site www.yalebooks.com/lynn, which testifies to an editorial policy that is strange, to say the least.

Strategies of U.S. Law Enforcement Professionals Against Lawless Areas and Crime Hot Spots

Maurice Cusson

ABSTRACT

The article begins by painting a bleak picture of the American *inner city*: violence of all kinds culminating in frequent shootings and homicides by and against African Americans. Added to this are social disorganization, the powerlessness of local actors to control the thugs, exclusion, and poverty. In these areas where people fail to live together in peace, victims no longer call the police. By failing to respond or neglecting to intervene, the police are said to have displayed a *"laissez faire"* attitude in the *inner city*, unlike in other neighbourhoods. However, beginning in the 1990s, teams of reform-minded police officers in New York, Boston, and elsewhere launched innovative strategies that were evaluated by criminologists and later succeeded in significantly reducing violent crime, including homicides. In the first category of strategies, teams targeted crime hot spots, micro- locations in the urban area, such as street segments, where an increase in crime could be observed. For example, an analysis of the spatial distribution of 911 calls in a city showed that 50% of all crimes were concentrated in 5% of these crime hot spots. In each of these micro-locations targeted, police officers developed an appropriate action plan that included a greatly increased police presence and vigilance, interventions against disorderly conduct, incivilities, parking tickets, and other offences. These police officers also organized the implementation of situational prevention measures. The second strategy was developed in New York and called *ComStat*. It started with excellent digitized and updated crime statistics for real-time decision making. Then, police officers in neighbourhood stations found ways to deter criminals by checking, questioning, searching, and disarming offenders, mischief-makers, and other criminals. The third strategy addressed a unique manifestation of American violence: shootings and deadly settlements of scores. It involved real-time personal deterrence of gang members, confiscation of their weapons, and hit-and-run operations. These strategies have been the subject of numerous quasi-experimental evaluations, and the overall results

doi: 10.18278/ijc.9.1.8

have been positive: violent crime has significantly decreased in hot spots and areas where police have implemented one of these strategies. A fourth measure—initiated by legislators—was to decriminalise cannabis possession and trafficking to end the harassment and locking up of dealers. In this way, police officers were able to focus on fighting violent crime rather than wasting their energies on artificial offences. The article concludes by arguing that American police officers who incorporate these new strategies into their practice are now legitimate in claiming the title of *professional*, as they know the difference between effective strategies and ineffective or even counterproductive expedients.

Keywords: policing strategies, police professionals, lawless areas, crime hot spots, evaluations, *Crime Hot Spots Policing, ComStat, Focused Deterrence,* cannabis decriminalization, New York, Boston

Estrategias de los profesionales de las fuerzas del orden de EE. UU. contra áreas sin ley y puntos críticos de delincuencia

Resumen

El artículo comienza pintando un panorama sombrío del centro de la ciudad estadounidense: violencia de todo tipo que culmina en frecuentes tiroteos y homicidios por y contra afroamericanos. A esto se suma la desorganización social, la impotencia de los actores locales para controlar a los maleantes, la exclusión y la pobreza. En estas áreas donde las personas no logran vivir juntas en paz, las víctimas ya no llaman a la policía. Al no responder o no intervenir, se dice que la policía mostró una actitud de «laissez faire» en el centro de la ciudad, a diferencia de otros barrios. Sin embargo, a partir de la década de 1990, equipos de policías con mentalidad reformista en Nueva York, Boston y otros lugares lanzaron estrategias innovadoras que fueron evaluadas por criminólogos y luego lograron reducir significativamente los delitos violentos, incluidos los homicidios. En la primera categoría de estrategias, los equipos se centraron en puntos críticos de delincuencia, microubicaciones en el área urbana, como segmentos de calles, donde se podía observar un aumento de la delincuencia. Por ejemplo, un análisis de la distribución espacial de las llamadas al 911 en una ciudad mostró que el 50 % de todos los delitos se concentraron en el 5 % de estos puntos críticos de delincuencia. En cada una de estas microubicaciones seleccionadas, los agentes de policía desarrollaron un plan de acción apropiado que incluía una presencia y vigilancia policial mucho mayor, intervenciones contra la alteración del orden público, incivilidades, multas de estacionamiento y otros delitos. Estos policías también organizaron la implementación de medidas de prevención situacional. La segunda estrategia se desarrolló en Nueva York y se llamó ComStat. Comenzó con excelentes estadísticas criminales digitalizadas y actualizadas para la toma de decisiones en tiempo real. Luego, los oficiales de policía en las comisarías de barrio encontraron formas de disuadir a los delincuentes controlando, interrogando, registrando y desarmando a los delincuentes, malhechores y otros delincuentes. La tercera estrategia abordó una manifestación única de la violencia estadounidense: tiroteos y acuerdos de cuentas mortales. Implicaba la disuasión personal en tiempo real de los pandilleros, la confiscación de sus armas y operaciones de atropello y fuga. Estas estrategias han sido objeto de numerosas evaluaciones cuasiexperimentales y los resultados generales han sido positivos: los delitos violentos han disminuido significativamente en los puntos conflictivos y las áreas donde la policía ha implementado una de estas estrategias. Una cuarta medida, iniciada por los legisladores, fue despenalizar la posesión y el tráfico de cannabis para acabar con el acoso y el encarcelamiento de los traficantes. De esta forma, los agentes de policía pudieron concentrarse en combatir los delitos violentos en lugar de malgastar sus energías en delitos artificiales. El artículo concluye argumentando que los policías estadounidenses que incorporan estas nuevas estrategias en su práctica ahora tienen legitimidad para reclamar el título de profesionales, ya que conocen la diferencia entre estrategias eficaces y expedientes ineficaces o incluso contraproducentes.

Palabras clave: estrategias policiales, profesionales de la policía, áreas sin ley, puntos críticos de delincuencia, evaluaciones, Vigilancia de puntos críticos de delincuencia, ComStat, disuasión enfocada, despenalización del cannabis, Nueva York, Boston

美国执法专家针对不法之地和犯罪高发区的策略

摘要

本文首先描绘了美国"内城"（inner city）的荒凉景象：各类暴力集中于此，表现为非裔美国人发起的（以及针对非裔美国人的）频繁枪击事件和他杀。此外还存在社会混乱、地方行动者在控制罪犯方面的无能为力、排斥和贫困。人们在这些地方无法和平共处，受害者不再呼叫警察。与其他邻区不同的是，因无法对此加以响应或忽视干预，"内城"的警察被认为展现"自由放任"的态度。不过，自20世纪90年代起，纽约市、波士顿以及其他地区具有改革思想的警察团队启动了创新策略，后者经犯罪学家评估并显著减少了暴力犯罪事件，包括他杀。第一类策略中，警察团队以城市地区的犯罪高发区和微型地点为目标，例如街区这类犯罪情况可能增加的地方。例如，一项关于城市911呼叫电话的空间分布分析显示，50%的犯罪事件集中在5%的犯罪高发区。这些微型地点中，警方采取适宜行动计划，包括大幅提升警力和警戒、混乱行为干预、不文明现象、违章停车以及其他违法行为。警方还组织了场景预防措施的执行。第二类策略在纽约市提出，被称为ComStat。这类策略以优秀的数字化及更新的犯罪统计数据为出发点，用于实时决策。随后，片区公安局警察通过一系列方法威慑罪犯，包括对犯罪分子、违法人员和其他罪犯进行检查、盘问、搜查以及解除武装。第三类策略针对美国暴力的独特情况：大规模枪击和死亡案件。这包括针对犯罪成员的实时个人威慑、武器没收以及肇事逃逸操作。这类策略一直是许多准实验评估的主题，并且整体结果是积极的：犯罪高发区的暴力犯罪数量显著减少。第四类策略由立法者发起，用于对大麻持有及交易一事去犯罪化，以期结束对交易商的骚扰和监禁。如此一来，警察能聚焦于打击暴力犯罪，而不是浪费精力在人为违法行为（artificial offences）上。本文的结论主张，将这些新策略融入实践的美国警察如今能合法获得专家的称号，因为他们知道有效策略与无效策略甚至是起反作用的权宜之计之间的差异。

摘要：治安策略，警察专家，不法之地，犯罪高发区，评价，犯罪高发区治安，ComStat，集中威慑，大麻去犯罪化，纽约市，波士顿

Violent crime emerges in some parts of American cities as some of the most serious crime problems in the country, particularly for African Americans living in these troubled urban areas. In the latter, crime proliferates in the form of violent robberies, gang fights, score-settling, and murders, but also drug trafficking and the gang wars that follow. Americans refer to these neighbourhoods where outlaws rule in a variety of ways: *inner cities, slums, black ghettos*. (The French equivalent are *zones de non-droit, quartiers sensibles, cités interdites*, and *zones de développement prioritaire*.)

Intense research has been conducted on Chicago, where homicides are committed with terrifying annual frequency. As an example, between 1965 and 1989, the area of the city with the highest number of homicides had a rate of 75.0 per 100,000 inhabitants (in comparison, the quietest area of Chicago had a rate of almost zero: 0.34 per 100,000). The most affected areas also suffer from other woes: unemployment, poverty, lack of commerce and services, social disorganization. The inhabitants of these lawless areas are reportedly powerless to take charge of their lives, to act effectively to solve their own problems, to trust others, and to control the violence of their children and adolescents. Reasonable adults thus seem to be reduced to impotence and do not dare reprimand or punish the thugs around them. In Chicago, this passivity and ineffectiveness in the exercise of informal social control is seemingly strongly correlated with homicide rates.[1]

African Americans live in large numbers in the *inner cities,* where they struggle to coexist with Latinos and poor whites. Yet African American homicide rates are six times higher than those of whites. Across the United States, between 1979 and 2018, the average homicide rate was 27 per 100,000 population for blacks, compared to 4 per 100,000 for whites.[2]

In these areas, there may be many motives for the killings. A drug dealer could be taken out by a competitor or shot dead because he dared to venture into enemy territory. Members of gang X might drive into gang Y's territory and riddle their enemy's lair with bullets. A young man could be provoked by a fellow gang member, leading them to come to blows, and then one of them might raise his pistol and shoot. In the environment where these two young men lived, one does not go out without a loaded pistol. Moreover, the code of honour dictates that one must be respected at all costs and should not tolerate offence or humiliation. Three other cases of homicide exist: a robber shouts, his wallet or his life, the victim resists and pays with his life, or the robber is killed because the victim was armed. A burglar breaks into a house at night. When confronted by the owner of the house, he shoots him, unless he is shot by the owner himself. A drunken and angry spouse beats his wife to death because she wants to break up with him.

The term *black ghetto* highlights the close relationship between the problems of a lawless area and the miserable lives of African Americans who live in constant fear of violent death. More than 80% of homicides involve a murderer and a victim who know each other and belong to the same social environment. This is also the case among African Americans: in the United States, between 1976

---

1 Block, R.; Block, R. 1992. Homicide Syndromes and Vulnerability. Violence in Chicago Community Areas over 25 Years. In *Studies on Crime Prevention*, Vol. 1, No. 1, National Council for Crime Prevention. Sampson, R. J. 2012. *Great American City*: Chicago: University of Chicago Press.

2 My thanks to Claire Chabot for providing me with these figures. See also Chabot, C. 2021. *Ending the convergence of black and white homicide rate ratios in the United States, 1979-2018.* Doctoral dissertation in criminology. University of Montreal.

and 2005, 94% of black homicide victims were killed by blacks.[3] Thus, in *black ghettos*, people seemingly fail to live together in peace. The victims have given up calling the police, who are absent and hate to set foot in this hostile environment. When the police dare to go there, they turn a blind eye and stand by when a fight breaks out. What doesn't help the police and the investigators is that the gangs keep a lid on the situation by intimidating the victims, the parents, the teachers, the young girls, the small shopkeepers, and the good students. For their part, the judiciary reportedly doesn't bother investigating crimes committed by black murderers on black victims. As a result, the latter conclude that the only defense they have against violent people in their neighborhoods is armed retaliation or revenge. Also, residents of an *inner city* only call the police as a last resort. A black man who kills a black man is likely to get away with it because such crimes are not considered a priority by investigators and because police too often fail to prove the murderer's guilt. Indeed, police officers are seen as racist by African Americans. On the one hand, law enforcement officers reportedly racially profile and target black drug dealers, and on the other hand, police officers seemingly do not move when it comes to ensuring the safety of African Americans. In the eyes of *inner city* residents, the police tolerate behaviors in their neighborhoods that they would not condone in a white neighborhood. It appears clearly that the relationship between cops and African Americans is atrocious, marked by fear of the other. They are terrorized by the police, some of whom are ready to shoot a black person at the first sign of trouble. Indeed, it is estimated that the police are responsible for nearly 1,000 killings of citizens in the United States each year.[4]

While violent criminals are rarely punished in these lawless areas, millions of small-time drug dealers (mostly African Americans) are arrested and incarcerated each year, one of the reasons for the overcrowding of American prisons.

The social-economic-institutional factors that account for the high rates of homicide by and against African Americans in the *inner city* have been documented. Social factors include ineffective social control within families and neighbourhoods and the criminogenic influence of gangs; economic factors involve inequality, unemployment, and poverty; institutional factors, encompassing the shortcomings of incompetent policing, which alternates between absence, passivity, and abuse of force; and finally, justice, which is inaccessible except when it comes to incarcerating a drug dealer.[5] The causality also goes in the opposite direction: the high crime rate of a lawless district ends up being known elsewhere, which leads employers to stop hiring candidates from those poor neighbourhoods, resulting in unemployment and poverty.

---

3   I would like to thank Claire Chabot for giving me this figure.

4   Jobard, F. 2019. The use of force by the police. In Cusson, M. Ribaux, O. Blais, É. and Raynaud, M-M. 2019. *New treatise on security*. Montreal: Hurtubise and Quebec: Septentrion.

5   Anderson 2012. *Code of the Street*. New York: Norton and Sampson, R. J. 2012. *Great American City*.

Faced with this disastrous equation, how have law enforcement authorities responded? Very unevenly. In many cities in the South and West, including St. Louis, Missouri, and New Orleans, police authorities turn a blind eye, allowing their officers to alternate between passivity and excessive force.[6] In contrast, as in New York and Boston, from 1990 onwards, police chiefs supported by criminologists tackled the problem head on, and they have innovated, implemented, and then evaluated quasi-experimentally with positive results. Thus, in several cities, police organizations have implemented *Crime Hot Spots Policing*. In New York, the program was named *ComStat* and, in Boston, *Focused Deterrence*. Then, on a completely different note, in some 20 American states, legislators decriminalized the possession and sale of cannabis, so that in these states, the police now focus on cracking down on real crime rather than wasting their time arresting and incarcerating small-time drug dealers.

The crime hotspot as a primary target

In 1989, a team of criminologists led by Lawrence Sherman published a landmark article in which the researchers succeeded in identifying with great precision in an urban area micro-locations affected by excessive crime, *crime hot spot*. The researchers had compiled hundreds of thousands of telephone calls to the police in the city of Minneapolis. These calls were recorded with the callers' street addresses, which made it possible to determine precisely where the call came from. Once this was done, a digital map of the city was used to identify street segments, intersections, and other micro-locations where more crimes had been committed. It was discovered that nearly 50% of all criminal activity in the city was concentrated in as little as 3% of Minneapolis's street addresses. A similar finding was made in several other cities. Weisburd went so far as to state a "law of criminal concentration. It states that in a large city, 50% of crime is concentrated in 5% of the city's micro-locations.[7]

A crime hot spot is not necessarily where the offenders live, but rather where they converge to find their victims or steal their possessions. It is more often their hunting ground rather than where they live.

A crime hotspot is a micro location—a segment of a street, a crossroads, a shopping center, a council flat, a car park, a nightclub, a stadium, a railway station—where crimes, misdemeanours and incivilities abound. In the words of Marcus Felson, in this place, active offenders come into contact with victims in the absence of a "guardian," that is to say, a protector, a supervisor, a policeman. It is a crime hot spot where active offenders converge to find vulnerable victims, loca-

---

6   See: Roth, R. *American Homicide*. Cambridge: Harvard University Press.

7   In New York City, Boston, Minneapolis, Tel Aviv, Seattle, Lowell, the percentages of crime hotspots responsible for 50% of crime range from 3% to 6%: see Weisburd et al. 2018: *Place Matters and* Sherman & al. 1989; Hot Spots of Predatory Crime. *Criminology vol 27.*

tions exposed to theft and impunity (as guards, police officers, controllers, supervisors and private security are absent or passive).

In these hot spots, vulnerable people have unfortunate encounters with armed and brawling criminals. Buildings—shopping malls, slums, small businesses, low-income housing—remain unprotected against intruders, burglars, vandals. There is no access control, no concierge, no alarm system, and no one in charge of the security of the location.

In Seattle, crime hotspots—far from being evenly distributed across the city—tend to be located in close proximity to each other in the same neighbourhood. Thus, a lawless area is defined as an area of the city that contains several crime hotspots, including areas that are not affected by crime.

The hot spot—rather than the neighbourhood—is a prime target for preventive and enforcement operations, simply because police strike the bull's eye when they focus on these micro-locations: law enforcement officers track down offenders and have the opportunity to protect many victims and secure poorly protected buildings. That's why Weisburd and his colleagues insist that crime hot spots should be a priority for an urban police force. The target should not be the neighbourhood or the area, but the micro-location where crime and incivilities are concentrated. And the smaller the area targeted by police interventions, the more effective the action is likely to be. Rather than spreading out over a territory in which there are areas where there is nothing occurring, we prevent and deter where the criminal activity is taking place. For it is in these places that victims are calling out for help. Offenders need to be monitored and controlled, and the need for situational prevention is felt and apparent.

Based on this knowledge of crime hotspots, small teams of police officers in American cities have been developing response plans tailored to each of the hotspots identified as priorities in their city since 1990. In Lowell, Massachusetts, the city police launched a series of operations in 17 hotspots in the city. Three captains are in charge of the teams. Together with their colleagues, they take stock of the available information and come up with an appropriate plan of action. Most of the time, it is obvious that a police presence must be restored where it had been neglected. A significant number of police officers are now patrolling the area. They make themselves accessible to plaintiffs and victims. They do not hesitate to intervene in the occurrence of incivility, traffic violations, disturbances at night and fights. They do not hesitate to intervene in cases of incivility, traffic violations, night-time disturbances and fights. They have situational prevention measures implemented: repairing light fixtures, installing remote surveillance cameras, demolishing a dilapidated, abandoned and squatted building, fencing off a vacant lot used as a meeting place for drug dealers and their clients, advising victims of burglaries to install better locks.

As a result, these 17 crime hotspots were compared to 17 others also affected by crime. They were made comparable through randomization. And where increased police presence and situational prevention measures had been put in place, the numbers of violent robberies had significantly decreased compared to the experimental group: 42% less in the experimental group; in addition, there was a decrease (-34%) in non-family assaults.[8]

Lowell was far from the only city in which law enforcement succeeded in curbing crime by tackling hot spots. In fact, between 1990 and 2017, there has been an accumulation of targeted intervention projects on crime concentrations. Of the batch, 78 were the subject of published experimental evaluations, allowing Braga to compile, in 2018, a review of 65 scientific articles describing and evaluating these 78 projects. It was found that 62 of these policing operations resulted in significant decreases in the number of crimes.[9]

ComStat in New York: precise statistics and quick decision-making

In 1994, Bill Bratton became Chief of Police of New York. At that time, the city was ravaged by a crime made of violent robberies, shootings, burglaries, murders . . . that year, the city's homicide rate peaked at 30 per 100,000 population (in comparison, in France, there are, depending on the year, 1 or 2 homicides per 100,000 inhabitants). Added to this was a police force plagued by racketeering, corruption, and sloppiness. Supported by a strong team of deputies, Bratton remobilized the police force and launched a radical new strategy whose centerpiece was called *ComStat*. The new system began by digitizing the city's crime statistics to provide decision-makers with accurate, timely, digitized, and mapped information. This data was provided on a weekly basis to the headquarters and the chiefs of the 74 *precincts* in the metropolis. Police analysts used geomatics software to map the various types of crime in the area to describe the increase or decrease in crime. These data and maps were distributed to the headquarters and to each district station. *ComStat* pinpointed the previous week's crime hotspots and the types of crime that were occurring there. *ComStat* provided access to reliable, up-to-date crime figures from the top to the bottom of the police hierarchy for the various crimes committed in each neighbourhood and at the crime scene (as opposed to annual crime statistics aggregated at the national, provincial, or large city level, which are of almost no operational value).

Bratton directed *ComStat*. Every week, early in the morning, he called his deputies and the neighbourhood station chiefs to a meeting (to which journal-

---

8   Braga and Bond 2008. Policing Crime and Disorder, a Randomized Control Trial. *Criminology*, Vol. 46.

9   Braga, A. B. Turchan, A. V. Papachristos, D. M. Hureau, 2019. Hot spots policing of small geographic areas effects on crime. *Campbell Systematic Review*.

ists were invited). On large screens, the crime statistics of the previous week were presented and thanks to a *Mapinfo* type software, everyone could see and locate the micro-locations where burglaries, robberies, shootings, etc. had been committed. The two deputies of the chief were constantly questioning one or other of the neighbourhood captains: What do you know about this shooting that was heard in your neighbourhood? Do you have any information about the perpetrators? Do you have any background information on them? Have you arrested any of them? Have any offenders in the area been stopped and searched? If so, how many guns were confiscated? And the captain, when questioned, had an interest in giving specific answers. The important matter was getting the information to the decision-makers so that the necessary action could be taken quickly. All these exchanges were public. *ComStat* was the opposite of the cult of secrecy and confidentiality that had previously prevailed in the NYPD.

In the areas of New York City identified by *ComStat* as problematic, Bratton encouraged his officers to implement a strategy inspired by the work of Wilson and Kelling. In 1982, Wilson and Kelling wrote a famous article entitled "Broken Windows." The two authors illustrate their points with an anecdote. On a rundown street in a neglected neighbourhood, there is a derelict building with a recently broken window. At the sight of this window, two kids get the idea of breaking more windows. Then other vandals come and continue the destruction. During this time, nothing is done, nothing is repaired. No one to watch, no one to intervene. Eventually the street takes on a sinister, intimidating air. Some people would prefer to avoid it, but being a shortcut, they venture at their own risk. One day, a group of thugs, knowing that they were safe, attacked a passer-by and snatched her purse. It's the beginning of a black series.

Bratton concludes that it is important to take incivilities, disorder, and damage seriously. And that we must listen to the people who complain about nighttime noise, people who urinate in front of their door, and thugs who make obscene remarks to passers-by. In order to ensure safety, the police have a duty to deal with incivilities and disorder. Police officers have a duty to maintain order. In such a way that honest people will stop being afraid and will dare to intervene, to blame, to reprimand a youth that is too turbulent and offensive. How to achieve this? The police officer will make a point of approaching the individual he or she has caught in the act of contravention or incivility. He will question him and, if the answers do not satisfy him, he will want to see his identification, then he will search the suspect. Experience has shown that in the process he may find false papers or a gun that is being carried illegally. And then the policeman will make a proper arrest. This procedure is called "stop and frisk." It was a real deterrent. However, over time, police officers began to abuse this practice and misuse it. Instead of reacting to tickets or incivilities, law enforcement officers judged on the basis of the customers' faces and, not surprisingly, the colour of their skin. And, over time, they started stopping and questioning individuals constantly. So much so that in 2011, in New York City, 700,000 "stop and frisk" cases were recorded in a single year, resulting in only 12% of arrests based on serious grounds. The practice had degenerated into harassment. Bratton likened the abuse to "overmedication": the patient is cured and no longer needs the drug, but the incompetent doctor insists: keep taking your pills. It was therefore necessary to put an end to such abuses. It was in 2014 that Bratton, having returned to office, put a stop to this wave of unwanted stops: that year, the number of "stop and frisk" dropped by 98%.[10]

ComStat and the practices and policies inaugurated by Batton were successful. We have seen that in 1990, the homicide rate in the American metropolis was 30 per 100,000 inhabitants. However, by 2009, that rate had dropped to 6 per 100,000. The robbery rate had also dropped by 80%, as had the burglary rate. Combined, the most serious crimes (murder, burglary, auto theft, robbery) had dropped by 46%. On the other hand, in other American cities, no decrease similar to that of New York was recorded.[11] The conclusion is that a system such as *ComStat*, which combines an excellent 911 call recording system, patrol officers who systematically write event reports, data digitization, fact classification, geolocation and timely communication of information to local decision-makers, who immediately send a surplus of reactive police officers to the field, who are attentive to any offence and who adopt situational prevention measures, is effective. Another conclusion is that contrary to a persistent prejudice, crime varies not only under the influence of social and economic factors, but also under the effect of police action or inaction, of the competence or incompetence of police officers and, finally, of innovations in policing.

Boston, "face-to-face" deterrence and pacification

The early 1990s were a period of great urban violence in the Boston metropolitan areas. Residents of underprivileged neighbourhoods would often hear shootings at night, and passersby in the morning would regularly see young men's bodies lying on the ground. In an attempt to provide a solution to this situation, criminologist David Kennedy worked with local police officers and first calculated that between 1990 and 1994, Boston had suffered a total of 155 homicides involving teenagers or young adults under the age of 21, often members of violent gangs.

The first investigated solution was called the *Ceasefire* initiative. David Kennedy gathered police officers, local community leaders, a prosecutor, probation and parole officers to launch a *focused deterrence* operation named *Ceasefire*. After

---

10 Bratton, B. Knobler, P. 2021. *The Profession*. New York: Pinguin Press P, 337.

11 Silverman, E.B. 1999. *NYPD Battles Crime*. Boston: Northeastern University Press. Zimring, F. E. 2006. *The Great American Crime Decline*. Oxford: Oxford U. Press. Zimring, F. E. 2012. *The City that Became Safe*. Oxford: Oxford University Press. Bratton, B. Knobler, P. 2021. *The Profession*. New York: Pinguin Press.

gathering information, including shooting, victims, and suspects records. Hence, they gained great knowledge of victims' and perpetrators' background and of the dynamics of violent territories across the city. The working group then called in gang members involved in nighttime gunfights. They encouraged gang members to look for peaceful coexistence with other city gangs, additionally warning them severely on potential consequences of their actions by authorities, were they to continue.

At the same time, the Boston Police Department launched a sting operation whenever a murder was committed during gang wars. A large team of police officers was mobilized to arrest as many members of the two warring gangs as possible. Where nighttime shootings occurred, police presence was immediately intensified, and gang members were tracked down and arrested as soon as possible.

Resulting from this action, the annual average of homicides involving victims younger than 24 years old fell from 44 between 1991 and 1995 to 25 in 1996 and 15 in 1997. Deterrence, gun confiscation, and interventions in the neighbourhoods were effective and this model was emulated elsewhere. This led to 24 *focused deterrence* operations inspired by Boston's experiment, of which the currently-studied results seem to announce significant crime-level reduction.[12]

Decriminalization of cannabis: dealers become sellers

While police departments in New York, Boston, and elsewhere were implementing the aforementioned strategies, legislators in some 20 American states were progressively decriminalizing the possession and sale of cannabis. Arguably, this was not without consequence in the *inner cities,* which were centres of intense drug trafficking.

For almost half a century, the American repressive apparatus waged a relentless war on cannabis trafficking: "The War on Drugs." As a result, millions of small-time drug dealers —mostly African Americans—ended up incarcerated. This massive incarceration movement continued into the early 21st century. In 2006, for example, there were 1.9 million *drug arrests* in the United States and 48% of the federal prison population were drug dealers.[13]

These aggressive repression policies worsened the already tense relationship between the police and the population of an *inner city*, especially where there

---

12 Kennedy, D. (2001). *Reducing gun violence: the Boston gun project's operation ceasefire*. Washington: Dept. of Justice, Office of Justice Programs, National Institute of Justice. Kennedy, D. (2009). *Deterrence and Crime. Prevention,* Routledge. Braga et al., 2018. "Focused Deterrence Strategies and Crime Control: An Updated Systematic Review and Meta-Analysis of the Empirical Evidence," *Criminology and Public Policy*, Vol. 17, No. 1, 2018.

13 Caulkins, Jonathan P. and Peter Reuter. 2017. Dealing with Drugs More Effectively and Humanely. In *Crime and Justice - Reinventing the Criminal Justice System*, ed. Daniel Nagin and Michael Tonry. University of Chicago Press, Chicago, 46(1): 95-158.

were concentrations of African Americans. Not long ago, in Washington, D.C., 30 percent of African Americans under the age of 25 had at least one prior conviction. These young people had criminal records that prevented them from getting regular jobs.[14]

The failure of crackdown policies seems to be unanimously accepted. Easy profits ensured a constant supply of dealers' workforce, replacing incarcerated ones. Law enforcement proved powerless on the demand side as well. The numbers of cannabis users remained at high levels with fluctuations unrelated to law enforcement. Most criminologists agreed that the criminalization of acts such as dealing small quantities of drugs leads to injustices and produces perverse effects. Criminologists mostly argue that carrying and trafficking cannabis are offences that do not deserve such repression, especially for the quite harmless effects of cannabis on consumers compared to that of alcohol. It appears that investing in cannabis trafficking repression leads to a diversion of police and judicial resources away from real crimes.[15] This has partially justified the decriminalization of cannabis sale and possession in the 20 states that have already done so.

Decriminalization has not been followed by a significant increase in cannabis while former drug dealers no longer risk jail sentences. Gangs face profits reduction while the police entertains better relations with underprivileged neighborhoods' inhabitants. More time can be allocated to other crimes. Our hypothesis seems thus plausible: where cannabis is legalized, violent crime seems to have declined in *inner cities*, but this remains to be tested against the figures.[16]

A conclusion that looks like a summary

The last decades saw a rise in U.S. law enforcement authorities' efforts to reduce violence in lawless metropolitan areas. Criminologists have observed their significant success, as violent crimes have been lowered. Innovative police officers not only targeted crime hotspots, but focused on deterrence operations against gangs and implementing situational prevention measures for pre-crime situations.

Over time, lessons were learned from failures and successes of such policies. Restoring peace and security, these initiatives show that the fight against crime can

---

14 Caulkins, Jonathan P. and Peter Reuter. 2017. Dealing with Drugs More Effectively and Humanely. In *Crime and Justice - Reinventing the Criminal Justice System*, ed. Daniel Nagin and Michael Tonry. University of Chicago Press, Chicago, 46(1): 95-158.

15 Caulkins, Jonathan P. and Peter Reuter. 2017. Dealing with Drugs More Effectively and Humanely. In *Crime and Justice - Reinventing the Criminal Justice System*, ed. Daniel Nagin and Michael Tonry. University of Chicago Press, Chicago, 46(1): 95-158.

16 Brochu, S., N. Brunelle, and C. Plourde. (2016). *Drugs and crime. A complex relationship* (third edition), Montreal, Les Presses de l'Université de Montréal. Reuter (2013). "Why Has US Drug Policy Changed So Little over 30 Years?" in Tonry, M. [ed.], *Crime and Justice: A Review of Research*, vol. 42. *Crime and Justice in America, 1975-2025*. Chicago: University of Chicago Press. On artificial incrimination, see Gassin, R. Cimamonti, S. Bonfils. *Criminology*. Seventh edition. Paris: Dalloz. And Cusson, M. 2021. *Security, Liberty and Crime*. Quebec City: Septentrion.

be effective. Therefore, fighting the roots of crime, such as poverty, inequality, exclusion is not the only solution available. These results prove that police strategies can be fruitful, far from counterproductive expedients of the past.

Four strategies stand out from thirty years of experimentation. The first requires to identify precisely micro-sites with high crime frequency, analyze the phenomenon's cause and monitor, control, and sometimes arrest involved individuals. The second strategy, *ComStat,* is similar to the first. It begins with statistical vigilance to detect in real time the emergence of localized criminal problems and then seeks ways to deter criminals through undelayed, direct actions against them. The third is a manifestation of violent law enforcement practices. It involves live, personal deterrence of gang members, shootings, confiscation of weapons, and hit-and-run operations. The fourth measure—initiated by legislators—was simple, but necessary: decriminalize cannabis possession and trafficking to stop harassing and locking up dealers. Through such evolution, the police could focus more effectively on high-end criminal networks.

These four strategies encourage us to learn a simple but insufficiently taught lesson : focusing on proper crime matters more than petty criminals. Little, drug-trafficking related crimes will require too many officers for uncertain results. Crime hotspots should be the sole object of law enforcement, in order to ensure the main goals: deter and remove opportunities from thieves.

Featured Titles from Westphalia Press

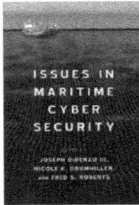

Issues in Maritime Cyber Security Edited by Nicole K. Drumhiller, Fred S. Roberts, Joseph DiRenzo III and Fred S. Roberts

While there is literature about the maritime transportation system, and about cyber security, to date there is very little literature on this converging area. This pioneering book is beneficial to a variety of audiences looking at risk analysis, national security, cyber threats, or maritime policy.

**The Death Penalty in the Caribbean: Perspectives from the Police
Edited by Wendell C. Wallace PhD**

Two controversial topics, policing and the death penalty, are skillfully interwoven into one book in order to respond to this lacuna in the region. The book carries you through a disparate range of emotions, thoughts, frustrations, successes and views as espoused by police leaders throughout the Caribbean

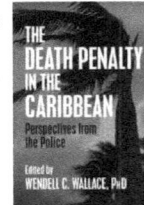

**Middle East Reviews: Second Edition
Edited by Mohammed M. Aman PhD and Mary Jo Aman MLIS**

The book brings together reviews of books published on the Middle East and North Africa. It is a valuable addition to Middle East literature, and will provide an informative read for experts and non-experts on the MENA countries.

Unworkable Conservatism: Small Government, Freemarkets, and Impracticality by Max J. Skidmore

Unworkable Conservatism looks at what passes these days for "conservative" principles—small government, low taxes, minimal regulation—and demonstrates that they are not feasible under modern conditions.

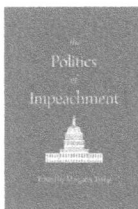

**The Politics of Impeachment
Edited by Margaret Tseng**

This edited volume addresses the increased political nature of impeachment. It is meant to be a wide overview of impeachment on the federal and state level, including: the politics of bringing impeachment articles forward, the politicized impeachment proceedings, the political nature of how one conducts oneself during the proceedings and the political fallout afterwards.

Demand the Impossible: Essays in History as Activism
Edited by Nathan Wuertenberg and William Horne

Demand the Impossible asks scholars what they can do to help solve present-day crises. The twelve essays in this volume draw inspiration from present-day activists. They examine the role of history in shaping ongoing debates over monuments, racism, clean energy, health care, poverty, and the Democratic Party.

International or Local Ownership?: Security Sector Development in Post-Independent Kosovo
by Dr. Florian Qehaja

International or Local Ownership? contributes to the debate on the concept of local ownership in post-conflict settings, and discussions on international relations, peacebuilding, security and development studies.

Donald J. Trump's Presidency: International Perspectives
Edited by John Dixon and Max J. Skidmore

President Donald J. Trump's foreign policy rhetoric and actions become more understandable by reference to his personality traits, his worldview, and his view of the world. As such, his foreign policy emphasis was on American isolationism and economic nationalism.

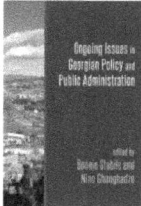

Ongoing Issues in Georgian Policy and Public Administration
Edited by Bonnie Stabile and Nino Ghonghadze

Thriving democracy and representative government depend upon a well functioning civil service, rich civic life and economic success. Georgia has been considered a top performer among countries in South Eastern Europe seeking to establish themselves in the post-Soviet era.

Poverty in America: Urban and Rural Inequality and Deprivation in the 21st Century
Edited by Max J. Skidmore

Poverty in America too often goes unnoticed, and disregarded. This perhaps results from America's general level of prosperity along with a fairly widespread notion that conditions inevitably are better in the USA than elsewhere. Political rhetoric frequently enforces such an erroneous notion.

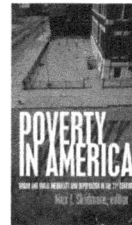

westphaliapress.org

www.ingramcontent.com/pod-product-compliance
Lightning Source LLC
Chambersburg PA
CBHW081646270326
41933CB00018B/3367